PATRICK JOSEPH KENNEDY
b. 1857   d. 1929

m.1887

Mary Augusta Hickey
b. 1857   d. 1923

JOSEPH PATRICK KENNEDY
b. 1889   d. 1969

m. 1914

ROSE ELIZABETH FITZGERALD
b. 1890

JOHN FRANCIS FITZGERALD
b. 1863   d. 1950

m. 1889

Mary Josephine Hannon
b. 1865   d. 1964

JOSEPH PATRICK, JR.
b. 1915   d. 1944

JOHN FITZGERALD
b. 1917   m. 1953   d. 1963

Jacqueline Lee Bouvier
b. 1929

ROSEMARY
b. 1918

KATHLEEN "KICK"
b. 1920   m. 1944   d. 1948

William John Robert Cavendish
Marquess of Hartington
b. 1917   d. 1944

EUNICE MARY
b. 1921   m. 1953

Robert Sargent Shriver, Jr.
b. 1915

PATRICIA
b. 1924   m. 1954   div. 1966

Peter Lawford
b. 1923   d. 1984

ROBERT FRANCIS
b. 1925   m. 1950   d. 1968

Ethel Skakel
b. 1928

JEAN ANN
b. 1928   m. 1956

Stephen Edward Smith
b. 1927

EDWARD MOORE
b. 1932   m. 1958   div. 1982

Virginia Joan Bennett
b. 1936

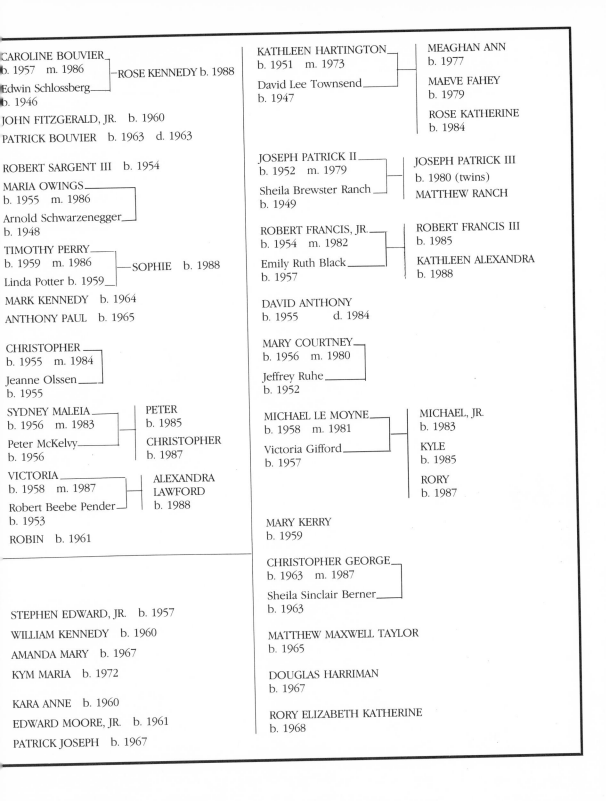

CAROLINE BOUVIER
b. 1957   m. 1986 ┐
                 ├─ROSE KENNEDY b. 1988
Edwin Schlossberg┘
b. 1946

JOHN FITZGERALD, JR.   b. 1960

PATRICK BOUVIER   b. 1963   d. 1963

ROBERT SARGENT III   b. 1954

MARIA OWINGS
b. 1955   m. 1986 ┐
                  │
Arnold Schwarzenegger┘
b. 1948

TIMOTHY PERRY
b. 1959   m. 1986 ┐
                  ├─SOPHIE   b. 1988
Linda Potter b. 1959┘

MARK KENNEDY   b. 1964

ANTHONY PAUL   b. 1965

CHRISTOPHER
b. 1955   m. 1984 ┐
                  │
Jeanne Olssen┘
b. 1955

SYDNEY MALEIA   PETER
b. 1956   m. 1983   b. 1985
                  │
Peter McKelvy   CHRISTOPHER
b. 1956   b. 1987

VICTORIA   ALEXANDRA
b. 1958   m. 1987   LAWFORD
                  │ b. 1988
Robert Beebe Pender┘
b. 1953

ROBIN   b. 1961

STEPHEN EDWARD, JR.   b. 1957

WILLIAM KENNEDY   b. 1960

AMANDA MARY   b. 1967

KYM MARIA   b. 1972

KARA ANNE   b. 1960

EDWARD MOORE, JR.   b. 1961

PATRICK JOSEPH   b. 1967

KATHLEEN HARTINGTON   MEAGHAN ANN
b. 1951   m. 1973   b. 1977
                        │
David Lee Townsend   MAEVE FAHEY
b. 1947   b. 1979

                            ROSE KATHERINE
                            b. 1984

JOSEPH PATRICK II   JOSEPH PATRICK III
b. 1952   m. 1979   b. 1980 (twins)
                        │
Sheila Brewster Ranch   MATTHEW RANCH
b. 1949

ROBERT FRANCIS, JR.   ROBERT FRANCIS III
b. 1954   m. 1982   b. 1985
                        │
Emily Ruth Black   KATHLEEN ALEXANDRA
b. 1957   b. 1988

DAVID ANTHONY
b. 1955   d. 1984

MARY COURTNEY
b. 1956   m. 1980 ┐
                  │
Jeffrey Ruhe┘
b. 1952

MICHAEL LE MOYNE   MICHAEL, JR.
b. 1958   m. 1981   b. 1983
                        │
Victoria Gifford   KYLE
b. 1957   b. 1985

                           RORY
                           b. 1987

MARY KERRY
b. 1959

CHRISTOPHER GEORGE
b. 1963   m. 1987 ┐
                  │
Sheila Sinclair Berner┘
b. 1963

MATTHEW MAXWELL TAYLOR
b. 1965

DOUGLAS HARRIMAN
b. 1967

RORY ELIZABETH KATHERINE
b. 1968

THE KENNEDY ENCYCLOPEDIA

AN A-TO-Z ILLUSTRATED GUIDE TO AMERICA'S ROYAL FAMILY

T—H—E

Kennedy

ENCYCLOPEDIA

CAROLINE LATHAM & JEANNIE SAKOL

NAL BOOKS

NEW AMERICAN LIBRARY

A DIVISION OF PENGUIN BOOKS USA INC., NEW YORK

PUBLISHED IN CANADA BY
PENGUIN BOOKS CANADA LIMITED, MARKHAM, ONTARIO

Published simultaneously in Canada by
Penguin Books Canada Limited.

The author gratefully acknowledges the following permissions:

"P.T. 109" written by Mary John Wilkin and Fred Burch.
Copyright © 1961 Cedarwood Publishing. Copyright Renewed.
International Copyright Secured. All Rights Reserved.
Used By Permission.

"CAMELOT" © 1960 by Allan Jay Lerner and Frederick
Loewe. CHAPPELL & CO., publisher and owner of allied
rights throughout the world. All Rights Reserved.
Used By Permission.

NAL TRADEMARK REG. U.S. PAT. OFF. AND FOREIGN COUNTRIES
REGISTERED TRADEMARK—MARCA REGISTRADA
HECHO EN DRESDEN, TN, U.S.A.

SIGNET, SIGNET CLASSIC, MENTOR, ONYX, PLUME, MERIDIAN and NAL BOOKS
are published *in the United States* by New American Library,
a division of Penguin Books USA Inc.,
1633 Broadway, New York, New York 10019, and
in Canada by Penguin Books Canada Limited,
2801 John Street, Markham, Ontario L3R 1B4

Library of Congress Cataloging-in-Publication Data

Latham, Caroline.
  The Kennedy encyclopedia : an A-to-Z illustrated guide to
America's royal family / Caroline Latham and Jeannie Sakol.
      p.   cm.
  ISBN 0-453-00684-1
  1. Kennedy family—Dictionaries.   2. United States—
Biography—Dictionaries.   I. Sakol, Jeannie.   II. Title.
E843.L37   1989
973.922'0922—dc20
  [B]   89-33616
                                                               CIP

Designed by Barbara Huntley

First Printing, November, 1989

          1   2   3   4   5   6   7   8   9

PRINTED IN THE UNITED STATES OF AMERICA

ACKNOWLEDGMENTS

Our sincere thanks go to the many people who helped and encouraged us with this book. Among them are: Melody Miller, Deputy Press Secretary to Senator Edward M. Kennedy; Mary Paris, Executive Assistant to Congressman Joseph P. Kennedy II; Henry J. Gwiazda and Alan B. Goodrich of the John Fitzgerald Kennedy Library; the research staff of the New York Public Library; Madeline Djerejian of Black Star Photos; Barbara Kloberdanz, Assistant to New York City Council President Andrew J. Stein; and to Madeleine Amgott, Linda Lipman, and Marie Silverman Marich. Once again the logistics were smoothed by Tony and his always reliable Hudson Valley Express. Our editor, Kevin Mulroy, has been supportive and helpful. Particular ongoing gratitude goes to our agent, Alice Martell.

ACKNOWLEDGMENTS

INTRODUCTION

We had just finished an encyclopedic volume about Britain's royal family when we began our research for *The Kennedy Encyclopedia*. The similarities between the two subjects were startlingly clear. We Americans have democratic principles, but we still miss the glamor, the pageantry, and the unifying presence of a royal family. So we have done our best to compensate for our lack of royalty by our focus on the Kennedy family. It is no accident that so many writers have used the metaphor of royalty to describe the Kennedys, referring to Ted Kennedy as the heir apparent, or young Joe Kennedy as the reluctant prince. Politically, we may have varying opinions of the achievements and effects of the Kennedys on our government, but we *are* united in our fascination with the personalities involved, and with the impact of a single family on a nation of more than two hundred million people. Although the reality of American politics has never been kind to dynastic dreams since the days of the Adamses, the Kennedys have succeeded in establishing the legend of their ongoing dominance, if not the reality.

Surely the Kennedys are all that legends are made of. The descendants of Irish immigrants who came to this country with little more than vague hopes for the future, the children of Joe and Rose Kennedy took their place in world affairs with all the aplomb of an upper class born and bred for leadership. Their enormous success in the public arena was from the start notably combined with a private dedication to the family, both real and ideal, which increased its mystique in the eyes of outsiders. Today, the twenty-nine grandchildren of Joe and Rose bear witness that "being a Kennedy" still means something special, still carries that faint echo of the lost Camelot—still arouses interest in the future of another generation.

For decades the world has been fascinated by every detail available about the Kennedy family: their triumphs and tragedies, their accomplishments and their failures, their passions and their follies. From the first Kennedy to come to America (Patrick, in 1848) to the newest arrival (baby Rose Kennedy Schlossberg), the legend of the once and future Kennedys still enchants us.

Caroline Latham and Jeannie Sakol
Hudson, New York
November 1988

THE KENNEDY ENCYCLOPEDIA

The A List

According to young Edward Kennedy's fellow students at Harvard in the 1950s, he and a friend kept a list of potential dates, which they rated from A, the top choice, to E, only in emergencies. Ted prided himself on rarely having to stoop below a B.

"Abraham, Martin and John"

In October 1968, pop singer Dion released a recording of the song "Abraham, Martin and John," about the assassinations of two presidents, Abraham Lincoln and John F. Kennedy, and the civil rights leader Martin Luther King, Jr., with a verse about "Bobby" as well. The song was an instant hit.

Addison's Disease

In 1947, on a visit to England, John F. Kennedy collapsed suddenly and was rushed to the London Clinic. There his illness was diagnosed as Addison's disease, from which he had probably suffered for some time. Addison's disease is caused by an insufficiency or failure of the adrenal glands, a small pair of glands located near the kidney that secrete the hormone adrenaline. The symptoms of adrenal insufficiency include dizziness, nausea, and weight loss, with eventual circulatory collapse without proper treatment. Classically, Addison's disease is caused by tuberculosis of the adrenal glands, a problem from which Jack Kennedy never suffered, and thus he sometimes explained that he didn't have the "real" Addison's disease, but a different sort of adrenal insufficiency, exacerbated by the malaria he caught in the Pacific during World War II.

The question of whether candidate Kennedy suffered from Addison's disease became an issue of the 1960 campaign, because it raised fears about his fitness for the demanding office of the presidency. At one time Addison's disease was considered fatal, but in the 1930s, treatment with adrenal hormone extract came into use, and long-term survival became possible. By 1950, it was discovered that cortisone was an even better method of treatment, and Jack Kennedy remained on cortisone for the rest of his life, his symptoms for the most part under control. For political reasons, however, he continued to deny that he had the "real" Addison's disease.

The "Aging" Kennedy

Friends of Senator Edward M. Kennedy, who remember him as he first appeared in the Senate as a fresh-faced young man of thirty, comment in surprise that Kennedy is turning gray.

Says Kennedy's press aide, Melody Miller, "Isn't it wonderful that we've finally had a chance to see a Kennedy age?"

Aircraft Carrier John F. Kennedy

On May 27, 1967, the aircraft carrier *John F. Kennedy* was launched at Newport News, Virginia. An 88,000–ton vessel belonging to the class known as CVA 67, the ship cost two hundred million dollars to build and was the largest conventionally powered ship in the fleet. The *John F. Kennedy* was christened by the late President's daughter, Caroline, with other members of the Kennedy family in attendance. The aircraft carrier is still in service, based in its home port of Norfolk, Virginia.

Herve and Nicole Alphand

Herve Alphand was the French ambassador to the United States during the years that John F. Kennedy was President. The ambassador and his charming wife, Nicole, became personal friends of the Kennedys and thus among the most important figures in Washington diplomatic and social circles. Jacqueline Kennedy felt comfortable with the cultured and stylish Nicole, and both the Kennedys enjoyed her special brand of elegant hospitality. According to Washington observer Barbara Howar, Ambassador Alphand sometimes entertained his guests with his lengthy rendition of a chicken laying an egg.

Caroline christens the aircraft carrier John F. Kennedy. (Dennis Brack, Black Star)

Amagiri

The *Amagiri* was a Japanese destroyer carrying troops through the Blackett Strait on the night of August 1, 1943. It had made the trip to the Japanese base at Kolombangara and was returning through the straits at a speed later estimated at forty knots. In the darkness, the *Amagiri* rammed into the unseen PT-109, commanded by Lieutenant John F. Kennedy, and sliced the smaller lighter craft in half. Two crew members of the PT-109 were killed at the time of the collision, but Kennedy managed to save the other ten by leading the swimming group to nearby small islands and living on coconuts while they tried to signal Allied troops.

Nearly ten years later, when John F. Kennedy was campaigning for the Senate in 1952, the

Japanese commander of the *Amagiri*, Kohei Hanai, wrote him a letter wishing him success in the election, adding, "I am firmly convinced that a person who practices tolerance to your former enemy like you, if elected to the high office of your country, would no doubt contribute not only to the promotion of genuine friendship between Japan and the United States but also to the establishment of the universal peace."

This letter was released by Kennedy staffers to the press and drew favorable reaction from the voters of Massachusetts. Hanai, who later became mayor of a town in northern Japan, expressed his shock and sorrow at the death of President Kennedy in 1963. "I think his death is a great loss to Japan," said the President's former enemy.

Ambassador to the Court of St. James

In December 1937, Joseph Patrick Kennedy was appointed United States Ambassador to the Court of St. James, the first Irish-American ever to hold the post. He traveled to London the following March and presented his credentials to King George VI at Buckingham Palace. The entire Kennedy family, except for the children at college, moved into the Ambassador's Residence at 14 Prince's Gate, a huge house in Knightsbridge that had been given to the American government by J. P. Morgan. Joseph Kennedy was initially a very popular figure in England, and his intimacy with Prime Minister Neville Chamberlain made him an effective ambassador. But after Chamberlain's appeasement policy toward Nazi Germany failed and the Prime Minister was forced to resign in the early days of Great Britain's war on Germany, Kennedy found himself less welcome in the office of the new Prime Minister, Winston Churchill. At the same time, Ambassador Kennedy's unequivocal support of the policy of isolationism for the United States made him a political liability for President Roosevelt. The President began to conduct his relations with the government of Great Britain without involving his ambassador, and after a confrontation with the President failed to remedy the embarrassing situation, Joseph Kennedy resigned in February 1941. For the rest of his life, however, he preferred to be addressed as "the Ambassador."

American Red Cross

From the time that World War II broke out, Kathleen Kennedy had wanted to return to England, to help that country with its war effort, and to be with her friends there. She was deeply attached to the country—and to Billy Cavendish, Marquess of Hartington, the titled Englishman she was later to marry. In the summer of 1943, she was accepted by the American Red Cross to work in the rest-and-recreation clubs for the American G.I.'s in England. In part through the influence of her father, Kathleen was posted to a club one block away from Harrods department store, which put her smack in the middle of London and close to the friends she wanted to see. Although her schedule at the Red Cross was a heavy one, allowing her only one and a half days off per week, she managed to return to her former social life without harming her job performance. Her responsibilities at the Red Cross boiled down to acting like a normal American girl, dancing and chatting with lonely American soldiers and reminding them of their sisters and girlfriends back home. The lively and friendly Kathleen was superb at such a job.

The Kennedy family descends on London, left to right: *Eunice, Jack, Rosemary, Jean, Joe Sr., Teddy, Rose, Joe Jr., Pat, Bobby, Kathleen. (Courtesy of the Kennedy Library)*

Elizabeth Dunn Anderson

Elizabeth Dunn Anderson was the governess employed by Joseph P. and Rose Kennedy when their younger children were small. She was first hired in 1936 to work at Hyannis Port, looking after Bobby, Jean, and Teddy. Among other duties, she was expected to help stimulate their interest in American history.

Announcing the Candidacy

Senator Robert F. Kennedy announced his candidacy for the presidency on St. Patrick's Day, March 17, 1968. With his wife and nine of their ten children watching, he spoke to the press in the Senate Caucus Room. His opening words were "I am announcing my candidacy for the presidency of the United States": exactly the same words spoken from the same podium by his brother John F. Kennedy eight years earlier.

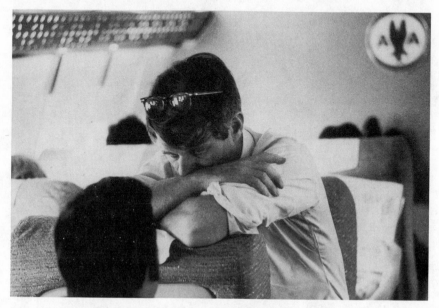

Bob Kennedy engages in a quiet conversation on the campaign trail. (Steve Schapiro, Black Star)

Army-McCarthy Hearings

The Army-McCarthy hearings, televised for thirty-six days in the summer of 1954 to a nation of observers, revolved around charges by the Army that Senator Joseph R. McCarthy and his chief counsel, Roy Cohn, had improperly sought special treatment for their friend and former employee, Army Private G. David Schine. Robert F. Kennedy participated in the proceedings as counsel to the Democratic minority of McCarthy's Senate Subcommittee on Investigations. Kennedy's job was to draft pertinent questions for Democratic senators to pose to witnesses such as Schine and Cohn. McCarthy's defense strategy was to mount his own offensive against not just the Army but the entire U.S. government for its communist leanings. Although the Republican majority of the subcommittee found McCarthy not guilty, the minority charged him with "inexcusable actions." The hearings marked the beginning of the end of McCarthy's power in Washington.

Arnold's Cigars

Kennedy family in-law Arnold Schwarzenegger is fond of expensive cigars, and is said to smoke five or six a day. His favorite is an import called Dom Perignon, after the classic champagne, with a price tag of thirty-five dollars each.

Arrest of Dr. Martin Luther King, Jr.

During the final weeks of the 1960 Kennedy campaign for the presidency, news headlines told of the arrest of Dr. Martin Luther King, Jr., and scores of other demonstrators as they tried to integrate a restaurant located within an Atlanta department store. All the other demonstrators were quickly released, but Dr. King was sentenced to four months of hard labor in a Georgia penitentiary and held without bail until he began to serve his sentence.

John F. Kennedy decided to make a public response to the injustice done to the civil rights leader. He personally telephoned the pregnant and distraught Coretta King to offer his sympathy and support. Then the candidate's brother Bob called the judge who had sentenced King and cajoled him into agreeing to let King out on bail pending his appeal (which was ultimately successful). The fact that the Kennedys had reacted so quickly and so supportively to Dr. King's arrest—and that Vice-President Nixon made no response at all—was not lost on black voters, who overwhelmingly supported Kennedy.

The Artificial Leg

In a 1988 interview in *People* magazine, Ted Kennedy, Jr., talked frankly about the stages he had gone through in adapting to the artificial leg he has had since he lost a leg to bone cancer at the age of thirteen.

As a kid I was embarrassed a lot about having an artificial leg. I felt like I was different. And I felt a need to conceal it. If I were to go swimming or do something where I'd have to take my leg off, I wouldn't feel like a whole person anymore. People would stare. My reaction was to stare back, give them a dirty look or curse them under my breath. It took me years to feel like, "It's their problem and not mine."

Inga Arvad

Danish-born Inga Arvad was a reporter and feature writer on the staff of the Washington *Times-Herald* in 1941. She soon met fellow employee Kathleen Kennedy and Kathleen's brother Lieutenant John F. Kennedy, who was then in Washington working at the Office of Naval Intelligence. A romance blossomed quickly between the beautiful blonde and the young officer. Jack Kennedy seemed to be very much in love with Inga, who was several years older than he and a worldly and talented woman. His father knew all about the relationship and countenanced it as long as it went no further than a diversion, but it was hidden from his mother, who would have been horrified because Inga was a Protestant and already twice-married, once to an Egyptian diplomat and once to a Hungarian movie director. Early in 1942, a picture of Inga attending the 1936 Olympic Games in Berlin with Adolph Hitler came to light, and rumors quickly branded Inga a German spy. Inga's own account was that she met Hitler when she worked as the German correspondent for a Danish newspaper and covered the wedding of Hitler's friend and colleague, Hermann Goering. Her association with Hitler, she explained, was based solely on the desire to interview top leaders of the Third Reich. At one point, it seemed as if Lieutenant Kennedy might be forced to leave the Navy because of his involvement with Inga, especially when the FBI began to follow her and tape her conversations. Perhaps because of Joseph P. Kennedy's intervention, Jack was merely reassigned to duty in Charleston, South Carolina, and then the South Pacific. Reluctantly, he accepted his father's insistence that it was impossible for a Kennedy to have a serious relationship with a Protestant divorcée suspected of being a Nazi spy, and Jack broke off with Inga in March 1942, although they continued to correspond for some time. He affectionately called her "Inga-Binga" and seemed upset and depressed when she married another man in 1947—comforting himself with the thought that she didn't really love her new husband. He was Tim McCoy, a former star of Hollywood westerns, with whom Inga had two sons. She died of cancer in 1973.

As We Remember Joe

After the wartime death of John F. Kennedy's eldest brother, Joseph P. Kennedy, Jr., in August 1944, Jack decided to put together a small volume of tributes to the memory of his brother; the book was called *As We Remember Joe*. He asked his brothers and sisters, and also some of Joe's friends, to write down their reminiscences. Contributors included family members Kathleen and Ted, London School of Economics professor Harold Laski, Kennedy aide Eddie Moore and his wife, Mary, journalist Arthur Krock, Joe's college friend Ted Reardon, and several servicemen from Joe's unit. Jack himself wrote the introduction, commenting:

I think that if the Kennedy children amount to anything now or ever amount to anything, it will be due more to Joe's behavior and his constant example than to any other factor. He made the task of bringing up a large family immeasurably easier for my father and mother, for what they taught him, he passed on to us, and their teachings were not diluted through him, but rather strengthened ...

The book was privately printed in an edition of five hundred copies, at a cost of about five thousand dollars, and the first copy presented to Rose and Joe Kennedy on that sad Christmas of 1944. Joe found it so affecting he was unable to read more than a few lines at a time.

Asked to Leave Harvard

In 1951, when Edward M. Kennedy was a freshman at Harvard, he had a tough time with Spanish and feared he might fail the course. He arranged for a classmate to take a test for him, but the substitution was detected and both young men were asked to leave Harvard. Ted spent two years in the Army and then reapplied to Harvard. The university permitted him to return, and he graduated in the class of 1954.

Assassination of President John F. Kennedy

On November 22, 1963, at 12:36 P.M., Central Standard Time, President John F. Kennedy was shot by a sniper, later identified as Lee Harvey Oswald, as he rode in an open car, a 1961 Lincoln, in a motorcade through Dallas, Texas. Immediately after the shooting, the President's car sped up and drove directly to Parkland Hospital. Doctors there attempted to resuscitate the President, but he never regained consciousness and was soon pronounced dead. Assistant Press Secretary Malcolm Kilduff made the terse announcement: "President John F. Kennedy died at approximately 1 o'clock Central Standard Time today here in Dallas. He died of a gunshot wound in the brain. I have no other details regarding the assassination of the President."

A horrified nation stayed glued to the television set as further details became available. Texas Governor Connally, riding in the same car, was severely wounded in the chest, ribs, and arm. The shots seemed to have come from the windows of the Texas Book Depository, a multistory building on the motorcade route. The President was hit first in the throat and then the back of the head, the second shot causing a huge wound and loss of brain tissue. Mrs. Kennedy, who was unhurt, then crawled out on the rear of the car to try to get the help of Secret Serviceman Clint Hill. Taken by surprise, the Secret Service made no effort to return the gunfire, although they quickly surmised the location of the sniper. Later that day, the assassin was identified as Lee Harvey Oswald, who had also shot a police officer within an hour of the President's murder. The following day, Oswald was formally charged with both crimes.

Meanwhile, the body of the slain President was returned to Washington aboard Air Force One, accompanied by his widow, his staff members, and the new President, Lyndon B. Johnson, and his wife. They were met at Andrews Air Force Base by Robert F. Kennedy and a naval ambulance that took the coffin to Bethesda Naval Hospital, where a postmortem was performed and the body then prepared for burial. On Saturday morning, the coffin was taken to the White House, to lie in state in the East Room. On Sunday, the slain President was moved to the Rotunda of the Capitol Building, where he lay in state as hundreds of thousands of mourners passed by to pay their last respects. The funeral was held on Monday, November 25.

Assassination of Robert F. Kennedy

Robert F. Kennedy once commented, "If anyone wants to kill me, it won't be difficult," and sadly, he proved to be correct. RFK was campaigning in the California primaries for the presidential election of 1968 when he was assassinated by Sirhan Sirhan. On the night of the voting, Kennedy, who was staying in a suite at the Ambassador Hotel in Los Angeles, learned that he was projected to be the winner in the Democratic presidential primary, and just after midnight he went downstairs to speak to his jubilant friends and supporters gathered in the hotel's Embassy Room. Afterward, he headed for another meeting room in the hotel, where he would hold a press conference. He chose to pass through a back hallway that took him past the kitchen. At 12:16 A.M. on June 5, 1968, Sirhan Bishara Sirhan stepped forward and fired six shots at Robert Kennedy from a .22 caliber Iver-Johnson revolver. Two of the bullets struck their target, one behind the right ear. Members of the Kennedy entourage, including Rosie Grier and Rafer Johnson, moved quickly to subdue the gunman. They then protected him from the angry crowd, saying, "We want him alive."

Senator Kennedy was rushed to Central Receiving Hospital, where doctors worked to stabilize him, and thence to Good Samaritan Hospital, where he underwent nearly four hours of neurosurgery. Doctors hoped to remove the bullet fragments that had lodged in his brain, but the damage was too massive for surgery to help. Robert Kennedy lived little more than a day longer, with his wife constantly at his side holding his hand, his brothers and sisters in the room, his three oldest children paying a brief visit. He died at 1:44 A.M. on the morning of June 6, 1968. The news was released by his Press Secretary, Frank Mankiewicz, who read the following statement:

Senator Robert Francis Kennedy died at 1:44 A.M. today, June 6, 1968. With Senator Kennedy at the time of his death was his wife, Ethel; his sisters, Mrs. Patricia Lawford and Mrs. Stephen Smith; his brother-in-law Stephen Smith; and his sister-in-law, Mrs. John F. Kennedy. He was forty-two years old.

In his distress, Mankiewicz had forgotten to mention that Senator Edward M. Kennedy had also been at his brother's bedside.

Assistant to the United States Attorney for New York

After Robert F. Kennedy graduated from law school in 1951, the first job he had was as an assistant to Frank Parker, the United States Attorney for New York. He got the job, which paid forty-two hundred dollars a year, on the recommendation of Kennedy family friend Senator Joseph McCarthy. Kennedy began work in November with the Internal Security Division, pursuing charges of misconduct against former members of the Truman administration. He left the following spring to help his brother Jack campaign for the Massachusetts Senate seat.

Adele Astaire

Adele Astaire, sister and dancing partner of famed dancer Fred, was a relative by marriage of the Kennedy family. Adele and Fred were born in Omaha, Nebraska, and started touring the vaudeville circuit together when they were children. In the 1920s, they became a successful stage act in New York and London. Then Adele fell in love with Lord Charles Cavendish, the younger son of the ninth Duke of Devonshire. When she married him in the early 1930s, she gave up show business and left her brother quite worried about whether he had any future on his own; he always maintained that Adele was the star of the act, and he considered her his favorite dancing partner. A decade later, Adele became the aunt-in-law of Kathleen Kennedy when Kathleen married her nephew, Billy Cavendish, the Marquess of Hartington.

A

Lady Astor

Lady Astor was a noted English hostess of the 1930s at the Astor country house, Cliveden. Born Nancy Langhorne in Virginia, she married an English lord, descendant of the wealthy Astor family, and moved to his country. Lady Astor was a woman of beauty and accomplishment, who achieved the distinction of being the first woman member of Parliament in her adopted country. Lady Astor had met the Kennedys in the early 1930s. When Joseph Kennedy became Ambassador to the Court of St. James, she was a frequent guest at the Embassy. She took a great liking to Kathleen Kennedy and often invited her to weekend parties at Cliveden. Lady Astor was one of two friends Kathleen invited to attend her small wedding to the Marquess of Hartington in May 1944. Lady Astor was also present at Kathleen's funeral four years later.

Hugh Dudley Auchincloss

Hugh Dudley Auchincloss was Jacqueline Lee Bouvier's stepfather. He came from a socially prominent background, related by marriage to such august names as the Rockefellers, Vanderbilts, duPonts, and Saltonstalls; his mother was the daughter of one of the founders of Standard Oil. Schooled at Groton and Yale, Hugh obtained a law degree from prestigious Columbia University and practiced law in New York for a time. Later he worked for the Commerce Department and then the State Department, under President Herbert Hoover. In 1931, he founded the investment banking firm of Auchincloss, Parker & Redpath, headquartered in Washington. After two earlier marriages and three children, Hugh Auchincloss married the freshly divorced Janet Lee Bouvier in 1942 and provided a home for her daughters, his own three children, and the two children of their marriage. Jacqueline called her stepfather "Uncle Hughdie" and always displayed her sincere appreciation of all that he had done for the two Bouvier girls, but her deepest devotion was reserved for her own father, Jack Bouvier. Hugh Auchincloss, who suffered from emphysema, died on November 20, 1976. In his final years, he had been forced to sell both Merrywood and Hammersmith Farm.

The Baby Bassinet

Both of the children of President and Mrs. Kennedy passed their first months snugly sleeping in a lovely white wicker bassinet covered with white dotted swiss threaded by pink ribbons. The bassinet had originally been purchased for the infant Jacqueline Bouvier, a beautiful and chubby baby who weighed eight pounds at birth.

Bad Back

President John F. Kennedy's problems with his back may have begun when he tried to play football at Choate and Harvard, competing against much larger and heavier boys who used their weight as a weapon. By the time he was in his mid-twenties, he was a victim of chronic back pain, which at times became so severe it nearly incapacitated him. Just before he entered the training program for PT-boat officers, he had a serious flare-up that nearly kept him out of the program, and perhaps his back would have been less of a problem if he hadn't served on PT boats, with their constant pounding of the human body as the light craft skimmed over the waves. Friends who helped Jack Kennedy campaign in his 1952 Senate race remember that his back was so bad he was in continual pain and could scarcely walk—until he had to stride out on a stage and meet the voters. By 1954, Kennedy's agony was so severe that he could walk only with crutches, and he decided to look for some alternative to a life of pain and disability.

New York specialists recommended surgery to fuse some of his spinal discs, but warned that because of Addison's disease, from which he also suffered, there was a high risk of infection. Although he was given only a fifty-fifty chance of surviving the surgery, Jack Kennedy elected to undergo the operation. It took place in New York on October 10, 1954. That operation was not a success, and after months of further pain and discouragement, he underwent a second operation, on February 15, 1955. The second operation made it possible for him to walk again without severe pain, and he was able to return to the Senate that May. Thereafter, Kennedy had to observe special precautions to prevent a recurrence of serious back problems, sitting in his special rocking chair and swimming regularly, but he never again suffered from such severe disability.

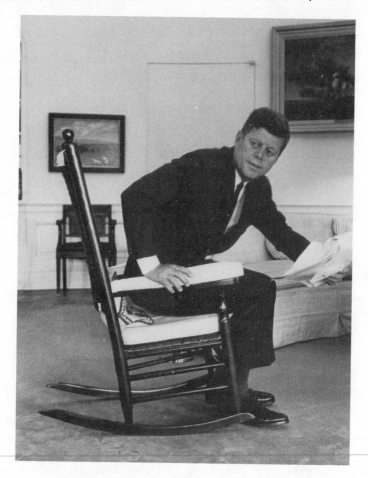

The President and his familiar rocking chair. (Fred Ward, Black Star)

Letitia Baldridge

Letitia Baldridge was Mrs. Kennedy's social secretary during the White House years. A lifelong Republican, she had, like Jacqueline Bouvier Kennedy, attended Miss Porter's School in Farmington, Connecticut, and Vassar College. She had been social secretary to Ambassador and Mrs. David Bruce in Paris, and then held the same post for Ambassador Clare Boothe Luce in

Italy. At the time she was hired by Mrs. Kennedy, Baldridge was the public relations director at Tiffany's. As she herself freely admits, her first press conference on behalf of the new First Lady was a virtual compendium of tactless remarks, but Baldridge later won kudos from the press, the public, and her bosses, President and Mrs. Kennedy, for her calm, poise, and talent for organizing huge social events, such as dinners for heads of state and receptions for hundreds of guests. She wrote about her experience in a book called *Of Diamonds and Diplomats*. After the assassination of the President, "Tish" Baldridge went to work at the Kennedy-owned Merchandise Mart. Today she is a consultant on matters of business and professional etiquette and has written several highly successful books on the subject.

Bay of Pigs

When President John F. Kennedy took office, he discovered that the Central Intelligence Agency was already in the process of implementing a plan to recruit a brigade of Cuban exiles to invade Castro's Cuba and thus encourage an expected uprising against his leadership. Although there were some private misgivings about the plan among Kennedy advisors, the President gave the final go-ahead for the invasion in early April—while cautiously deciding to reduce the planned scale of the invasion so as to minimize consequences to the U.S. of failure.

The invasion of the Bay of Pigs began on April 17, 1961, and was over two days later when the invading Cubans were totally defeated by Castro's forces. The Bay of Pigs was a severe embarrassment to the Kennedy administration in its early days: embarrassing because it was an obvious attempt to meddle in the internal affairs of another nation, and embarrassing because it was so ineptly executed. In retrospect, it was easy for everyone to see that the Bay of Pigs had been doomed to failure, and the President learned a hard lesson about the consequences of depending too much on "establishment" advisors. Henceforth, his own circle of intimates, such as his brother Robert, Ted Sorensen, Dick Goodwin, and Maxwell Taylor would be the voices to whom he listened most trustingly.

The brothers in the Oval Office. (Art Rockerby, Black Star)

The Beaverbrook Chair

In June 1956, the University of Notre Dame announced that Joseph P. Kennedy had endowed the Lord Beaverbrook chair of history, in honor of the British cabinet minister and newspaper publisher who had been a close friend of the Kennedy family.

Bedford-Stuyvesant

Bedford-Stuyvesant, or "Bed-Stuy," is a poor, largely black inner-city area of Brooklyn, New York. In 1965, when the newly elected senator from New York, Robert F. Kennedy, took a walk through the neighborhood, it was one of the worst slums in the country. RFK committed himself to a campaign to help Bed-Stuy. He enlisted friends and acquaintances, such as CBS head William Paley and Andre Meyer of the investment banking firm of Lazard Frères to

Senator Edward Kennedy and President of New York City Council Andrew Stein in Bedford-Stuyvesant. (Courtesy of Andrew Stein)

B

help him, and he used his political clout to bring in other public officials. Nonprofit corporations were set up to funnel development funds into the community. Robert Kennedy generated a commitment that was to have lasting effects.

Twenty years after RFK's death, it is still possible to see the improvements his program brought to the neighborhood, such as renovated houses, a public park designed by I. M. Pei, and a huge IBM plant providing local employment.

"Belle Mère"

"Belle Mère," a colloquial French expression for mother-in-law, was the term generally used by Jacqueline Kennedy to refer to her mother-in-law, Rose Kennedy.

Bellvue Hotel

When Jack Kennedy decided to run for Congress in 1946, he needed a base—and an address—in Boston's Eleventh District, which he hoped to represent. He initially moved into the Bellvue Hotel, a politicians' hangout near the State House on Beacon Hill (and pronounced by them the *Bella-View.*) Another resident at that time was his grandfather, John F. Fitzgerald, to whom Jack jokingly referred as the only person he knew in Boston. But the atmosphere at the Bellvue was not as congenial to young Jack as it was to his grandfather, and he soon moved to a small apartment on Bowdoin Street.

Bethlehem Steel

In 1917, Joseph P. Kennedy made his contribution to the war effort by leaving his post at the Columbia Trust (having his father, P. J. Kennedy, elected to succeed him as president) and going to work as assistant general manager of the Bethlehem Steel shipyard at Fore River in Quincy, Massachusetts. His salary was twenty thousand dollars a year, plus a share of the profits in the company cafeteria. Kennedy's job at the shipyard that built so many vessels for the U.S. Navy brought him into frequent contact with Assistant Secretary of the Navy Franklin Delano Roosevelt. Kennedy later characterized Roosevelt as a tough negotiator on the government's behalf: "When I left his office, I was so disappointed and angry that I broke down and cried," he remarked about one of their meetings. By the time the war ended, Joe's work in speeding up production had left him so tired he was on the brink of a breakdown, so Bethlehem Steel sent him to a health farm to recuperate. His long hours and managerial ingenuity made him so successful at his high-pressure work at the shipyard that the president and founder of the company, Charles M. Schwab, offered Joe Kennedy a high executive post at Bethlehem after the war. But Kennedy decided that the best opportunities for the postwar future lay in the stock market. Thus he turned down Schwab's offer and went to work at Hayden, Stone for half the salary.

Big Steel Bows to the President

In April 1962, Secretary of Labor Arthur J. Goldberg (who had once been general counsel for the steelworkers' union) helped negotiate a new contract between labor and management in the steel industry that held wage increases at a minimum. The union had bowed to the President's plea to make the new contract noninflationary, thus setting a good example for other major industries. A few days after the contract had been signed, Roger M. Blough, the chairman of the board of United States Steel, went to the White House and handed President Kennedy a statement announcing that steel prices would increase by six dollars a ton.

President Kennedy was infuriated. He was quoted as saying, "My father always told me that all businessmen were sons-of-bitches, but I never believed it till now." He brought the full pressure of the government to bear on U.S. Steel and its rival, Bethlehem Steel, which had quickly copied the price increase. Defense Department purchases of steel were switched to companies that had not announced any rise in prices, the Justice Department announced an investigation to see if antitrust laws had been violated, and public opinion was mobilized against "big steel." One week after his first visit to the White House, Blough went back and told the President he was rolling back the price increase.

Kirk Le Moyne Billings

Kirk Le Moyne Billings, always called "Lem," was a close intimate of the Kennedy family. He met young Jack Kennedy at Choate in 1932, and the two boys became instant best friends. Billings came from a fine old Social Register family, but his father, a Pittsburgh physician, died young and there was no money for Lem's education. He attended Choate on a scholarship, which made him enough of an outsider to be good company for Jack Kennedy, one of the few Catholic boys in the school. They remained close friends even after they left Choate, and the fact that Lem went to Princeton was one of the reasons that Jack decided to start college there rather than Harvard. Jack delighted in finding new nicknames for his friend, including "Delemma," "Le Moan," and "Pneumoan." Lem was for a time in love with Jack's sister Kathleen, although his chief role in her life was as a confidante to hear about her involvement with other young men.

Lem Billings remained close to the Kennedy family for the rest of his life, turning them into a full-time career. He was an usher at their weddings, an escort for wives and widows, a trusted confidante of the candidates. He served as a trustee for the family financial trusts, as a godfather to the children, as a familiar face at all the happy family parties and the sorrowful public events. Jackie Kennedy once joked that Lem Billings had been her houseguest since the day she was married.

After the deaths of Jack and Bobby Kennedy, Lem gradually grew close to the next generation of the family, serving for many of the younger children as a sort of living link to the past, the happy days when Joe, Jack, and Kathleen seemed to have the world at their feet. He took a special interest in young Bobby Kennedy, seeing in him a likely inheritor of the family political tradition. Lem Billings died on May 27, 1981, and his young friend Robert Kennedy, Jr., delivered the eulogy at his funeral.

B

Billy Whiskers

When Jack Kennedy was a little boy, his favorite book was *Billy Whiskers*, the story of an amiable goat, his wife Mrs. Whiskers, and their twin sons, the kids. The book, written by Frances Trego Montgomery, was first published in 1909, and followed by many sequels tracing the further adventures of the Whiskers family.

A Birthday Calendar for the Kennedy Family

JANUARY 9
Michael Kennedy, Jr.

JANUARY 11
Max Kennedy

JANUARY 14
P. J. Kennedy

JANUARY 17
Robert F. Kennedy, Jr.

JANUARY 24
Jean Olsson Lawford

FEBRUARY 11
John F. Fitzgerald

FEBRUARY 17
Mark Shriver

FEBRUARY 20
Kathleen Kennedy; Jean Kennedy Smith; Vicki Gifford Kennedy

FEBRUARY 21
Jeff Ruhe

FEBRUARY 22
Edward Kennedy

FEBRUARY 27
Michael Kennedy; Kara Kennedy

MARCH 22
Sheila Rauch Kennedy

MARCH 24
Douglas Kennedy

MARCH 29
Christopher Lawford

APRIL 11
Ethel Kennedy

APRIL 28
Robert Shriver

APRIL 30
Amanda Smith

MAY 6
Patricia Kennedy Lawford

MAY 29
John F. Kennedy

JUNE 15
David Kennedy

JUNE 25
Rose Kennedy Schlossberg

JUNE 28
Stephen Smith, Jr.

JULY 2
Robin Lawford

JULY 4
Kathleen Kennedy Townsend; Christopher Kennedy

JULY 6
Kyle Frances Kennedy

JULY 10
Eunice Kennedy Shriver

JULY 14
Patrick Kennedy

JULY 19
Ed Schlossberg

JULY 20
Antony Shriver

JULY 22
Rose Fitzgerald Kennedy

JULY 28
Joseph P. Kennedy, Jr.; Jacqueline Bouvier Kennedy Onassis

JULY 30
Arnold Schwarzenegger

AUGUST 7
Patrick Bouvier Kennedy

AUGUST 25
Sydney Lawford

AUGUST 29
Timothy Shriver

SEPTEMBER 2
Robert F. Kennedy III

SEPTEMBER 4
William Smith

SEPTEMBER 6
Joseph P. Kennedy

SEPTEMBER 8
Kerry Kennedy

SEPTEMBER 9
Joan Bennett Kennedy; Courtney Kennedy Ruhe

SEPTEMBER 13
Rosemary Kennedy

SEPTEMBER 24
Joseph P. Kennedy II; Stephen Smith

SEPTEMBER 26
Edward Kennedy, Jr.

OCTOBER 4
Joseph and Matthew Kennedy

Black Jack

Black Jack was the name of the riderless horse that followed the coffin of President Kennedy in his funeral procession. The horse, a black gelding, was saddled in the usual way, with an English saddle and a yellow-banded Army horse blanket. But in the silver stirrups were a pair of tall riding boots reversed, and a sword was hanging from the saddle: traditional symbols of a fallen military leader. Black Jack, named after the affectionate term used for General John "Black Jack" Pershing, was led by an Army officer, and many observers noted the horse's restlessness— which also seemed a suitable symbol at the funeral of the young President cut down in his prime.

Bobby Pays the Bill

The Kennedy family always liked to tease Robert F. Kennedy about his frugal ways, and no one liked to joke about that more than his father. In 1958, Joseph P. Kennedy told the press about the luncheon he had enjoyed at Washington's Metropolitan Club, at Bobby's expense. Using his son's guest privileges at the exclusive club, Joe and a friend ate lunch there, and afterward Joe simply signed Bobby's name to the check. The Ambassador said he had scrutinized the menu to find the most expensive dishes and consumed them with great relish. "I usually don't eat much for lunch, and look for bargains. But this is a rare opportunity that must not be wasted."

Bombing Incident in London

Caroline Kennedy had her own brush with tragedy when she was visiting the London home of family friend Hugh Fraser, a member of Parliament. On October 24, 1974, the seventeen-year-old Caroline heard a bomb explode under the red Jaguar she would have entered moments later. Although she was unhurt, a pedestrian, one of Fraser's neighbors, was killed by the explosion. Caroline calmly told *The New York Times*, "I am fine."

B

Bone Cancer

In 1973, young Edward M. Kennedy, Jr., noticed a bump on his right leg that hurt when he touched it and made it painful for him to play active games at school. The lump was swiftly diagnosed as bone cancer, and on November 17, the twelve-year-old underwent an operation to amputate his leg above the knee. His parents were with Ted when he awoke from the surgery, and then Senator Kennedy had to leave his son's bedside to attend the wedding of his niece Kathleen Kennedy and give away the bride. The surgery was followed by chemotherapy. The treatment of the cancer was successful, and since then Ted has learned to use an artificial leg so expertly that he can ski, play ball, and dance more agilely than most young men his age.

Boston Cream Pie

One of the best-loved desserts of the Kennedy family is Boston cream pie. The simple but rich dessert, basically a yellow cake filled with a custard layer and sometimes covered with a chocolate glaze, was frequently served in the home of Rose and Joseph Kennedy, and Rose later shared her recipe with her grown daughters and daughters-in-law. Boston cream pie symbolizes a Kennedy family get-together and remains a favorite with the younger generation.

ROSE KENNEDY'S BOSTON CREAM PIE
"The Favorite of the Kennedy Family as the Children Were Growing Up"

1 cup cake flour
1 ¼ teaspoons baking powder
few grains of salt
4 eggs, separated
1 cup sugar
1 ½ tablespoons cold water
1 ½ tablespoons lemon juice
1 teaspoon vanilla

FILLING
3 tablespoons cornstarch
⅔ cup sugar
few grains of salt
3 egg yolks
1½ cups milk, scalded
2 tablespoons butter
1 teaspoon vanilla

Preheat oven to 325°. Sift the flour three times with the baking powder and salt. Beat the egg whites until stiff but not dry. Beat in ½ cup of the sugar gradually. Beat the egg yolks, water, and lemon juice together until very thick and pale yellow. Beat in the remaining ½ cup sugar. Combine the yolks and whites, folding until blended. Add the vanilla; fold in the flour mixture. Pour into a buttered 9-inch cake pan; bake one hour. Cool on a rack, turning out of the pan in ten minutes. Wrap and set aside for 24 hours. Split it horizontally and fill.

Mix the cornstarch, sugar, and salt. Beat the egg yolks until thick. Combine with the cornstarch mixture, beating until perfectly smooth. Pour in the hot milk gradually. Add the butter and vanilla. Cook in the top of a double boiler over boiling water until thick, stirring all the time to prevent scorching. Cool this filling, then spread it thickly on one layer of the cake, cut side up. Top with second layer. Dust generously with confectioner's sugar. (Rose Kennedy did not use a chocolate glaze.)

B

"Boston Johnny"

"Boston Johnny" was a nickname given John F. Fitzgerald when he was a congressional representative in Massachusetts, because of his long, vigorous, and ultimately successful fight to re-open the Charlestown Naval Yard.

Boston Latin School

Boston Latin School is a prestigious Boston educational institution for boys established in 1635, making it the oldest public school in the country. It boasts many famous alumni, including Cotton Mather, John Hancock, Benjamin Franklin, Ralph Waldo Emerson, and Henry Adams. But, in keeping with the Boston tradition of democracy, the school has also accepted boys of working-class families who had the will to succeed in the WASP world that dominated Boston. Academic standards are high, but even more important is the inculcation of "school spirit," a set of values and attitudes shared by leading New England families. John F. Fitzgerald entered Boston Latin School in 1879 and graduated in the class of 1884. Joseph P. Kennedy was enrolled in Boston Latin School in 1901, graduating in 1908.

John Vernou Bouvier III

John Vernou Bouvier III, born in 1891, was the scion of a socially prominent family from East Hampton, Long Island, who became a stockbroker. The eldest of five children born to lawyer and broker John V. Bouvier, Jr., and his wife, Maude Frances Sergeant, he graduated from Yale in 1914 and worked briefly for the Wall Street brokerage firm of Henry Hertz & Co. In 1922 he went into business for himself, borrowing the money from relatives to buy a seat on the New York Stock Exchange. His ultimate lack of success in the financial world was summed up by the friend who said Jack had managed to turn a $750,000 inheritance into a $100,000 estate. Dark-haired and romantically dashing, he was nicknamed "The Black Sheik," "The Black Orchid," and "Black Jack." His marriage to the former Janet Lee produced two children: Jacqueline Bouvier, born in 1929, and Lee Bouvier, born in 1933. The Bouviers were divorced in 1940, but Jack never remarried. His daughters remained devoted to him all his life, despite the rumors of womanizing and hard-drinking that perennially surrounded him. He died of cancer of the liver on August 2, 1957; according to his nurse, his last word was "Jackie." After a funeral at St. Patrick's Cathedral in New York, he was buried in East Hampton.

Miche Bouvier

Miche Bouvier was the cousin of Jacqueline Lee Bouvier, son of her father's younger brother, William Sergeant "Bud" Bouvier. On December 22, 1929, when baby Jacqueline was christened at the Church of St. Ignatius Loyola in New York City, Miche acted as her godfather when her parents' first choice for the position, her grandfather James T. Lee, got stuck in traffic and didn't appear at the ceremony.

Brearley School

The private Brearley School in New York was the school attended by Caroline Kennedy after the slain President's family moved to their Fifth Avenue apartment in that city.

Broken Ankle

In November 1955, when Jacqueline Kennedy was still a relatively new Kennedy in-law, she tried to join in one of the rough-and-tumble family games of touch football. The result was a broken ankle that hospitalized her for a time. That was the end of Jackie's attempt to meet the family on their own terms; thereafter, she wisely stuck to the areas in which she excelled.

Bronxville

In May 1929, Joseph P. Kennedy bought a house for his family, at 294 Pondfield Road in Bronxville, a posh suburb north of New York City. The previous owner of the six-acre Westchester County estate with separate cottages for the chauffeur and gardener was financier Joseph A. Goetz, and the price was $250,000. The Bronxville house, built of brick in the Georgian style, had originally been constructed for the man who founded the Busch brewing empire, and it had all the amenities, including a basement projection room where the latest Hollywood movies were shown to family and friends. The house on Pondfield Road was the Kennedy family's primary residence until 1941, when Joe Kennedy decided he no longer needed a base in New York and that he would prefer to divide his time between his homes in Palm Beach and Hyannis Port.

Brown University

Brown University in Providence, Rhode Island, seems to be a favorite with the younger generation of the Kennedy family. Among those who have attended the beautiful old school in the historic district of Providence are John Kennedy, Jr., Kerry Kennedy, Patrick Kennedy, and Rory Kennedy.

Lenny Bruce

The outrageous comedian Lenny Bruce had a performance scheduled in New York for the night of November 22, 1963, the evening of the day President Kennedy was assassinated. Since President Kennedy had been one of the prime targets of Bruce's foul-mouthed satire, the crowd of two thousand people wondered how the comedian would handle the situation. Could the bad boy of comedy suddenly turn tender and tear-jerking? Or would he top himself by a tasteless tirade against the President whose untimely death the whole country mourned? According to Bruce's friend, writer Terry Southern, Bruce too pondered these questions, unable to decide how to approach the issue. His solution was to work from the satirical premise that politics and show business were, as one writer about Bruce put it, "two sides of the same hustle." He strode out on the stage looking grieved and depressed, shook his head in deep sympathy, and exclaimed sadly, "Phew . . . Vaughn Meader!"—in sorrowful acknowledgment of the blow to the career of the man who achieved fame through his hit record satirizing the Kennedy family.

Brumus

Brumus was the name of the large black Newfoundland dog that was a family pet in the Robert F. Kennedy household. Brumus was known to eat food off guests' plates, give them occasional nips, and sometimes use a trousered or stockinged leg as a substitute for a lamppost. Despite Brumus's shortcomings, Bobby Kennedy was devoted to the dog. When he became attorney general, he began the practice of taking Brumus to the office with him. This practice was in defiance of government regulations specifying that "dogs and other animals shall not be brought upon governmental property for other than official purposes." Bobby explained his actions by saying, "Brumus usually stays at home with the children. But the children are away on vacation and he gets very lonely. So I bring him down here and get pretty girls to take him for a walk." J. Edgar Hoover complained about the presence of Brumus at the Justice Department, Arthur Krock wrote a snippy newspaper column on the subject, and all Washington waited to see what would happen next. Robert Kennedy finally agreed to leave Brumus at home at Hickory Hill.

Buffet at the Mayflower

On the January day in 1961 that President John F. Kennedy was inaugurated, his father decided to hold a luncheon before the event at the Mayflower Hotel. Joseph Kennedy turned the organization of the event over to Jacqueline Kennedy's newly appointed social secretary, Letitia Baldridge, telling her to invite only the immediate family. When Joe entered the Mayflower, he was taken aback to see a crowd of several hundred people milling around. "Who are all these people?" he demanded angrily of Baldridge. "Your family," she answered firmly. "They are *not*!" Joe Kennedy exploded. "Who are all these freeloaders? I want to know exactly why you asked them." The annoyed social secretary told him to go find out for himself, so he walked up to some of the strangers and asked who they were. Needless to say, they were all indeed family members; the Kennedy-Fitzgerald-Bouvier-Auchincloss group was so large no one could remember all the names and faces. Joe Kennedy quickly returned to Baldridge to apologize. "You're right, they are all family . . . and it's the last time we'll get them all together, too, if I have anything to say about it."

Dr. George Bulkey

Dr. George Bulkey was the White House physician who began to treat President Kennedy's bad back in 1963. In an effort to discontinue the novocaine injections prescribed by Dr. Janet Travell, Bulkey first consulted with a team of orthopedists and then worked out an exercise program aimed at restoring flexibility in the spine. By the time Kennedy left for Dallas in November 1963, there had been marked improvement, and the President was able to go through an entire gymnastic routine without discomfort.

The Bull Moose Party

Early in the twentieth century, former President Theodore Roosevelt broke away from the Republican party and organized his own splinter group, the Bull Moose party. John F. Fitzgerald, President Kennedy's grandfather, got off a classic line at Roosevelt's expense, calling the party "one-ninth moose and eight-ninths bull."

William Bullitt

William Bullitt was the United States Ambassador to France in 1939. Bullitt's colleague at the embassy in London, Joseph P. Kennedy, arranged for his son Jack to spend a month at the Paris embassy in the spring of 1939, as an educational experience. Bullitt saw to it that his staff extended every courtesy to young Jack.

Bumper Stickers

The Kennedys have been the subject of innumerable bumper stickers, some of them classics:

BE THANKFUL ONLY ONE CAN WIN
A reference to the full family participation in Jack Kennedy's 1960 presidential campaign.

KENNEDY AND CAMUS IN 1968
A reference to Bobby Kennedy's fondness for the works of the French author.

B

McGeorge Bundy

McGeorge Bundy was a close political advisor to John F. Kennedy. Bundy, born in 1919, obtained his degree from Yale and then taught at Harvard, rising to become the dean of the Faculty of Arts and Sciences. Bundy helped advise Kennedy during the 1960 campaign, and when Kennedy entered the White House the following January, "Mac" Bundy became the head of the National Security Council staff. A World War II army officer who was on the Normandy beaches on D-Day plus one, Bundy was considered one of the brightest of his generation. He continued to serve on the NSC for a time during the Johnson administration, then accepted the position of head of the Ford Foundation from 1966 to 1979. He currently teaches history at New York University.

"Bunny"

Jacqueline Kennedy sometimes called her husband "Bunny." According to a frequently quoted remark, she turned to him as they were watching the televised returns of the 1960 election in the wee hours of the morning and said, "Oh, Bunny, you're President now!"

Burning of RFK Assassination Photos

In April 1988, the state of California released much of its documentation of the investigation of Senator Robert F. Kennedy's assassination in Los Angeles on the night of June 5, 1968. Among the more than 50,000 pages of material was a certificate attesting to the fact that 2,410 photographs taken during the investigation were burned on August 21, 1968, little more than two months after the shooting. The Los Angeles Police Department said they did not know why the photographs were destroyed. Scholars have labeled the burning "incredible" and suggested it might be the result of something more sinister than mere incompetence.

James MacGregor Burns

James MacGregor Burns was a Harvard historian who wrote the first of the major biographical studies of John F. Kennedy, published in 1959. Burns had the advantage of full cooperation from his subject and therefore access to thousands of private documents. Ironically, Burns's previous book, a biography of Franklin D. Roosevelt, had been defeated as a candidate for the Pulitzer Prize by Jack Kennedy's own *Profiles in Courage*.

B

The Butterball Problem

When Ambassador Joseph P. Kennedy and his wife, Rose, were guests of King George VI and Queen Elizabeth at Windsor Castle for a weekend in 1939, they chatted during Sunday lunch with the two young Princesses, Elizabeth and Margaret Rose. Joe noticed that Princess Margaret said almost nothing, but concentrated on eating her lunch. The Queen explained that her younger daughter was embarrassed by the fact that she was usually the last to finish her meal. Joe lightened the atmosphere by telling the Royal Family about his young son Teddy, who had the opposite problem: He ate so fast, and so much, that he was turning into a butterball.

"Buttons"

"Buttons" was President Kennedy's favorite nickname for his daughter, Caroline.

Cabinet of President John F. Kennedy

DEAN RUSK, Secretary of State
ROBERT S. MCNAMARA, Secretary of Defense
DOUGLAS DILLON, Secretary of the Treasury
ORVILLE FREEMAN, Secretary of Agriculture
ARTHUR GOLDBERG, Secretary of Labor (#1)
W. WILLARD WIRTZ, Secretary of Labor (#2)
STEWART UDALL, Secretary of the Interior
ABRAHAM RIBICOFF, Secretary of Health,
  Education and Welfare (#1)

ANTHONY J. CELEBREZZE, Secretary of Health,
  Education and Welfare (#2)
LUTHER HODGES, Secretary of Commerce
ROBERT F. KENNEDY, Attorney General
J. EDWARD DAY, Postmaster General
DR. LUTHER L. TERRY, Surgeon General

"Cadillac Eddie"

When Edward M. Kennedy was in law school at the University of Virginia, he was given the nickname "Cadillac Eddie" by his fellow students, because he always showed up at parties in a flashy car with an attractive girl.

Alice Cahill

Alice Cahill was the governess hired by Joseph and Rose Kennedy in the late 1920s to look after their younger children.

C

29

Camelot

It was not until after the death of President John F. Kennedy that the concept of Camelot began to be associated with his administration, and the person who made the explicit association with King Arthur's Court, with its high ideals and progressive manners, was Jacqueline Kennedy. By ironic coincidence, two days before the President's assassination, the Kennedys held a ball at the White House and the Marine Band had played selections from *My Fair Lady* and *Camelot*, both favorites of the President. The music included the tune that was later to seem a nostalgic summing-up of the Kennedy Presidency:

> *Don't let it be forgot*
> *That once there was a spot*
> *For one brief shining moment*
> *That was known as Camelot*

In an interview given just weeks after the President's death, Mrs. Kennedy told journalist Theodore H. White, "When Jack quoted something, it was usually classical, but I'm so ashamed of myself—all I keep thinking of is this line from a musical comedy." She then quoted the lines from *Camelot*, citing them as favorites of the President. "There'll be great Presidents again—and the Johnsons are wonderful, they've been wonderful to me—but there'll never be another Camelot again."

White later told biographer C. David Heymann that he realized the comparison was a "misreading of history," but added that it seemed a small favor to grant the former First Lady "So the epitaph of the Kennedy administration became Camelot—a magic moment in American history when gallant men danced with beautiful women, when great deeds were done, and when the White House became the center of the universe."

The Campaign Humor of RFK

RFK told a group of farmers, "I'm the best friend the farmer has. I'm already doing more for the farmer than any of them, and if you don't believe me, just look down at my breakfast table. We are consuming more milk and more bread and more eggs, doing more for farm consumption, than any other candidate."

When asked in 1968 how he felt about a Johnson-Kennedy ticket, Bob replied, "I'd be willing, but I'm not sure that Mr. Johnson would accept the Vice-Presidency."

Told by advisors that the crowd in an Indiana town where he was to speak were extremely conservative, he said, "Make like, not war. See how careful I am."

Responding to charges that he was "ruthless," Bob Kennedy joked, "People say I am ruthless. I am *not* ruthless. And if I find the man who is calling me ruthless, I shall destroy him."

When the wind blew a piece of paper out of his hand during a campaign appearance in a prairie state, he told the laughing crowd, "Give me that back. That's my farm program."

The "carpetbagger" issue was raised in his campaign for the New York Senate seat, and Bob addressed it with humor. "People ask me why I came to New York. Well, a few months ago I read in the papers that California had passed New York in population. So I turned to my wife and I said, 'What can we do?' So we moved to New York and in just one day we increased the population by ten and a half. I challenge any other candidate to make that statement!"

C

Another witticism also made use of a reference to Bob's wife. He told the press he had no interest in the Oval Office and then added, in a jab at President Johnson, "And neither does my wife Ethel Bird."

In his last speech, to friends and campaign workers gathered at the Ambassador Hotel in Los Angeles on the night of his victory in the California primary, RFK joked, "I want to express my gratitude to my dog Freckles."

Tom Campbell

Tom Campbell was a member of the Harvard class of 1912 and one of Joseph P. Kennedy's best friends in his early manhood. A fellow Irish Catholic who came from Lowell, Massachusetts, Tom was well known for his wit, and he played on the football team as well.

Albert Camus

Albert Camus was a French writer and philosopher who won the Nobel Prize for Literature in 1957. His best-known works are *The Stranger, Resistance, The Rebel,* and *The Notebooks.* In his writings, he expounds a fatalistic view of the world, depicting human beings trying to grapple with the horrors of war, oppression, violence, and all forms of suffering. After the assassination of President Kennedy, his brother Robert turned to the works of Camus for insight into the tragedy that had befallen him and the entire nation. Eventually he found some measure of consolation in Camus' compassionate fatalism. One of his favorite quotations from Camus often turned up in his political speeches: "Perhaps we cannot prevent this from being a world in which children suffer, but at least we can reduce the number of suffering children, and if we do not help, then who will?"

Michael Canfield

Michael Temple Canfield was the first husband of Lee Bouvier, sister of Jacqueline Kennedy Onassis. Canfield was a New York stockbroker and the son of Cass Canfield, the publisher at Harper and Row. Michael Canfield was a Harvard alumnus and an ex-Marine and worked for a brief period at Harper and Row. After his 1953 marriage to Lee, he joined the U.S. diplomatic service and was posted to London. It was there that the marriage broke down, and there that Lee met her second husband, Prince Stanislaus Radziwill. The Canfield marriage was subsequently annulled.

Frances Anne Cannon

Frances Anne Cannon was an attractive and intelligent Sarah Lawrence student who became romantically involved with John F. Kennedy when he was a student at Harvard in 1938. Apparently

C

Jack's family took the romance seriously, for they expected that Jack would propose to Frances. However, she soon announced her engagement to writer John Hersey. Several years later, it was Hersey who wrote the story of the sinking of the *PT-109* that was published first in the *New Yorker* and later in *Reader's Digest*, making Jack Kennedy's name well known to the American public and giving him the national exposure he needed to embark on a political career.

Canterbury Preparatory School

Canterbury Preparatory School, in New Milford, Connecticut, was the first boarding school to which young Jack Kennedy was sent, in the fall of 1930. The school was founded in 1915 by a group of Roman Catholic laymen, and it was the first (and last) Catholic school Jack ever attended. He was unable to finish the school year because of a serious bout of illness. Over the summer he studied with a tutor to catch up with his class; the following fall he entered Choate.

The Caroline

The *Caroline* was the private plane used by John F. Kennedy when he campaigned for President. Named after Jack's daughter, the Convair plane was actually leased by one of Joseph P. Kennedy's businesses to the candidate for a nominal sum. The *Caroline* later did duty in the senatorial campaigns of Edward and Robert Kennedy as well.

The Caroni River

In the early 1980s, RFK's son Bobby Kennedy organized a trip for himself, brothers Michael and Max, old family friend Lem Billings, Dr. Tim Haydock, and a few other companions, to be the first rafters ever to run the Caroni River in Venezuela. The party was dropped in by helicopter to begin the trip down the uncharted river. The river and its rapids had looked deceptively tranquil from a reconnaissance, but within hours, the three enormous rafts used by the group were being tossed around like corks. They went over a sixty-foot waterfall and were sucked into a whirlpool thirty feet deep. "I was dying," young Bobby wrote in a later account of the trip. Several of the group lost teeth and suffered facial gashes, which Dr. Haydock stitched up. With their equipment and food washed away, the men improvised a helicopter pad so that they could be rescued a few at a time. But it was several days before all twenty-four members of the party were safely back in Caracas. Bobby, who was among the last to leave, relished describing how they ran out of food and were forced to eat caterpillars, termites, and the roots of jungle plants to survive. It was a trip no one would ever forget—or repeat.

C

Igor Cassini

Igor Cassini was a journalist who wrote the "Cholly Knickerbocker" gossip column for the *New York Journal-American*. He was acquainted with the Bouvier girls, and selected Jacqueline as "Deb of the Year" in 1947, then bestowed the same title on Lee three years later. Igor's brother was couturier Oleg Cassini, who designed many of Jacqueline Kennedy's clothes during the White House years. Igor became the director of a New York public relations firm, Martial and Company, that numbered among its clients the Dominican Republic. As it turned out, Cassini's interest went beyond the gentle encouragement of Dominican tourism to the conduct of United States foreign policy, as he attempted to induce the Kennedy government to back the dictatorship of Generalissimo Trujillo. In 1963, Cassini was indicted by the Attorney General's Office for failing to register as a foreign agent and was subsequently fined $10,000 and placed on six months' probation. Cassini's wife was Charlene Wrightsman, daughter of the Kennedy's friends Charles and Jayne Wrightsman, and she wrote to the President, asking him to intervene to protect Cassini. Several weeks later, she died from an overdose of sleeping pills.

Oleg Cassini

Fashion designer Oleg Cassini made many of the outfits Jacqueline Kennedy wore in public when she was First Lady. Cassini, who often garnered headlines himself, due to his marriage to Gene Tierney (who is rumored to have had an affair with Jack Kennedy in the late 1940s, just as she was divorcing Cassini) and well-publicized courtship of Grace Kelly, had known the Kennedy family socially for many years. In the 1950s, Cassini regularly dined with Joseph P. Kennedy every Tuesday night at New York's chic restaurant, La Caravelle; he had briefly dated Eunice, made clothes for Rose Kennedy, had met Jacqueline Kennedy at the time of her marriage and served as an escort occasionally when her husband was too busy to attend a party. After Kennedy won the 1960 election, his wife invited Cassini to come to Palm Beach and show her some sketches of his ideas. After their meeting, Jacqueline Kennedy decided to use Cassini as a quasi-official designer, and to base her look in the White House on his designs. She did not exclusively wear Cassini clothes—her dress for the Inaugural Ball, for example, was one that she had already ordered from Bergdorf Goodman, and on her trip to France she wore a Givenchy design as a tribute to that country's couture genius—but she followed Cassini's basic vision. He continued to create most of her clothes throughout her entire White House years. Although Cassini has now retired from the couture business that bears his name, he maintains his celebrity status by making public appearances in such extravaganzas as *Night of 100 Stars*. He wrote an autobiography in 1987, entitled *In My Own Fashion*.

William Cavendish, Marquess of Hartington

William John Robert Cavendish, the Marquess of Hartington, was the eldest son and heir of the tenth Duke of Devonshire, one of the richest and most powerful men in England. Always

C

called Billy by his friends, he was educated first at Eton and then at Trinity College, Cambridge. Billy met Kathleen Kennedy at a garden party at Buckingham Palace in the summer of 1938, and they saw each other frequently until Ambassador Kennedy sent his family back to the safety of the United States in 1939, on the eve of World War II. Not completely sure of their feelings for one another, Billy and Kathleen corresponded, but they did not meet again until the summer of 1943, when she wangled a return to England with the American Red Cross.

Their reunion convinced them both that they were truly in love, but the problem of their religious differences loomed large. Billy's family had been Protestants (members of the Church of England) for centuries, and Kathleen's family did not want her to take a husband outside the Catholic Church. Finally, Kathleen decided she would marry without the Church's blessing, and the couple was wed at a registry office in London on May 6, 1944. On September 9 of that year, Billy was killed by a German sniper as he led his men across a field; according to reports, his last words were, "Come on, you fellows, buck up." He was buried where he fell, in Heppen, Belgium. A marker was later placed in his memory at the Devonshire family home, Chatsworth.

Vincent Celeste

Vincent Celeste was the Boston Republican who ran against Senator John F. Kennedy in the 1958 election in Massachusetts, when Kennedy sought to retain the Senate seat he had won six years earlier. Kennedy's resounding victory over Celeste, with more than 75 percent of the vote, was a positive factor for his presidential candidacy two years later.

Neville Chamberlain

Neville Chamberlain was the Prime Minister of Great Britain at the time Joseph P. Kennedy became the United States Ambassador to his country. The son of a previous Prime Minister and leader of the Conservative party, Chamberlain was deeply committed to the policy of appeasement as a way of dealing with the threat of Nazi domination of Europe. Ambassador Kennedy made a number of speeches and public statements in defense of Chamberlain's policy, and continued to support Chamberlain even after the Prime Minister's September 1938 meeting with Hitler, which some British politicians saw as a serious moral and political defeat for Great Britain. After signs of increasing brutality of the Nazis toward the Jews and the unexpected German invasion of Czechoslovakia, popular support for the policy of appeasement vanished, but Kennedy still wholeheartedly backed Chamberlain's efforts to avoid war by refusing to confront Hitler. When Germany invaded Poland in September 1939, Chamberlain had no choice but to declare war on Germany. It soon became clear that the country had little confidence in Chamberlain as a wartime leader, and he resigned in May 1940, to be succeeded as Prime Minister by Winston Churchill. Chamberlain died of cancer in the fall of that year. He was visited in the final days of his life by his friend, Joseph Kennedy.

C

Chappaquiddick

Chappaquiddick is an island off Martha's Vineyard. On the night of July 18, 1969, a 1967 Oldsmobile driven by Ted Kennedy went off Dyke Bridge near Chappaquiddick and sank in a shallow ocean-fed pond. A passenger, Mary Jo Kopechne, was drowned. The accepted facts about the incident are these. Kennedy and Kopechne had both attended a party, given for the young women who had been a part of the RFK election staff in 1968, at a cottage rented by Kennedy's cousin, Joe Gargan. After the accident, Kennedy returned to the party to get Gargan and another man, former U.S. Attorney Paul Markham. Kennedy was in the lobby of his motel in Edgartown, the largest town on the Vineyard, at 2:30 A.M., and thereafter went to his room to make seventeen phone calls. He did not report the accident to the police until later that day, after the body of Mary Jo Kopechne had been found.

Kennedy's own account of the matter was given to the police the following day. He described attending the party and then getting in his car to drive Miss Kopechne to the ferry that would take her to Edgartown.

On July 18, at approximately 11:15 P.M., I went over to Chappaquiddick. Later, I was driving my car on Main Street, Chappaquiddick, to get the ferry back to Edgartown. I was unfamiliar with the road and turned right onto Dyke Road instead of bearing hard left on Main Street. After proceeding for approximately half a mile on Dyke Road, I descended a hill and came upon a narrow bridge. The car went off the side of the bridge. There was one passenger with me, one Miss Mary, a former secretary of my brother, Senator Robert F. Kennedy. The car turned over and sank into the water, and landed with the roof resting on the bottom. I attempted to open the door and the window of the car, but had no recollection of how I got out of the car. I came to the surface and repeatedly dove down to the car in an attempt to see if the passenger was still in the car. I was unsuccessful in the attempt. I was exhausted and in a state of shock. I recall walking back to where my friends were eating. There was a car parked in front of the cottage and I climbed in the back seat. I then asked someone to bring me back to Edgartown. I remember walking around for a period of time and then going back to my hotel room. When I fully realized what had happened this morning, I immediately contacted the police.

There has, of course, been a great deal of speculation about what really happened that night at Chappaquiddick, but investigations by the police and the press have uncovered no further information. Senator Kennedy, along with his wife, his sister-in-law Mrs. Robert Kennedy, and family friend Lem Billings attended Mary Jo Kopechne's funeral in Pennsylvania. Shortly thereafter, Joan Kennedy suffered a miscarriage. Ted Kennedy pled guilty to the charge of leaving the scene of an accident and was given a suspended sentence of two months in jail. The parents of the dead girl admitted they had unanswered questions about what had happened the night of their daughter's death. Senator Kennedy went on national television to try to put a stop to the rumors swirling around the incident, saying he had no involvement with Mary Jo Kopechne but adding that his conduct on the night of the accident was indefensible. Chappaquiddick raised questions about the character of Edward M. Kennedy that still linger in the minds of some voters twenty years later.

Charlie

Charlie was the name of the Welsh terrier that was Caroline Kennedy's pet from the time she was a baby. Photos of Caroline and Charlie were a press favorite in the Kennedy White House years. Charlie was cared for by White House kennel keeper Traphes Bryant.

C

Children of Mary

The Children of Mary is a sodality of the Order of the Sacred Heart. Membership in the sodality is the highest honor a young Catholic girl can achieve, bestowed on her in recognition of her conquest of pride and self-will and her achievement of interior silence. Rose Fitzgerald became a Child of Mary on May 22, 1909, at the Blumenthal Convent of the Sacred Heart in Valle, Holland. One of her pledges at the time she received the honor was "to make the effort necessary to practice those family virtues suited to my position as daughter, wife, mother, such as kindness, gift of self, abnegation and evenness." Another of her pledges was "in the face of changes of fortune, to hold my soul free." For the rest of her life, Rose has done her best to honor those sacred pledges.

The Choate School

The Choate School was an elite preparatory school for boys where generations of upperclass members of the Eastern establishment sent their sons before they went on to college at Harvard or Yale or Princeton. Choate was founded in 1896 by Episcopalian Judge William G. Choate, who modeled the school after England's Eton. To give his older sons every social and educational advantage, Joseph P. Kennedy enrolled them in Choate, located at Wallingford, in the heart of Connecticut's rolling hill country. Joe Junior went in 1928 and Jack followed in 1931. Although academic studies came hard to Joe, he worked diligently and achieved a fine record at Choate, winning the Harvard Trophy given to the boy who best combined scholarship and athletic excellence. Young Jack was a lazier student, albeit a more natural one, and didn't equal his older brother's academic record. He was also a less able athlete, due to his smaller size and frequent illnesses, and there too he found himself in his brother's shadow. Jack Kennedy graduated from Choate in 1933. Nearly thirty years later, when John F. Kennedy became President of the United States, the school unveiled his portrait, calling him Choate's most distinguished alumnus. Kennedy wryly observed, "This is the most ironic celebration of which I have ever heard." Today, the school is coeducational, having merged with a girls' school, and is called Choate Rosemary Hall. Despite the President's ties to the school, Choate has not been a popular choice with the next generation of the Kennedy family.

Winston Churchill

Winston Churchill, the great leader of the Conservative party, was the second Prime Minister of Great Britain in office during the time Joseph P. Kennedy was Ambassador to the Court of St. James. Churchill became Prime Minister in early May 1940, when his party lost faith in its previous leader, Neville Chamberlain. Churchill had insisted all along that Great Britain would have to go to war with Germany, and he also believed strongly that Great Britain could win the war, no matter how daunting the task initially appeared. His bellicose sentiments and deep commitment to winning the war at any cost were incompatible with the personal views of

C

Joe Kennedy, who felt that Great Britain had little chance of winning the war and believed that trying to fight it would bring an unacceptable level of loss of life and unaffordable expense. Kennedy had fully supported Chamberlain's policy of appeasement, and he subsequently espoused an isolationist point of view that tried to keep the United States out of the war. The lack of rapport between Churchill and Kennedy made Kennedy an ineffective ambassador, and President Roosevelt began to conduct foreign policy through other intermediaries. The situation culminated in Kennedy's resignation in February 1941.

Citizens Energy Corporation

The Citizens Energy Corporation was founded by RFK's son Joseph P. Kennedy II in 1979. The Massachusetts-based organization, with offices in Boston across the street from the Massachusetts State House, supplies inexpensive heating oil to poor families and provides funds for landlords to insulate rental housing to hold down fuel costs to tenants; it also offers research grants to foreign countries that are developing new energy resources and refineries. Commented Joe, "Citizens Energy is unique in that the assistance it provides is made possible solely through its own business activities in the oil industry. Over the years, we have become a respected participant in all sectors of the complex oil industry, conducting business on three continents." Joe served as the president of Citizens Energy until his election to Congress in 1986. At that time, his place was taken by his younger brother Michael.

"Cocky Tom"

Thomas Fitzgerald, the grandfather of Rose Fitzgerald Kennedy and first of the family to reach the New World, was nicknamed "Cocky Tom" because of having a cocked (or crossed) eye.

Cohasset Golf Club

In 1922, Joseph P. Kennedy, then a prosperous stockbroker at Hayden, Stone and Company, rented a summer house for his family at Cohasset, Massachusetts, where many of his old friends from Harvard as well as his current business associates also summered. In what he assumed would be a routine action, Kennedy applied to the Cohasset Golf Club for a summer membership, so he could play golf there with his friends. To his embarrassment and chagrin, he was rejected because of his Irish Catholic background. That event probably brought about the end of Joe Kennedy's attachment to Boston as a place to live and work. Within a few years, he had moved his base of operations to New York and subsequently bought a family home in the prosperous New York City suburb of Bronxville.

C

Roy Cohn

Roy Cohn was an attorney with a flamboyant career who was for many years an adversary of Robert F. Kennedy. Cohn, born in New York City in 1927, graduated from Columbia University in that city before he was twenty, and then got his law degree from the same institution after World War II. He worked with the U.S. Attorney's office in Manhattan, where one of his assignments was to assist in the prosecution of the notorious Rosenberg spy case. The success of that effort, which saw both Rosenbergs convicted and sentenced to death, gave him a reputation for getting results.

Roy Cohn was hired in 1953 by Senator Joseph McCarthy to act as chief counsel for the Senate Subcommittee on Investigations and thus was Robert F. Kennedy's boss for a time. Cohn and Kennedy clashed from the very beginning of their working relationship, with the result that Kennedy soon resigned his position. Later, when RFK accepted the position of counsel to the Democratic minority on the subcommittee, he and Cohn became open adversaries. At one point during the Army-McCarthy hearings, the two men nearly got into a fist fight. Cohn protested that it was unfair for Kennedy to work in the hearings because of his "hatred for one of the principals," a reference to himself. Kennedy answered that if he had a dislike for anyone in the case, it was certainly justified. Kennedy then told the press that Cohn had threatened to "get" Senator Henry Jackson, a Democratic member of the subcommittee and friend of the Kennedys, by claiming that Jackson had written something favorable toward the Communists. Cohn denied that he had made any such threat.

After the hearings were concluded, leaving Cohn's reputation somewhat tarnished, he left public life and returned to his native New York to go into private practice. He wrote best-selling books, won awards, and acted on behalf of such famous clients as Donald Trump, Bianca Jagger, and Mafia don Carmine Galante; it was rumored that Aristotle Onassis consulted Cohn about a divorce from his second wife, Jacqueline Bouvier Kennedy Onassis. Cohn was also engaged in a long-running fight with the IRS and owned almost nothing under his own name. Roy Cohn died in 1987, apparently due to AIDS. The end of his life had been clouded by his troubles with the IRS, hints of criminal wrongdoing, disbarment, and the hostility of Washington and New York socialites whom he had once counted as good friends.

Columbia Trust Company

The Columbia Trust Company was a small bank in East Boston of which P. J. Kennedy had been one of the founders in 1892. His son, Joseph Kennedy, had run errands for the bank in his childhood, and he went to work there in 1912, as soon as he graduated from Harvard, as a clerk for the treasurer, Alfred Wellington. In less than a year, he left the job at Columbia Trust for the broader experience of a brief stint in the civil service as a Massachusetts bank examiner. In 1914, Joe stepped in on his father's behalf and waged a proxy fight to defend the Columbia Trust against a hostile takeover by the First Ward National. The result was that twenty-five-year-old Joseph P. Kennedy became the president of the bank. His father then resigned as vice-president, and Joe's former mentor Alfred Wellington became his subordinate in the posts of treasurer and vice-president. Joe Kennedy ceased to take an active role in the management of the bank when he went to work at Bethlehem Steel's shipyard during World War I. In

1946, the Columbia Trust Company was sold to Boston's Shawmut Bank for slightly more than five hundred thousand dollars. The Kennedys were still the principal stockholders of the small bank.

Concord Academy

The Concord Academy, in Concord, Massachusetts, was the boarding school attended by Caroline Kennedy for four years. Her graduation from Concord Academy on June 5, 1975, was attended by her mother, her grandmothers Rose Kennedy and Janet Auchincloss, her brother John, and her uncle, Senator Edward M. Kennedy.

Conspiracy Theories

Immediately after the death of President John F. Kennedy, the publication of various conspiracy theories surrounding his assassination began, and time has licensed even greater elaboration. Each theory has its partisans, along with some evidence that seems to point in that particular direction. Among the most frequently discussed conspiracy theories:

- the murder of JFK was arranged by Fidel Castro, in retaliation for the President's agreement to CIA plans to assassinate the Cuban leader
- JFK's assassination was an act of Mafia vengeance, because the Kennedy administration was coming down too hard on organized crime
- the planner of JFK's assassination was New Orleans Mafia figure Carlos Marcello, trying to stop Attorney-General Robert F. Kennedy's attempts to deport Marcello
- the CIA was responsible for the murder of JFK, whom they feared would limit their powers and no longer back their plans for such actions as the Bay of Pigs invasions
- the Teamsters were behind the assassination of JFK, because of the anti-union activities of the Attorney-General and Jimmy Hoffa's feud with the Kennedys

- Vice-President Lyndon B. Johnson, backed by a group of ruthless Texas oilmen, was the one who instigated the assassination of the President, so that Johnson would become President, and policies more favorable to Texas oil could be enacted.

The physical evidence in the Kennedy assassination, as well as that related to the subsequent murder of Lee Harvey Oswald, is constantly being resifted in order to arrive at "final proof." The troubling elements of the evidence—or lack thereof—include the absence of any record of Oswald's interrogation; the lack of test evidence that Oswald had recently fired a rifle; the disappearance of certain records regarding the autopsy of President Kennedy, and the disappearance of the tissues of the President's brain, which might have proved beyond a shadow of a doubt which way the bullet came from; and the switch of coffins for the President, apparently between Dallas and Washington.

As the twenty-fifth anniversary of the assassination indicated, interest in conspiracy theories about the death of President Kennedy continues unabated.

C

Coronation of Pope Pius XII

Eugenio Cardinal Pacelli was elected Pope in early 1939, after the death of Pope Pius XI. He took the name of Pius XII and set the date of March 12, 1939, for his coronation. Since the Italian Cardinal had been a guest at the Kennedy home in Bronxville, New York, several years earlier, President Franklin Roosevelt decided to send Ambassador Joseph P. Kennedy to the papal coronation as his personal representative. Kennedy, then at the London embassy, took his wife and all his children, with the exception of Joe Junior, who was in Spain observing the Civil War. The Kennedys had front row seats for the impressive pageant, sitting directly before the altar when the new Pope conducted his first mass. The following day, the family was granted a private audience with the Pope, and a few days later, the Pope officiated at seven-year-old Teddy's first communion.

Correspondence Between Kennedy and Khrushchev

After the summit meeting in 1961, President John F. Kennedy and Russian Premier Nikita Khrushchev began a correspondence that continued regularly until Kennedy's death. The cor-

President Kennedy at the Vienna Summit with Premier Khrushchev. (Courtesy of the Kennedy Library)

C

respondence, not yet made public, is credited with helping to ease tensions between the two superpowers and contributing to the peaceful outcome of the 1962 Cuban missile crisis.

Countess Kennedy

In 1952, Rose Kennedy was made a Papal Countess by Pope Pius XII, whom she had known as Eugenio Cardinal Pacelli and entertained in 1936 for tea at her home in Bronxville, New York, during the Cardinal's American visit. The scroll conferring the honor was delivered to her by Francis Cardinal Spellman, and cited her exemplary life and many charities. Mrs. Kennedy's first public statement after learning of the honor (held by only two other American women) was, "I am overwhelmed by emotion and happiness. My first emotion is to feel that I am not worthy of something like this." Thereafter Rose was entitled to sign her name as "Countess Rose Kennedy"—and often did in European guest books.

Crimson "H"

All the sons of Joseph P. Kennedy were encouraged to excel in sports, and most of all they wanted to win Harvard University's coveted crimson "H" in football, awarded only to players who participated in the annual game against Yale. Joe Junior had made the varsity team but was not sent in to play during the Yale game, leaving his father in a rage and vowing never to contribute another penny to his alma mater. Jack was really too light and frail to be a good football player, but he also tried to win his letter, and also failed. It was Bobby Kennedy who finally achieved the distinction that had eluded his older brothers. Although he was very small for a football player, Bobby played with almost suicidal intensity; his coach later said, "You'd have to kill him to make him quit." Bobby was thus given the chance to go in as a substitute for one play during the Yale game in his senior year. That was all it took to win the right to wear the crimson "H."

Walter Cronkite

Walter Cronkite, the veteran news anchor for CBS, was the steady presence to whom millions of Americans turned for coverage of the events of President John F. Kennedy's assassination and last rites. For four days, uninterrupted by commercials or other programming, Cronkite presided over CBS reportage of the national tragedy, bringing the country closer together as he shared his own feelings with his viewers. The moment many viewers still recall is the six-second pause, during which Cronkite removed his glasses and cleared his throat as he fought to retain his composure, after his somber announcement of the President's death. Cronkite, who was later named in public opinion polls as the "most trusted man in America," showed us that even newsmen can shed tears over so significant a loss.

C

Cuban Missile Crisis

By October 1962, the U.S. government intelligence sources had collected incontrovertible evidence of a build-up by Russian forces on the island of Cuba. Aerial photos showed missile sites, and subsequent serial surveillance revealed missiles on Russian ships heading toward Cuban ports. With the agreement of his Cabinet, President Kennedy decided to make a measured response to the provocation. The U.S. announced a blockade of Cuban ports, to prevent the missiles from reaching their destination. While American vessels steamed to the area to intercept the Soviet ships, Kennedy called Khrushchev and urged the Russian Premier to reconsider his course. After a period of great tension throughout the world, the Russian ships allowed themselves to be peacefully turned back, and soon thereafter, the Cubans dismantled the bases that had been prepared for the nuclear missiles.

The President takes time for a walk with his son.
(Courtesy of the Kennedy Library)

C

James Michael Curley

James Michael Curley was a consummate politician who was an opponent of John Fitzgerald in Massachusetts politics. Nicknamed the "Purple Shamrock," Curley started out as a member of Boston's Common Council, was elected to the state legislature, and was elected to the Board of Aldermen while he was serving sixty days in jail for taking a civil service exam for a friend. After serving a term as a Massachusetts congressman, Curley decided to run for the office of Boston's mayor in 1913. Fitzgerald ran against him, but was forced to withdraw by Curley's threats to make public Fitzgerald's relationship with an entertainer in a saloon.

Decades later, Curley was to cast a momentary shadow on the career of John Fitzgerald's grandson, John F. Kennedy. When Kennedy was a congressman from Massachusetts, Curley—then serving his fourth term as the mayor of Boston—was found guilty of using the mail to defraud, and sentenced to a short term in federal prison.

Curley's supporters organized a petition to request clemency, on the grounds that at the age of seventy-two he was too old and ill to survive the ordeal of imprisonment. Jack Kennedy was asked to sign the petition, backed by nearly one-quarter of the voters in his district, and after careful consideration, declined. He was the only member of Congress from Massachusetts whose name was not on the petition. At the time, veteran political observers predicted that the action meant the end of Kennedy's political career. But when Curley's sentence was finally commuted by President Truman and he returned home in the best of health to indulge in a mammoth celebration, public opinion changed and Jack Kennedy's stand appeared courageous and morally correct.

Curley was the model for the protagonist of the best-selling political novel by Edwin O'Connor, *The Last Hurrah*. The movie version starred Spencer Tracy as the Curley character.

The Curragh

The *Curragh* is the fifty-five-foot sailboat owned by Senator Edward Kennedy and usually docked at Hyannis Port. He often takes the *Curragh* out on Nantucket Sound for an afternoon, with friends and family aboard to share the fun.

D

Danceuse

The young Jacqueline Bouvier was a skilled rider, and she had her own horse, a mare named Danceuse. The chestnut mare was a highly trained show horse that had previously belonged to Jackie's mother. In the summer, Danceuse was stabled in East Hampton, in the winter at Durland's on Manhattan's West 66 Street. When Jacqueline went away to prep school, Danceuse went with her.

Marion Davies

Marion Davies was the actress with whom publisher William Randolph Hearst had a long-standing liaison that was tantamount to a marriage. Through his consulting work for Hearst, Joseph P. Kennedy had become acquainted with Davies, and during the 1960 Democratic convention in Los Angeles, he and Rose were guests at her house, which put Joe close to the action at the convention hall but out of sight of the press. According to a story told by Frank Saunders, Joe Kennedy's chauffeur, a framed picture of Marion Davies was always on Joe's bedside table.

Meyer Davis

As far back as the 1920s, Meyer Davis and his orchestra were a feature of many important so-cial events all over the country. The Kennedys were no exception to the rule that a good society party required music by Meyer Davis. He played at the 1927 wedding of John V. Bouvier III and Janet Lee, and then a generation later, at the wedding of their daughter Jacqueline to John F. Kennedy. Meyer Davis was also asked to play at President Kennedy's Inaugural Ball.

The Day Caroline Stole the Show

President-elect Kennedy held a number of press conferences in the period between his election and his inauguration, to discuss key appointments and policies of his new Administration. At one of them, his pajama-clad daughter Caroline stole the show when she suddenly walked out on the patio of the Kennedy house in Palm Beach in a pair of her mother's high heels and said, "I want my daddy."

The Day John F. Kennedy Decided to Become President

According to accounts subsequently made public by Kennedy friends and family members, the day that John F. Kennedy decided he would run for the office of President can be pinpointed exactly. It was Thanksgiving, November 25, 1956, the year that Jack had almost won the vice-presidential nomination at the Democratic convention. The family was assembled for the traditional celebration at the compound in Hyannis Port. After dinner, Jack and his father went into a small study and debated the question of whether he should run for President in the next election, 1960. Jack listed all the reasons against it, and Joseph P. Kennedy countered every one with a reason to reach a positive decision. When they emerged, the decision that John F. Kennedy would run for the presidency had been made—although it was not officially announced until more than three years later, on January 20, 1960.

The Dearos

When John F. Fitzgerald was active in Boston politics, he always tried to please the crowd by referring to the Irish section of Boston as the "dear old North End." President Kennedy's grandfather repeated the phrase so frequently his supporters became known as "the dearos."

Death of a President

William Manchester, who had already written an adulatory biography of John F. Kennedy called *Portrait of a President*, was selected by the Kennedy family to write an authorized account of

D

the assassination of the President, to be entitled *Death of a President*. Manchester began his work about a month after the tragedy in Dallas, and he received full cooperation from the family, including lengthy interviews with the President's widow. Reportedly, Mrs. Kennedy had agreed to the project in the hope of forestalling other writers, such as Jim Bishop, from doing the same thing, less tastefully. She talked to Manchester fully and frankly, in the days after the assassination when her own emotions were still desperately painful.

Mrs. Kennedy's candor was probably a mistake, because when she saw the manuscript she was horrified by the appearance of remarks she had not intended for publication. Moreover, she was distressed to learn that excerpts of the book would be sold to *Look* and that Manchester would earn $665,000 from that one sale alone. Jacqueline Kennedy filed suit against Manchester and his publishers, Harper and Row, to block publication of the book. Robert Kennedy tried to protect his sister-in-law by supporting her in her fight to suppress the book. Jackie's friend Pete Hamill later commented, "RFK didn't really believe that Mrs. Kennedy's objections were worth the trouble, but she was his brother's widow—and the Kennedys have nothing if they do not have a ferocious sense of family loyalty."

In the end, Manchester made a few minor changes to remove the passages that most offended Mrs. Kennedy, and *Death of a President* became an international best-seller. Many people criticized the Kennedys for their actions in trying to halt publication of the book, which were characterized as an attempt at censorship, but the affair was eventually forgotten. The book, however, has become a classic, and in 1988, on the twenty-fifth anniversary of the assassination, it was reissued to reach a new generation of readers.

Debut of Jacqueline Lee Bouvier

Jacqueline Lee Bouvier was presented to society in two separate events during the summer of 1947. The first was a reception for 300 people at Hammersmith Farm in Newport, the home of her mother and stepfather, Hugh and Janet Auchincloss; the same party also served to celebrate the christening of Jackie's young half-brother, Jamie Auchincloss.

The second party for Jacqueline's debut was a formal dinner dance the following month, at Newport's posh Clambake Club. Later that season, Hearst newspaper columnist Igor Cassini, in his syndicated "Cholly Knickerbocker" column, named Jacqueline "Debutante of the Year," calling her "a regal brunette who has classic features and the daintiness of Dresden porcelain."

Debut of Rose Fitzgerald

Rose Fitzgerald was officially presented to Boston society on January 2, 1911, at a party held in her parents' rambling white house at 39 Welles Avenue in the Dorchester section of the city. The daughter of Boston's mayor wore not a single piece of jewelry to adorn her simple gown of white chiffon trimmed with yellow silk ribbon threaded through the hem—just a simple ribbon in her hair. Rose carried a sweet corsage of violets and lilies-of-the-valley. Her mother was a total contrast in a sophisticated gown trimmed with bands of black Chantilly

D

lace. The Fitzgerald house had been transformed into a bower of roses, and the young people at the party (one of whom was Rose's suitor Joseph Kennedy) went upstairs for a sit-down dinner. Many of the 450 guests were struck by the debutante's natural beauty, her direct and friendly manner, and her air of great self-possession.

Debut of Kathleen Kennedy

On April 7, 1938, Ambassador and Mrs. Joseph P. Kennedy introduced their daughter, Kathleen, to London society in a reception at the Dartmouth House.

Debut of Rosemary and Kathleen Kennedy

On June 2, 1938, Rosemary and Kathleen Kennedy made their debut at a ball given at the U.S. Embassy in London. Although Kathleen had already been honored with an afternoon reception that April, Rosemary has missed the earlier occasion, and it was customary for families of debutantes to host more than one affair during the season. More than three hundred guests danced the night away to the music of an English swing band, and the pretty and high-spirited Kathleen became one of the leading debs of the season. Rosemary, whose dancing partners were recruited for her by her sister and brothers, soon retreated to the quiet life at the Montessori school she attended outside London.

Decisions for a Decade

In March 1968, Doubleday published a book by Senator Edward M. Kennedy entitled *Decisions for a Decade: Policies and Programs for the 1970s*. The book critiqued past governmental policies and suggested new directions the government must take in the coming decade.

Democratic Convention of 1940

In the Presidential election year of 1940, Joseph P. Kennedy, Jr., then a student at Harvard Law School, accepted the suggestion of his grandfather, Boston politician John F. Fitzgerald, and decided to run for the position of Massachusetts delegate to the Democratic presidential convention. He campaigned vigorously throughout the district he wanted to represent, and came in a respectable second in the balloting, which gave him a seat at the convention held in Chicago that July. At the time Joe Junior had been elected a delegate, President Franklin D. Roosevelt had not yet announced whether he intended to run for a third term. Joe, like most of the Massachusetts delegation, was pledged to support the Presidential candidacy of Postmaster General

D

James Farley. By the time of the convention, Roosevelt had made the decision to seek a third term, and the Democratic National Committee promptly put pressure on all delegates to make the President's endorsement unanimous. After thinking the matter over, and asking his father (then the United States Ambassador to Great Britain) for his opinion, Joe opted to honor his campaign pledge and cast his vote for Farley. After the first ballot, Farley released his handful of delegates to support Roosevelt, and Joe then voted for the President. Afterward, many observers were impressed by the young Kennedy's political courage under fire. Farley himself sent a cable to Joseph P. Kennedy in London: "I WILL EVER BE GRATEFUL TO YOUR SON JOE FOR HIS MANLY AND COURAGEOUS STAND AT LAST NIGHT'S CONVENTION." The convention confirmed Joe's belief in his son's bright future in politics.

Democratic Convention of 1956

The Democratic Convention for the presidential election of 1956 was held in Chicago in the stifling heat of mid-August. The convention opened with a film on the history of the Democratic Party, narrated by Massachusetts Senator John F. Kennedy. The eleven thousand delegates quickly selected Adlai E. Stevenson of Illinois as their candidate for President; at Stevenson's request, the nomination speech was made by Senator Kennedy, who called Stevenson "a man equal to our times." Said Kennedy, "The nominee of the convention must be something more than just a good candidate, a good politician, a good conservative or a good liberal, since he may guide the destiny of not only the country but the free world."

Stevenson subsequently took the highly unusual step of asking the convention to select his running mate by popular vote. It turned out that the unexpected contest was between Senators Estes Kefauver of Tennessee and John Kennedy of Massachusetts. The first ballot showed Kefauver with 483 votes, Kennedy with 304; on the second ballot, Kefauver had 755 to Kennedy's 589. On the third ballot, Kefauver pulled ahead and Kennedy made a graceful concession speech, thanking the convention for its generosity and kindness toward him, and moving to nominate Kefauver by acclamation. The Stevenson-Kefauver ticket thus selected lost decisively in the November election to Eisenhower and Nixon.

Democratic Convention of 1960

The 1960 Democratic Convention took place in Los Angeles, in the sweltering heat of mid-July. Most of the Kennedy family stayed at the convention headquarters, but Ambassador Joseph P. Kennedy rented the home of Marion Davies, the consort of his late friend William Randolph Hearst, and stayed out of the public eye for those last few days of hectic political maneuvering. John F. Kennedy's name was placed in nomination by Governor Orville Freeman of Minnesota; Kennedy's chief opponent was Senate Majority Leader Lyndon Johnson, nominated by the Speaker of the House, Sam Rayburn. Johnson had used the opening days of the convention to criticize Kennedy sharply; Kennedy, with his usual light irony, told the delegates, "I come here today full of admiration for Senator Johnson, full of affection

D

for him, strongly in support of him—for majority leader of the United States Senate."

The first ballot brought John F. Kennedy the nomination, by a vote of 806 to 409 ballots. The following day, overriding the advice of many of his staff, Kennedy asked Johnson to be his running mate. The convention closed with a speech by Kennedy asking his party to help the country make the sacrifices necessary to move to a New Frontier. His wife Jacqueline did not attend the convention because of her pregnancy, but watched on television from their home in Hyannis Port and told the press she was very excited by her husband's nomination.

Democratic Convention of 1964

In 1964, it was clear that the Democratic candidate for President would be the incumbent Lyndon B. Johnson. The big question was who would be selected as his running mate. Initial speculation centered around Attorney General Robert F. Kennedy. Many in the party felt he would be an ideal vice-presidential candidate, but by the end of July, Johnson had decided against such a choice, because he felt he was politically strong enough to win the election without the help of the former President's brother; no love was lost between Johnson and Kennedy. Johnson knew that a film celebrating the accomplishments of President Kennedy would be shown at the convention, and that the President's widow, Jacqueline, might decide to attend, and he feared that an uncontrollable tide of emotion might sweep the President's brother onto the ticket. Thus he told RFK before the convention that he would not select him as a running mate, and in a television address a few days later, announced that no member of the Cabinet would be considered for the vice-presidency. Bob later told the other Cabinet members, "I'm sorry I took so many good men over the side with me." President Johnson's caution was justified, for at the convention, Robert F. Kennedy was given an emotional twenty-two minute standing ovation.

Democratic Convention of 1988

At the Democratic Convention of 1988, which nominated Governor Michael Dukakis of Massachusetts as its presidential candidate, one of the highlights was the brief speech by John F. Kennedy, Jr., introducing his uncle, Senator Edward M. Kennedy, as a featured convention speaker. John told the delegates, "So many of you have entered public service because of my father. Because of you, he is in a sense still with us, and for that I thank you." It was a moving movement that brought thunderous applause.

Devotion School

The two oldest sons of Joseph and Rose Kennedy, Joe Junior and Jack, started their educations at a public elementary school near their Brookline home. It was called Devotion School, so named in honor of a rich benefactor of Brookline, Edward Devotion. Jack Kennedy was enrolled in September 12, 1922, for kindergarten and also attended first grade there.

D

Devotion to the President

President John F. Kennedy greatly appreciated the devotion of his longtime secretary, Evelyn Lincoln. Once he joked, "If I had said to her, 'Mrs. Lincoln, I have just cut off Jackie's head, would you send over a box?' she would have replied, 'That's wonderful, Mr. President. I'll send it right away. Did you get your nap?'"

Dexter School

The Dexter School was a country day school, established in 1892 and originally the lower school of the prestigious Noble and Greenough Preparatory School, near the Kennedy home in Brookline, Massachusetts, where Joseph P. Kennedy enrolled his two oldest sons in 1924, in preference to a parochial school. Joe Junior and Jack were probably the only Catholic boys in the prestigious elementary school, which provided early education to members of such socially prominent Bostonian families as the Appletons and the Saltonstalls. Jack Kennedy attended Dexter for grades two, three, and four.

Angie Dickinson

Rumors have long circulated about an affair between President John F. Kennedy and the beautiful blonde actress Angie Dickinson, who was born into a Catholic family in North Dakota on September 30, 1932. Dickinson met members of the Kennedy family, including Jack, at a party at the Lawfords' house just before the Democratic Convention of 1960, in Los Angeles. Thereafter, she made appearances on behalf of the Kennedy campaign, attended the Inauguration, visited Hickory Hill, and went to the races at Hialeah with Joseph P. Kennedy; she and her then-husband, popular composer Burt Bacharach, were members of the Kennedy family circle. Long evasive about the exact nature of her relationship with the President, Dickinson wrote a 1975 article for *Ladies' Home Journal* in which she did finally go on record to deny the rumors. Then she added confusingly, "Jack Ken-

Angie Dickinson. (Movie Star News)

nedy was the most exciting man in the world at the time I knew him. And to hear that I was having a romance with him is, of course, flatter-ing. It was never rumored that he was in love with me, but Jack made no bones about the fact that he appreciated beautiful girls."

C. Douglas Dillon

C. Douglas Dillon was the secretary of the treasury in the Kennedy administration. He was in fact a Republican who had served in the Eisenhower administration as under secretary of state and donated large sums of money to Republican campaigns, including that of the candidate Kennedy defeated, Richard Nixon. Dillon, fifty-one years old at the time of his Cabinet appointment, came from a family that owned the investment banking firm of Dillon Read. He was a Harvard graduate with close ties to Wall Street but a pragmatic approach to fiscal policy. His willingness to become part of the team impressed both John F. and Robert Kennedy. Douglas Dillon was to become a Kennedy insider, so close to the family that Robert Kennedy named one of his sons after him.

Dinner at Mount Vernon

One of the most celebrated official entertainments of the Kennedy presidency took place in the summer of 1961, when President and Mrs. Kennedy hosted a dinner for the President of Pakistan, General Ayub Khan. It was decided to hold the dinner party at Mount Vernon, the home of America's first President, George Washington. The affair required very careful planning. One hundred and fifty guests had to be transported down the Potomac River from Washington, the food had to be prepared in the White House kitchens and driven to Mount Vernon in Army trucks, tents were erected to protect the guests from rain and wind, the grounds were sprayed to reduce the insect population, and portable toilets were concealed behind big trees in the yard. A few days before the party, Mrs. Kennedy toured Mount Vernon with White House Chief Usher J. B. West. "I suppose you're going to go back and jump off the White House roof," she teased. "No," he replied loyally, "not until the day after the dinner."

The state occasion began with mint juleps served in silver cups on the veranda of Mount Vernon, the same hospitality offered their guests by George and Martha Washington, and continued with a military drill by troops dressed in colonial uniforms. Dinner, served under a huge yellow tent, consisted of avocados stuffed with Maryland crabmeat, chicken and mushrooms served in a rice ring, and fresh raspberries. Afterward, the National Symphony Orchestra performed, before guests reboarded the boats for the return trip to Washington. The much-photographed Jacqueline Kennedy was wearing a white organza and lace gown designed by Oleg Cassini, with a pistachio-green satin sash, and wore her hair up with a big diamond ornament in the center.

D

Dinner for the King and Queen

One of the especially memorable events of Joseph P. Kennedy's tenure as American ambassador to Great Britain was the dinner party he and his wife, Rose, gave at the American embassy on May 4, 1939, for King George VI and Queen Elizabeth of England. After the embassy was checked for safety by Scotland Yard, the tables were decorated with orchids flown in from Paris and the best china and silver set out for the occasion. A photo of Rose Kennedy taken before the arrival of the royal guests shows her in a tiara and a white gown trimmed with silver sequins. All the Kennedy children were assembled to greet the King and Queen, and then the party went in to dinner, which featured fillet of sole and American strawberry shortcake for dessert.

Waiting for the King and Queen, left to right: *Rose, Teddy, Rosemary, Joe Jr., Joe Sr., Eunice, Jean, Jack, Bobby, Pat, Kathleen. (Courtesy of the Kennedy Library)*

D

Doggerel

During the 1960 Presidential campaign, some unidentified Republican came up with a bit of doggerel that sniped at the Kennedy family:

*Jack and Bob will run the show
While Ted's in charge of hiding Joe.*

Doll Collection

Over the years, Rose Kennedy amassed a large doll collection, which was kept on display in the basement of her Hyannis Port house. Rose, an inveterate traveler, picked up the dolls as souvenirs of the foreign countries she visited.

The collection began as a way to interest the children in learning about other countries, but even after the children were grown, Rose continued to bring home the beautifully dressed dolls.

Luella Hennessy Donovan

Luella Hennessy Donovan is a registered nurse who has been associated with the Kennedy family for decades. The young Luella Hennessy was hired by Joseph P. Kennedy in 1937 when the Kennedys' youngest child (Teddy) was five. One of her first major responsibilities was looking after the seasick Kennedy children when they traveled to London the following spring to join their father, the new U.S. envoy, at the American Embassy.

Scarcely was the youngest Kennedy grown than the first of the next generation began to arrive. Luella Hennessy went to the home of Robert and Ethel Kennedy to care for the first grandchild of Rose and Joe Kennedy, young Kathleen Kennedy, born on the Fourth of July, 1951, and thereafter she served as nurse for twenty-eight of the twenty-nine Kennedy grandchildren. Luella later married and then became the director of the Kennedy-Donovan Center, a treatment facility for handicapped youths and adults financed by the Lt. Joseph P. Kennedy, Jr. Foundation.

William O. Douglas

William O. Douglas was a former professor at Yale Law School who worked in Washington during the 1930s and met Joseph P. Kennedy, who marked him down as an able man. In 1937, when Kennedy's successor as chairman of the Securities and Exchange Commission resigned, Douglas had hoped to be appointed in his place, but Wall Street put up strong opposition and it seemed that President Roosevelt was reluctant to make the appointment. The discouraged Douglas decided to return to teaching at Yale and was ready to catch a train for New Haven when he got a call from Joe Kennedy suggesting that Douglas should sit by the telephone and wait to hear from the President. Later that day, the call came, and Douglas became chairman of the SEC. Within a year and a half, Roosevelt appointed him to the Supreme Court. Douglas always felt gratitude for the actions of Joe Kennedy in helping to secure him the SEC post. He remained a friend and supporter of the Kennedys for the rest of his life.

Morton Downey

Famed Irish tenor Morton Downey was a close friend of Joseph and Rose Kennedy. Like the Kennedys, Downey had a winter home in Palm Beach. Downey sang at the wedding reception of Jack and Jacqueline Kennedy, and Rose Kennedy always loved his rendition of "My Wild Irish Rose." To please her, he often sang her father's old campaign song, "Sweet Adeline." His son is the controversial TV talk-show host, Morton Downey, Jr.

Duke of Devonshire

The tenth Duke of Devonshire was Edward William Spencer Cavendish, who inherited the title in 1938, only months before the Kennedy family arrived in London when Joseph P. Kennedy became Ambassador to the Court of St. James. The Duke was married to Lady Mary Alice Gascoyne-Cecil, and their eldest son was William Cavendish, the Marquess of Hartington, who married Kathleen Kennedy in 1944. Among the houses owned by the Devonshire family were Chatsworth, the 150-acre estate in Derbyshire; Holker Hall in Lancashire; Lismore Castle in Ireland; a villa at Chiswick, outside London; Bolton Abbey in Yorkshire; and Churchdale and Hardwick Halls, both in Derbyshire. The Duke's younger brother Charles married Adele Astaire, the sister and first dancing partner of Fred. The tenth Duke was the head of the Freemasons in England, an organization with an anti-Catholic bias. After the tenth Duke's death, the title went to Billy's younger brother Andrew, who married one of the Mitford sisters, Deborah.

Eaton Place

The London residence of the tenth Duke and Duchess of Devonshire, the in-laws of Kathleen Kennedy, was in Eaton Place, known to fans of *Upstairs, Downstairs* as the site of the Bellamy household.

Peter Edelman

Peter Edelman was a member of Senator Robert F. Kennedy's staff. A native of Minnesota, he had attended Harvard Law School and worked as a clerk for Justice Arthur Goldberg before he joined the team at the Justice Department when Kennedy was attorney general. Edelman was the staff member who drafted the bills Kennedy introduced in the Senate, and later helped him write the position papers he used as a candidate for President in 1968. Today, Edelman teaches law at Georgetown University.

Editorial Career

In September 1975, Jacqueline Kennedy Onassis became a working woman when she embarked on a career as an editor. Her first job was at Viking Press, as a two-hundred-dollar-a-week editorial consultant. The association ended when the firm published a novel, set in the future, that involved the assassination of Edward M. Kennedy. It was called *Shall We Tell the President*, and was written by Jeffrey Archer. Mrs. Onassis felt that the publishers had attempted to counter criticism of the novel by implying that she had approved its content, and so she resigned.

In 1978, Mrs. Onassis joined Doubleday Books as a hands-on editor. Among the books she has signed and seen to publication are *Call the Darkness Light*, a serious novel about the plight of women workers in the textile mills of Lowell, Massachusetts; *In the Russian Style*, a handsome illustrated book featuring Russian furniture, art, and costume, on which she worked with the Metropolitan Museum of Art's Walter Hoving; *Dancing on My Grave*, by ballerina Gelsey Kirkland; and *Moonwalk*, the autobiographical best-seller by pop star Michael Jackson. Mrs. Onassis has an office in the Doubleday building on Fifth Avenue, and attends regular editorial meetings. One of her editorial colleagues is quoted as saying, "She is a serious professional in every way. She arrives a tad after 9:30 A.M., about the same time as the other editors, and works on a full load of manuscripts." In 1988, she received her first raise. Her current salary is estimated to be about $45,000 a year.

"Edward M. Kennedy Foundation"

During Edward Kennedy's first campaign for the Senate, in 1962, he realized he would be vulnerable to charges that his only qualification was his relationship to the President. Early in the campaign, one of his opponents taunted him by jokingly proposing the creation of an Edward M. Kennedy Foundation, "to benefit wealthy and undeserving young men who want to start at the top." Ted was able to weather such criticism and win the Senate seat.

83 Beals Street

After Joseph P. Kennedy married Rose Fitzgerald in 1914, he took his new bride to the home he had just purchased, a modest gray frame house in Brookline, a middle-class suburb of Boston. The seven-room house (plus two more tiny rooms in the attic for live-in help) cost $6,500, of which Kennedy had to borrow $2,000. The couple's first four children—including future President John F. Kennedy—were born in the house on Beals Street, sleeping in a simple bassinet for the first few months of their existence. The house was decorated in muted colors, with reproductions of great paintings on the walls. The living room was dominated by a grand piano that had been a wedding present, and the china used for tea was emblazoned with green shamrocks, a gift from Sir Thomas Lipton. In 1920, the family moved a few blocks away, to a bigger house on Naples Road, and the Beals Avenue house was sold to Kennedy's aide, Edward Moore.

On July 19, 1964, the former Kennedy home on Beals Street was designated a National Historic Landmark. The Kennedy family repurchased it from its owners, Mr. and Mrs. Louis Pollack, in 1966 for $60,500, and then donated it to the U.S. Government, which opened it to the public as a museum operated by the National Park System. Rose Kennedy helped guided the restoration of the house to the way it looked during Jack Kennedy's childhood, and she attended the official opening on May 29, 1969, the late President's fifty-second birthday.

E

Electing a President in 1960

The 1960 presidential election, a contest between Vice-President Richard M. Nixon and Senator John F. Kennedy of Massachusetts, was one of the closest in history. Nixon had the advantage of his links to a popular President and his experience as an insider in the Eisenhower administration. Kennedy had the advantages of charm and good looks, a ubiquitous family, and a campaign based on the recognition that the country had become smug and self-satisfied. Some analysts believed that the televised debates had given Kennedy an edge, but pre-election polls showed the race still too close to call. Election Day was November 8, 1960, and returns made the race a cliff-hanger that was not decided until well into the morning of the following day. Nixon sent a message conceding defeat and congratulating Kennedy, and President-elect John F. Kennedy, with his entire family, dressed and posed for pictures in the living room of Ambassador Joseph P. Kennedy's oceanfront home at Hyannis Port. Then they all drove to the National Guard Armory in Hyannis, Massachusetts, to appear before the press.

Eleventh Congressional District of Massachusetts

The Eleventh Congressional District in Massachusetts includes such diverse areas as Cambridge (home of Harvard and MIT), middle-class Somerville, and the heavily Irish working-class area of Charlestown. John F. Fitzgerald represented the Eleventh Congressional District before the turn of the century, and then for many years its representative was James Curley, Fitzgerald's old opponent. In 1945, Curley ran for and won another term as Boston's mayor, leaving the Eleventh District Congressional seat open. In the subsequent election of 1946, Fitzgerald's grandson, young John Fitzgerald Kennedy, won the tough fight for the Democratic primary against nine rivals in June, in light voter turnout. He then swept the November election in the heavily Democratic district by a landslide.

The Elvis Presley Connection

Sooner or later, nearly everything of significance in America ends up being connected to Elvis Presley—and the Kennedy family is no exception. When Elvis died in 1977, the magazine *Rolling Stone* wanted to send journalists to cover the funeral. They dispatched Pete Hamill to the scene, and at his suggestion, he was accompanied by apprentice photographer ... Caroline Kennedy! Unfortunately, she was recognized by members of the crowd, who were trying to take *her* picture. Moreover, the Presley family complained they had been misled into believing she was there as a representative of the Kennedys, rather than an employee of *Rolling Stone*.

E

The Empty Chair

When Robert F. Kennedy ran for the Senate in New York in the fall of 1964, his opponent was incumbent Republican Kenneth Keating. Television stations tried to arrange a Kennedy-Keating debate, but the candidates could not agree on a format. Keating then tried a different tactic: He bought a half-hour of TV time in which to debate an empty chair. He claimed he had invited Kennedy, and claimed that Kennedy had failed to appear. So, he explained, he invited Republican Senator Jacob Javits to join him instead. Apprised of Keating's tactic, Kennedy surprised his Republican opponent by showing up at the TV studio and trying to gain entrance to the set. Keating's aides promptly turned him away. Later, Bob Kennedy made jokes about the event. "There were Javits and Keating on television really giving it to this empty chair. I've never seen either of them better. They kicked that chair all over the room." Public opinion came down on Kennedy's side, and the "empty chair" debate was later considered to be a significant factor in his win in November.

The Enemy Within

In 1960, Harper and Row published a book by Robert F. Kennedy called *The Enemy Within*, about his investigation of labor racketeering. Kennedy wrote the first draft and then asked Harvard fellow John Seigenthaler to help him cut and polish it. The book made a brief appearance on the best-seller list, and the author donated the profits to the Joseph P. Kennedy, Jr., Foundation to help its work with the mentally retarded. After the 1960 election, Jacqueline Kennedy gave RFK a specially bound copy and wrote on the flyleaf: "To Bobby, who made the impossible possible and changed all our lives." President Kennedy also gave Bob a leather-bound copy of the book and wrote: "To Bobby, the brother within, who made the difficult easy." In 1961, Robert Kennedy signed a contract with Twentieth Century-Fox for a movie version of the book and selected Budd Schulberg to write the screenplay. But the project was eventually abandoned.

Enrolling James Meredith in the University of Mississippi

On January 21, 1961, black student James Meredith applied for admission to the all-white University of Mississippi at Oxford. Meredith later said his decision to apply was influenced by President Kennedy's stirring Inaugural Address, and that had Nixon been elected, he would not have gone ahead. The university rejected Meredith, who promptly sued, with the support of Medgar Evers and the state NAACP. He won the suit, but the university countered with delays and harassment. Finally the matter went to the Supreme Court, which handed down a ruling on September 10, 1962, that Meredith must be admitted to the university forthwith. The governor of Mississippi, Ross Barnett, countered with a public pronouncement that the state would

E

never yield to "the evil and illegal forces of tyranny."

The Justice Department, under Attorney General Robert F. Kennedy, committed the federal government to protect Meredith when he tried to register that fall, and federal marshals attempted to maintain order on the campus in the face of angry mobs. In the end, it took a decision by President Kennedy to send in the Army. Backed by the presence of U.S. Troops, Meredith was finally able to enroll, and had the courage and endurance to remain on campus until he graduated. Later, he wrote to Robert Kennedy about the fight to enroll him in the university, "I am a graduate of the University of Mississippi. For this, I am proud of my country, the United States of America. The question always arises, was it worth the cost? I believe that I echo the feeling of most Americans when I say that 'no price is too high to pay for freedom of person, equality of opportunity, and human dignity.'"

The Eternal Flame

Jacqueline Kennedy was involved in choosing every detail of the funeral and burial arrangements for the assassinated President. One of her decisions was to place an eternal flame on the President's grave, as a symbol of the hope he brought to his country. On the day of the funeral, she and her brother-in-law Robert F. Kennedy lighted the flame with long electric wands.

Some months later, the flame was incorporated as a permanent memorial on top of the President's tomb. It still burns like a beacon on the Arlington hillside, now commemorating the graves of the two Kennedy brothers who lie side by side under the tall elms overlooking the nation's capital.

Ethel's Yearbook

Here's the way the Manhattanville College yearbook described Ethel Skakel: "An excited, hoarse voice, a shriek, a peal of screaming laughter, the flash of shirt tails, a tousled brown head—Ethel! Her face is at one moment a picture of guilelessness, and at the next alive with mischief."

Judith Immoor Campbell Exner

In 1975, Senate hearings investigating the link between organized crime and CIA attempts to assassinate Fidel Castro turned up the name of Judith Campbell as a woman reported to be "intimately linked" with both President John F. Kennedy and mobster Sam Giancana. At that time, Campbell, accompanied by her second husband, Dan Exner, called a press conference to deny knowledge of any involvement the underworld might have had with the CIA, but in the course of the conference she admitted a long-term intimacy with both Kennedy and Giancana. In 1977, Judith published a book, *My Story*, that contained details and corroboration

E

of both liaisons, and much of the content of her book was substantiated by subsequent press investigations.

According to Exner, she met John F. Kennedy in early 1960, when he was just beginning to campaign in the presidential primaries. She was introduced to him by Frank Sinatra, with whom she had been having an affair that ended, she said, when she refused to join him in engaging in group sex. After weeks of telephone courtship, Judith met Jack Kennedy one night at the Plaza Hotel in New York for "a wonderful night of lovemaking." Judith says she felt unhappy and guilty about her involvement with a married man, but she believed Jack's insistence that he and Jackie were hopelessly incompatible and had already agreed to get a divorce if he didn't win the election. Judith therefore continued to see Kennedy throughout his campaign and even afterward—about twenty times—in the White House. Evidence such as plane tickets and telephone logs seemed to support her story. She explained that the affair ended in 1962, when she became disillusioned by the President's self-centeredness: She felt she was being used by a man who had little time for more than sex. Throughout the entire period of her affair with Kennedy, she was also involved with Sam Giancana, whom she had also met through Frank Sinatra.

In 1988, Judith Exner once again went public, this time with what she said was the *whole* truth about her knowledge of the relationship between the Kennedy presidency and organized crime. She explained that she had feared she would be killed if she told the truth back in the 1970s, but since she had discovered she had terminal cancer, she no longer had any fears for her own safety and she wanted to set the record straight. In an exclusive story for *People*, for which she was paid at least fifty thousand dollars, Judith claimed that Jack Kennedy not only knew she was having a simultaneous relationship with Sam Giancana, he actually used her as a liaison between himself and the mob. She set up meetings for him with Giancana, and carried envelopes back and forth between the two men. She said she never saw the contents of the envelopes, but it was obvious from their size and weight that they were papers of some kind. According to Exner, she continued to see Sam Giancana and another mobster, Johnny Roselli, at Kennedy's request. When her romance with Kennedy faded, she remained close to Sam Giancana because he was the only one who understood the difficult position in which her activities had placed her, and he offered sympathetic support.

Exner's second revelations created a stir in the press, and there was some attempt to refute her claims; interestingly, the person who seemed most offended by these revelations, and most anxious to deny them, was the daughter of Sam Giancana. Yet the evidence Exner produced, along with the records documenting activities of the various individuals involved, lends credence to her story.

The Fatal Trip to Texas

The reasons for President John F. Kennedy's trip to Texas in November 1963 were primarily political. The next presidential election was only a year away, and Kennedy's staff was worried about the war among the Texas Democrats. Senator Ralph Yarborough, a liberal Democrat, was no longer speaking to Governor John Connally, a conservative Democrat, and Vice-President Lyndon Johnson seemed to be caught somewhere in the middle. Realizing that all factions would have to work together to produce another Democratic victory in 1964, President Kennedy decided a trip to Texas would be in order. The itinerary for his trip: San Antonio one afternoon, Houston for dinner, Fort Worth that night. Breakfast in Fort Worth the following day, lunch in Dallas, dinner in Austin, a private evening at the home of the Johnsons in Austin's hill country.

As Mrs. Kennedy began to regain her strength after the birth and death of the couple's son Patrick the previous August, she decided she would accompany her husband. She had rarely shown any interest in such political occasions, but the Kennedys had grown closer together in

the White House, and she wanted to help Jack in any way she could. So she packed the clothes that would make her stand out in the crowds: an ivory outfit, a dress in clear yellow, and the shocking pink Chanel style suit with a matching pillbox hat.

The trip seemed to go better than President Kennedy had dared hope. Although Connally had snubbed Yarborough once or twice, and Yarborough had declined Johnson's invitation to ride in his limousine, the warring Democrats were behaving reasonably well. And the crowds seemed friendly. Kennedy felt relaxed enough to adopt a humorous note in his speeches. At breakfast in Fort Worth, he apologized to the crowd for his wife's lateness, saying jovially, "Mrs. Kennedy is organizing herself. It takes her longer, but of course she looks better than we do when she does it." Jackie was dressed in the hot pink suit and feeling a bit warm in the Texas heat. She complained to her husband when she learned that the car they would be riding in for the Dallas motorcade would have its bubble top removed, because the wind was so hard on her coiffure, but the President told her that was the least of their worries: He was wondering how to get all the warring politicians to sit in the same car together. As the big Lincoln drove past the Texas Book Depository, Nelly Connally, the Governor's wife, leaned forward and said, "No one can say Dallas doesn't love and respect you, Mr. President."

Moments later, the shots rang out.

President and Mrs. Kennedy ride with the Connollys through the streets of Dallas. (Dallas Times-Herald, *Black Star*)

"Fatstuff"

The young Edward M. Kennedy, a hearty eater, was usually affectionately referred to as "Fatstuff" by his brothers and sisters.

F

Paul "Red" Fay

Paul Fay was a fellow student at the school in Melville, Rhode Island, where Lieutenant John F. Kennedy went through the course to teach the handling of PT boats. The Irish-American Fay, from San Francisco, became a close friend of Jack Kennedy, despite his first impression that Kennedy was a skinny, argumentative kid. That first impression led to Fay's favorite nickname for Jack Kennedy, "Shafty Boy." Fay was best man at Jack's wedding, and he and his wife, Anita, were frequent guests at the Kennedy houses in Hyannis Port and Palm Beach. During the Kennedy administration, Fay became under secretary of the Navy. Kennedy called his friend "Grand Old Lovable" and was perpetually entertained by Fay's rendition of "Hooray for Hollywood."

After President Kennedy's death, his old friend wrote a warm and touching account of the private Jack Kennedy he knew entitled *The Pleasure of His Company*. Fay submitted the manuscript to the family before publication and cut a number of passages that they considered unflattering because of placing the President in the context of a circle of friends who came across as uncultured jocks. Apparently, there was some resentment within the family that Fay had dared to reveal the private side of JFK, for when Fay offered a three-thousand-dollar donation to the Kennedy Library, Jacqueline Kennedy wrote a letter refusing the gift and calling it "hypocritical."

FBI Files on President Kennedy's Assassination

In late 1977, in response to a request made under the Freedom of Information Act, the Federal Bureau of Investigation released forty thousand pages of documents amassed during its investigation into the assassination of President John F. Kennedy. In January 1978, the FBI released another fifty-eight thousand pages. These raw data have been the basis for many conflicting theories of the assassination. Despite all the available evidence, no new theory has supplanted the official explanation that Lee Harvey Oswald, acting alone, killed the President.

The Fessenden School

Edward M. Kennedy attended the Fessenden School, in West Newton, Massachusetts. He later enrolled his son Patrick in the same school.

Feud Between Robert F. Kennedy and Lyndon B. Johnson

The feud between Robert F. Kennedy and Lyndon B. Johnson began during the early months of campaigning for the presidential primaries in 1960 and continued until Kennedy's death in 1968. Johnson had supported John F. Kennedy's bid for the vice-presidential nomination at the 1956 Democratic convention, but in 1960, Johnson was himself an announced candidate for the presidency, and he was capable of rough speaking. Bob resented Johnson's off-the-cuff remarks about Joseph P. Kennedy and about the state of Jack Kennedy's health; in return, Johnson suspected that a rumor that he was dying of a heart attack originated with Bobby's staff. Matters did not improve when Robert Kennedy made it obvious that he did not agree with his brother's choice of a running mate.

During the Kennedy presidency, the conflict between LBJ and RFK continued. Johnson, who as Vice-President considered himself the second most important man in Washington, was hurt and angry to find that most people gave Robert Kennedy that title. As is usually the case with Vice-Presidents, Johnson was on the fringes of the administration, and he blamed Bobby for the fact. After the assassination of President Kennedy, Johnson took power as President, and even then there were hard feelings. Robert Kennedy was reported to have been upset over the speed with which Lyndon Johnson had himself sworn into office, and his complete takeover of the White House in a matter of days; Johnson, for his part, felt that he was unfairly treated as some sort of usurper by the Kennedy circle. RFK's subsequent resignation as Attorney General was completely predictable. So was Johnson's refusal to consider Kennedy as a vice-presidential running mate in 1964. The breach between the two men had not yet healed by the spring of 1968, when Johnson had bowed to the inevitable and withdrawn as a candidate for the 1968 presidential nomination and Robert Kennedy was trying to win the nomination himself.

The Kennedys and the Johnsons. (Abbie Rowe, Black Star)

F

A Few of His Favorite Things

President John F. Kennedy was a man of definite tastes. His favorite cigars were Cuban, his favorite drink frosty daiquiris (also a favorite of his brother Ted, who whips them up for family gatherings). His favorite poem was "Ulysses" by Alfred Lord Tennyson, and his favorite song was "Greensleeves." His favorite dinner was steak, and his favorite meal on the run was a cheeseburger and a milkshake.

Fighting at Vinegar Hill

In 1798, the Irish farmers of County Wexford rose up against their British landlords in a brief rebellion that was soon crushed. The last and decisive fight in this rebellion came at Vinegar Hill, when a priest led the Irish farmers into ragged battle. Two Kennedy brothers fought at Vinegar Hill. John was wounded and later died of his injuries. His brother Patrick, who carried the dying man home, survived, and fathered a son who immigrated to Boston in 1848, the first of the Kennedys in America and the great-grandfather of President John F. Kennedy.

The Fifty-Mile Hike

During the Kennedy administration, the President called on all Americans to improve their nationally poor level of physical fitness and asked the Marines to lead the way by instituting a training practice of hiking fifty miles in twenty hours. Then someone suggested that the Kennedy administration itself ought to set a good example. The President's bad back prevented him from attempting such a feat, but Attorney General Robert F. Kennedy took up the challenge. One winter's day, he told his staff, "Well, I guess I'll have to do that fifty-mile hike tomorrow . . . and you're all going with me." The next morning it was only twenty degrees in Washington, and the hike took place through ice and snow. By early afternoon every one had dropped out except Bobby and his press aide, Ed Guthman. Guthman later recalled:

By nightfall it had gotten a lot colder and my legs were getting stiff. We took a break at about the forty-mile mark, and it was obvious that I couldn't go any farther. Bobby understood. But as he started to slog on, he turned and looked at me and said, "You're lucky your brother isn't the President."

Of course Bobby finished the hike.

Film Booking Offices (FBO)

Film Booking Offices (FBO) was the movie booking subsidiary established by the motion picture company, Robertson-Cole Company. In 1926, Joseph P. Kennedy bought a controlling interest in FBO from its English owners, putting him into the lucrative movie business at the time of its greatest expansion. Leaving his wife and children in Brookline, Massachusetts, Joe

F

went out to Hollywood to run the studio, which initially concentrated on turning out low-budget genre productions—Westerns, dog pictures, melodramas—and made very good profits. The focus was quantity rather than quality; FBO's top-grossing film was a dreadful white-hunter epic entitled *The Gorilla Hunt*. Within a few years, Kennedy used the profits from FBO's Grade B Pictures to merge the studio with his new acquisition, the Keith-Albee-Orpheum chain of theaters. Shortly thereafter, he merged Keith-Albee-Orpheum into the newly formed Radio-Keith-Orpheum (RKO), which was to become a major power in Hollywood.

Finch College

Finch College is a popular finishing school in New York City, where Kathleen Kennedy studied art and design from 1939 to 1941 (after being turned down at Sarah Lawrence).

Fire in the Senate Building

When Senator Robert F. Kennedy moved into his office in the Old Senate Office Building in January 1965, he tried to put his own stamp on the tiny rooms. His first step was to have logs brought in and a fire lit. What Kennedy didn't know was that the installation of an air conditioning system had blocked all the chimneys. Soon smoke was pouring out of his office into the corridors of the Senate Building, much to the embarrassment of the new senator from New York.

First Communion for Teddy

Edward M. Kennedy was seven when the Kennedy family attended the coronation of Pope Pius XII in 1939 as representatives of President Roosevelt. As Eugenio Cardinal Pacelli, the Pope had visited the Kennedy home in Bronxville, New York, in May 1936. The new Pope especially remembered Teddy, the youngest member of the family, who had sat comfortably in his lap and asked questions about his large crucifix. Three days after his coronation, Pope Pius XII gave Teddy his first communion, making young Kennedy the first American ever to be so honored.

First Lady

When President John F. Kennedy entered the White House, his wife, Jacqueline, made it clear to all staffers that she would prefer to be called simply "Mrs. Kennedy" rather than "the First Lady," the term generally used by her predecessors. "First Lady sounds like a saddle horse," she explained.

F

First Statement of
President Lyndon B. Johnson

When Air Force One arrived at Andrews Air Force Base on the night of November 22, 1963, bearing the body of slain President Kennedy and the new President, Lyndon B. Johnson, Johnson disembarked and spoke his first words to the grieving nation: "This is a sad time for all people. We have suffered a loss that cannot be weighed. For me it is a deep personal tragedy. I know the world shares the sorrow that Mrs. Kennedy and her family bear. I will do my best. That is all I can do. I ask for your help—and God's."

Bob Fisher

Bob Fisher was a classmate of Joseph P. Kennedy's at Harvard who became one of Joe's closest friends. Bob was an excellent athlete who played right guard on Harvard's football team and was named All-American in his senior year. The remainder of his life failed to fulfill his early promise, and Bob Fisher died in 1942, leaving behind debts that Joe Kennedy paid.

Edward C. Fitzgerald

Edward C. Fitzgerald was the seventh child of Thomas and Rosanna Cox Fitzgerald, born on March 1, 1867. Rose Kennedy's Uncle Eddie, a gregarious, generous man, never married, but was known throughout Boston's Irish community for his willingness to help others. He owned several taverns and a hotel, and was renowned for his own interest in drinking and eating well. He died on March 3, 1940.

Eunice Fitzgerald

Eunice Fitzgerald, a sister of Rose Fitzgerald Kennedy, was the fifth child and youngest daughter of John and Josie Hannon Fitzgerald, born on January 26, 1900. While she was still in her teens, Eunice came down with tuberculosis. Despite a valiant fight, and several stays in an excellent sanitarium in upstate New York, Eunice died at the family home in Dorchester on September 25, 1923, when she was only twenty-three years old.

George Fred Fitzgerald

George Fred Fitzgerald was the tenth child of Thomas and Rosanna Cox Fitzgerald, born on February 10, 1871. This uncle of Rose Kennedy was one of the younger brothers whose care

F

John F. Fitzgerald undertook. George had worked as a salesman for a brewery, and then, with his brother John's help, became a Democratic ward boss for Dorchester in 1903. His heavy drinking culminated in institutionalization and death on October 29, 1914.

Henry S. Fitzgerald

Henry S. Fitzgerald was the eleventh child and youngest son of Thomas and Rosanna Cox Fitzgerald, born on October 24, 1875. His older brother John was a father figure in his life, and his first job was as John's clerk. Henry, who looked very much like John, married Margaret Herlihy, and the newlyweds moved into a house in Dorchester a block away from John's house. The two brothers remained close until John's death in 1950; Henry died five years later, on February 22, 1955.

James T. Fitzgerald

James T. Fitzgerald was the oldest son of Thomas and Rosanna Cox Fitzgerald to survive into adulthood. Born on April 15, 1860, he was three years older than his more famous brother, John F. Fitzgerald. Jim settled in Charlestown and became the proprietor of Bunker Hill House, a large hotel, as well as several taverns. He was the most prosperous member of the family, and always contributed money to his brother John's campaigns; he was also the first of the family to spend a winter vacation in Palm Beach, a spot later to be identified with both the Fitzgerald and Kennedy families. Jim died in 1950, the same year as his younger brother John.

John Francis Fitzgerald

John Francis Fitzgerald was born in a tenement in Boston's North End on February 11, 1863, the fourth son of Irish immigrants Thomas and Rosanna Cox Fitzgerald. He attended Eliot Grammar School and then worked as a newsboy on a corner on posh Beacon Hill. In 1879 (about the time his mother died during her thirteenth pregnancy) young Johnny entered the prestigious Boston Latin School, from which he graduated in 1884 and entered directly into Harvard Medical School. Two weeks before the end of his first year of medical school, his father died. In order to keep the family together, John decided to leave school and go to work, hiring a housekeeper to look after the younger boys. He found a patronage job as assistant to Democratic ward boss Matthew Keany, which gave him an invaluable education in the inner workings of Boston politics. John subsequently worked as a clerk in the Customs House and was elected to Boston's City Council in 1892. Later that year, he won the office of state senator. One of his colleagues in the state senate was P. J. Kennedy, whose son would eventually marry Fitzgerald's daughter Rose.

In 1889, John married Mary Josephine Hannon, his second cousin, and the couple had six children: Rose Elizabeth (1890), Mary Agnes (1892), Thomas Acton (1895), John Francis, Jr. (1897), Eunice (1900), and Frederick (1904). John Fitzgerald was elected to Congress in 1894, where he served until the summer of 1900. After five years as the publisher of a small Boston Catholic weekly, John Fitzgerald ran for the post of mayor of Boston and took office on January 1, 1906. He was defeated in the election held two years later and subsequently found himself testifying before a grand jury investigating possible corruption in his administration. Yet John Fitzgerald, campaigning under the slogan "Manhood Against Money," was reelected two years later, by a narrow margin of fourteen hundred votes. At the end of that term, however, Fitzgerald's political career reached its end, and he was never again elected to public office, although he campaigned for the position of mayor in several more elections. He sold his large house in Dorchester and moved into the Bellvue Hotel, a gathering place for Massachusetts politicians.

Thereafter, Fitzgerald spent much of his time with his family, enjoying the love of his children and adoration of his grandchildren. He lived long enough to see his grandson Jack elected to Congress and to celebrate the victory by jumping up on a table and leading the singing of his old campaign song, "Sweet Adeline." John F. Fitzgerald died on October 2, 1950, of a coronary thrombosis after a long illness. His body lay in state at the house of his son, Thomas Fitzgerald, until the funeral on October 5, presided over by Archbishop Richard Cushing and attended by more than thirty-five hundred mourners, including the governor of Massachusetts and Speaker of the House "Tip" O'Neill. Fitzgerald was buried at St. Joseph's Cemetery in West Roxbury, Massachusetts.

Joseph Andrew Fitzgerald

Joseph Andrew Fitzgerald was the eighth son of Thomas and Rosanna Cox Fitzgerald, born on May 10, 1868. He fought in the Spanish-American War and, according to Fitzgerald-Kennedy biographer Doris Kearns Goodwin, returned with a severe form of malaria in which the parasites were localized in his brain. He was supported by his brothers until 1905, when John used his political clout to get him a job delivering the traffic report from the Warren Avenue Bridge to City Hall. Joe died on October 19, 1920.

Mary Josephine Hannon Fitzgerald

Mary Josephine (Josie) Hannon married John F. Fitzgerald on September 18, 1889, at St. Bernard's Church in Concord, Massachusetts. Her mother was a Fitzgerald, first cousin to John's father; the two first met when he paid a visit to her family in the farming community of Acton, Massachusetts, in 1878 and was struck by Josie's beauty and her attractively reserved manner.

Born on October 31, 1865, Josie finished grammar school and then went to work as a seamstress in a dress factory while John Fitzgerald continued to court her and try to overcome the opposition of her family to the marriage of second cousins. In 1890, a year after their wedding, Josie gave birth to their first child, Rose Elizabeth Fitzgerald. Five more children followed, but three of them died in their twenties and thirties. Josie Hannon Fitzgerald died on August 8, 1964, having lived long enough to see her grandson inaugurated President of the United States. Her funeral was conducted by Francis Cardinal Spellman and attended by more than a thousand mourners. She was buried in the family plot in West Roxbury, at St. Joseph's Cemetery.

F

Michael J. Fitzgerald

Michael J. Fitzgerald was the fifth son of Thomas and Rosanna Cox Fitzgerald, born on May 13, 1864, and given the same name as an older brother who had died before the age of one. Michael became a policeman, and when his brother John became mayor of Boston, he was given the position of health inspector. He married Elizabeth Theresa Degnan and had five children. Michael died on June 10, 1925.

Rosanna Cox Fitzgerald

Rosanna Cox (called Rosa) was an Irish immigrant to Boston who married Thomas Fitzgerald on November 15, 1857 and gave birth to twelve children—one of whom was John Francis Fitzgerald, the grandfather of President Kennedy. Rosa died suddenly of a cerebral hemorrhage on March 10, 1879, while in her thirteenth pregnancy, and was buried in the Fitzgerald family plot at Holy Cross Cemetery in Malden, Massachusetts.

Thomas Fitzgerald

Thomas Fitzgerald, the father of John F. Fitzgerald, was born in Ireland in 1822 and spent his early years helping his parents on their potato farm. When the potato crops failed in the late 1840s, the family immigrated to America together. After a brief attempt at farming, Thomas became a peddler of fish in Boston. In 1857, he married fellow Irish immigrant Rosanna Cox, with whom he had twelve children, eight of whom lived to adulthood. In the early 1860s, Thomas went into business with his brother James in a combination grocery store/saloon, and with the profits of that business was able to buy some tenements in Boston's North End and eventually to open his own grocery store. Thomas's wife, Rosanna, died in 1879. He lived on until 1885, leaving many of his twelve offspring still in their childhood at the time they were orphaned.

Fitzgerald Family Bible

Thomas Fitzgerald, the great-grandfather of President Kennedy and the first of that family to arrive in the New World, owned a leather-bound Bible in which he recorded all the births and deaths in his family. The Bible passed to his son John, who added the record of the lives of his own children, and their children as well. When John F. Kennedy was inaugurated President in January 1961, he chose to be sworn into office on the Fitzgerald family Bible.

Lord Peter Fitzwilliam

Lord Peter Fitzwilliam was the man Kathleen Kennedy fell in love with late in 1946 and finally decided she would marry. In the eyes of Kathleen's family, it was a disastrous decision. Not only was Lord Peter a Protestant, he was presently married to someone else. Dashing and charming, he was a war hero and a man of action who usually put his own pleasure ahead of other people's notion of duty. Despite her mother's threats that she would be disowned by the family if she married a divorced Protestant, Kathleen went ahead with her plans. Joe Kennedy agreed to meet with Lord Peter and Kathleen when he was in Paris in May 1948. While they were waiting for him to arrive, they decided to fly to Cannes for a few days. On May 13, as they headed south through a severe storm, their plane crashed and both were instantly killed.

The Fluffed Note in "Taps"

According to a military report released after the funeral of President John F. Kennedy, only two flaws marred the fastidiously planned ceremony: the manure in the road left by the horses, and the fluffed note by the bugler playing "Taps" at Arlington Cemetery.

The bugler was Keith Clark, who had been standing in the chilling rain of that November day for more than three hours before he lifted his horn to his lips at 3:08 P.M. and began to play the farewell notes. Not only was he stiff and cold, he couldn't hear himself play, because of the dying echoes of the 21-gun salute. His sixth note came out with a bump in it, like a sob of the horn. Many listeners thought the mistake was a deliberate emotional reaction to the moment that symbolized the country's farewell to the President, just before his coffin was lowered into the grave.

The bugle is now in the collection of the Smithsonian Institution.

Foreign Languages

Jacqueline Kennedy was a popular First Lady at home and abroad, in part because she could speak to many people in their native tongues. In addition to English, Mrs. Kennedy was fluent in French, Spanish, and Italian. Her husband, President Kennedy, spoke only English—unless you count his "Haarvaad" accent as a second language.

4 Smith Square

After World War II, Kathleen Kennedy (Lady Cavendish) decided she would prefer to return to live in England, where she was surrounded by many friends as well as the memories of her husband, who was killed in the war. Although always a welcome guest at the many homes of her in-laws, the Duke and Duchess of Devonshire, Kathleen wanted a house of her own. Thus she purchased a smart London town house at 4 Smith Square, in a neighborhood near Westminster Abbey. She furnished the house with lovely antiques she bought in the London shops.

Freckles

Freckles was the brown-and-white cocker spaniel that was the dog closest to the heart of Robert F. Kennedy (Brumus notwithstanding!). In 1968, Freckles often traveled with the Senator as he campaigned for the presidency. One member of the RFK staff commented, "If Freckles had a single admirer in the Kennedy campaign entourage, it was the candidate himself. Most thought it to be a pest and an abomination."

Freedom Riders

In the early summer of 1961, James Farmer of the Congress of Racial Equality organized a small group he called the Freedom Riders. The integrated group traveled through southern states to assert the constitutional rights of integration in interstate bus stations. When the group entered Alabama, things turned ugly. The Riders were beaten up and trapped in a local bus station. The Justice Department negotiated their release and provided transportation for them to New Orleans. But other, more militant Freedom Riders took their place. Martin Luther King, Jr., traveled to Alabama, and Attorney General Robert Kennedy sent five hundred U.S. marshals to protect him. In Birmingham and Montgomery, angry mobs attacked the Riders, and more concerted violence erupted when they arrived in Mississippi. But the Kennedy Administration stood firm, and that fall the attorney general asked the Interstate Commerce Commission to issue regulations to end segregation of interstate bus terminals. Within a year, the integration of bus terminals had been accomplished.

Orville Freeman

Orville Freeman was the secretary of agriculture under President John F. Kennedy. A traditional liberal, Freeman had been the governor of Minnesota. Formerly a supporter of Adlai Stevenson, Freeman made the nominating speech for Kennedy at the 1960 Democratic convention. When his appointment to the Cabinet was announced, reporters asked Freeman how he had gotten the job. In a joking reference to the heavy bias toward Harvard-educated appointees, Freeman answered, "I'm not really sure, but I think it's something to do with the fact that Harvard does not have a school of agriculture."

F

Robert Frost

John F. Kennedy was deeply moved by the poetry of Robert Frost, and he often used Frost's line about having "promises to keep and miles to go before I sleep" in his campaign speeches. Thus, he asked the elderly poet to write a poem for the Inauguration and appear at the ceremony to read it in person. When the moment came, the sun was shining on the white piece of paper so strongly that it virtually blinded Frost, and the nation observed its new Vice-President courteously trying to shield the paper with his top hat to enable to poet to read his work. Finally, Frost laid aside the paper and spoke the lines of another poem from memory.

"Frownies"

Rose Kennedy was careful about maintaining her youthful appearance as long as possible. She watched her figure, and wore big hats to keep the sun off her face. One of her favorite weapons in the war against age was her supply of "Frownies," skin-colored tapes that were applied to wrinkled areas to smooth them out and prevent further lines from being created. Her former secretary, Barbara Gibson, reported that Rose often wore her Frownies around the house, and she also sent them to friends she felt should know about them; the Duchess of Windsor was one such recipient.

The Fruitful Bough

The Fruitful Bough was a book of recollections about Joseph P. Kennedy edited by his son, Edward M. Kennedy. Ted took on the task during the months of his recuperation from a near-fatal plane crash in 1964, and got his title from a passage in the book of Genesis: "Joseph is a fruitful bough, even a fruitful bough by a well, whose branches run over the wall ..." The privately printed book was a gift to Kennedy family and friends, evoking memories of the founding father who was at that time bedridden and unable to talk because of his massive stroke in 1961.

The Funeral of President John F. Kennedy

The nation's final farewell to its slain President, John F. Kennedy, took place on November 25, 1963, the day of his young son, John's, third birthday. The President's body was lying in state in the Capitol Rotunda, upon the same catafalque that had held the coffin of President Lincoln, as hundreds of thousands of mourners filed silently past throughout the night to pay their respects. After the President's widow and two brothers knelt by the coffin for one last private moment, it was placed on a gun caisson drawn by seven matched gray horses and, as bands played "Hail to the Chief" and the Navy hymn, "Eternal Father, Strong to Save," moved

F

to the White House. There, in the long drive-way, the funeral procession formed. At 11:35 A.M., Mrs. Kennedy walked down the White House steps and took her place at the head of the procession. With Robert Kennedy on her right and Edward Kennedy on her left, the heavily veiled widow began the slow walk behind her husband's coffin as bagpipers from the Scottish Black Watch played a sad lament. Mrs. Kennedy was followed by President and Mrs. Johnson, then the two Kennedy children in a closed car. After them came the procession of heads of state from all over the world. They included such figures as President de Gaulle of France, Emperor Haile Selassie of Ethiopia, Prince Philip and former Prime Minister Harold Wilson of Great Britain, and King Baudouin of Belgium.

Thirty minutes later, the procession reached St. Matthew's Roman Catholic Cathedral, where Richard Cardinal Cushing was waiting at the door to greet the family and sprinkle holy water on the coffin. Then he conducted the traditional funeral mass in Latin. Gounod's "Ave Maria" was sung by Luigi Vena, who had performed the same selection at the wedding of the President. When the Mass was concluded, Cardinal Cushing again sprinkled the coffin with holy water, saying, "May the angels, dear Jack, lead you into Paradise." Then the Most Reverend Philip Hannan,

Auxiliary Bishop of Washington, spoke briefly about the President's life, concluding with a passage from his Inaugural Address. Funeral guests emerged clutching the card they had been given, a photograph on the front and a simple prayer on the back: "Dear God—please take care of your servant—John F. Kennedy."

Once again the funeral procession formed. Mrs. Kennedy and the rest of the Kennedy family stepped into waiting limousines, Caroline and John were sent home to the White House with their nurse Maud Shaw, and the final cortege got underway. For more than an hour, the caisson rolled through the streets of the nation's capital, followed by Black Jack, the riderless horse with high boots reversed in the stirrups, a traditional symbol of a slain military leader. The procession finally stopped on a hillside in Arlington Cemetery, below the Lee-Custis mansion, in a clearing framed by tall elms. There Cardinal Cushing conducted short graveside ceremonies. Cannons fired a twenty-one-gun salute and rifle volleys cracked. Fifty jets, one for each state of the Union, flew overhead, accompanying the President's plane, Air Force One. A bugler blew taps, as Mrs. Kennedy, with the help of her husband's brother Robert, lit the Eternal Flame.

The Funeral of Senator Robert F. Kennedy

The funeral of Senator Robert F. Kennedy took place on June 8, 1968. His body had been flown from Los Angeles to New York to lie in state at St. Patrick's Cathedral, surrounded by an honor guard that for a time included his eldest son, Joseph P. Kennedy II. The Requiem Mass there, attended by more than twenty-three hundred people, was conducted by Richard Cardinal Cushing, who had also presided over President Kennedy's funeral mass. The family had chosen

a white mass, in which the priests wear white vestments, to emphasize the promise of eternal life. Robert Kennedy's sons Joseph II, Robert Jr., and David served as acolytes at the Mass. Leonard Bernstein led members of the New York Philharmonic in the funeral march from Mahler, and friend of the Kennedy family Andy Williams sang "The Battle Hymn of the Republic" without accompaniment, his voice soaring out through the Cathedral in a moving moment. Senator

Leaving the White House, Jacqueline Kennedy and her two children pause on the steps before going to the Rotunda. (Fred Ward, Black Star)

Edward M. Kennedy, the last surviving male of his generation, delivered a moving eulogy for his slain brother.

My brother need not be idealized or enlarged in death beyond what he was in life. He should be remembered simply as a good and decent man, who saw wrong and tried to right it, saw suffering and tried to heal it, saw war and tried to stop it. Those of us who loved him and who take him to his rest today pray that what he was to us, and what he wished for others, will someday come to pass for all the world. As he said many times, in many parts of this nation, to those he touched and those who sought to touch him, "Some men see things as they are and say why. I dream things that never were and say, why not?"

After the mass, a thousand guests boarded a twenty-one-car special train at Pennsylvania Station. The four-hour trip to Washington took on the character of an Irish wake, during which the Kennedy family tried to cheer up friends and colleagues who mourned Robert Kennedy's loss. From Washington's Union Station, the funeral cortege moved through the darkness to Arlington, where at 11 P.M., Robert F. Kennedy was buried just forty-seven feet away from his brother, the slain President.

The Funeral of Dr. Martin Luther King, Jr.

Dr. Martin Luther King, Jr., was shot and killed on a balcony in Memphis, Tennessee, on the evening of April 4, 1968. Senator Robert F. Kennedy, traveling in Indiana to campaign for the Presidency, heard the news and made a moving speech to a predominantly black crowd in Indianapolis. "What we need in the United States is not division," he said. "What we need in the United States is not hatred. What we need in the United States is not violence or lawlessness, but love and wisdom, and compassion toward one another, and a feeling of justice toward those who still suffer within our country, whether they be white or black." Afterward, he telephoned Coretta Scott King, who asked him to help her bring King's body back to Atlanta. Kennedy arranged for a chartered plane for that purpose.

On the day of the funeral, Mrs. King received a visit from Jacqueline Kennedy. The two women went into the Kings' bedroom for a brief private talk. Mrs. Kennedy, accompanied by her friend Mrs. Paul Mellon, then attended Dr. King's funeral. A few months later, when Robert Kennedy was assassinated, Jacqueline Kennedy told one of his staff, "I'll tell you who understands death are the black churches. I remember at the funeral of Martin Luther King. I was looking at those faces and I realized they know death. They see it all the time and they're ready for it."

Ron Galella

Ron Galella is a free-lance photographer who for many years specialized in snapping pictures of Jacqueline Kennedy Onassis. In 1972, she took him to court to force him to stop bothering her and her children. Although Galella, who supported himself by selling his candid photos to various newspapers and magazines, claimed he was only trying to earn a living, the court found he was guilty of invading Mrs. Onassis's privacy. He was ordered by the judge not to go within one hundred yards of her home or the children's schools. In other locations, he could not get closer to the children than seventy-five yards, and had to stay at least fifty yards away from Mrs. Onassis. Thereafter, paparazzo Galella found other subjects for his camera work. The cost of Mrs. Onassis's victory was reported to be a $500,000 bill from her attorneys, Paul Weiss Rifkind Wharton and Garrison.

In 1981, Mrs. Onassis once again took Galella to court, for disregarding the injunction. He was fined $10,000 and prohibited from ever taking another picture of Jacqueline.

John Kenneth Galbraith

John Kenneth Galbraith was a renowned economist who became a supporter of John F. Kennedy's campaign for the presidency in 1960. Galbraith, born in Canada, had taught at the University of California at Berkeley before joining the administration of President Franklin D. Roosevelt. Galbraith taught a few years at Harvard and then went to England in the 1930s to study the new economics of John Maynard Keynes. In the postwar period, Galbraith worked briefly for the State Department and for *Fortune* magazine, before he returned to Harvard. He wrote several influential books, particularly *The Affluent Society* and *The New Industrial State.*

After supporting Adlai Stevenson's presidential aspirations in the 1950s, Galbraith helped John F. Kennedy campaign in 1960, and became a trusted Kennedy advisor. Early in 1961, President Kennedy appointed him ambassador to India, and Galbraith entertained Mrs. Kennedy and her sister, Princess Radziwill, on a much photographed visit to that country. Galbraith is currently the Paul M. Warburg Professor of Economics at Harvard, and continues to work as a writer as well.

Mary Barelli Gallagher

Mary Barelli Gallagher was Jacqueline Kennedy's personal secretary during the White House years. Formerly employed by Senator John F. Kennedy and then by Mrs. Kennedy's mother, Mrs. Hugh D. Auchincloss, Mrs. Gallagher was asked to join the White House staff after the 1960 election. After the assassination, she continued to work for Mrs. Kennedy in Washington until 1964, when the Kennedys moved to New York. In 1969, she wrote a book entitled *My Life with Jacqueline Kennedy*, which unflatteringly depicted her former boss as a free-spending woman determined to get her own way at all costs.

Ann Gargan

Ann Gargan was the youngest child of Joseph and Agnes Fitzgerald Gargan and thus the niece of Rose Kennedy. Ann was born in 1935, and her mother died in 1936, when Ann was not yet two. Her father died ten years later. Ann subsequently became a part of the Kennedy circle, and especially close to her uncle Joe. A deeply religious young woman, Ann entered a convent, in an order of nursing nuns, but was forced to leave because of ill health. Joe Kennedy offered her a home in her hour of need, and she later was able to repay the favor by acting as his companion and then his primary care-giver after his incapacitating stroke in 1961. Ann was with him when he died in 1969. On July 15, 1971, Ann Gargan married Thomas King, an Irish immigrant, in Boston; King died of a heart attack at Massachusetts General Hospital in February 1979.

Joseph Gargan

Joseph Gargan is the son of Joseph and Agnes Fitzgerald Gargan, and thus the nephew of Rose Kennedy. Born in 1930, Joe lost his mother at the age of six, when she died of a cerebral embolism and his father died ten years later. Rose and Joe Kennedy oversaw his upbringing and paid for his education, and thus he became close to his Kennedy cousins. His special friend was Teddy, the child closest to his own age, and the two remained friends into adulthood. Joe was with Ted at Chappaquiddick right after the accident, and stood by him loyally. Joe and his wife live in Hyannis Port, only a few blocks away from the Compound, and he oversees the care and maintenance of all the Kennedy homes on Cape Cod.

Mary Agnes Fitzgerald Gargan

Mary Agnes Fitzgerald was the second child of John and Josie Hannon Fitzgerald, born on November 10, 1892, and the sister closest in age to Rose Fitzgerald. The two young women attended the Blumenthal Sacred Heart Convent in Valle, Holland, together and remained close for the rest of their lives. An attractive young woman with blonde hair, Agnes stayed at home with her parents for many years, not marrying until 1929, when she was in her late thirties. Her husband was Joseph Gargan, a lawyer, Marine Corps captain, and former football hero at Notre Dame. Agnes and Joe had three children: Joseph Junior (1930), Mary Jo (1931), and Ann (1935). On September 17, 1936, Agnes died unexpectedly, of an embolism, in her sleep. Ten years later, her husband, Joe, died. Thereafter, Rose and Joe Kennedy oversaw the upbringing and education of the three Gargan children, who were especially close to their Kennedy cousins.

Jim Garrison

Jim Garrison was the District Attorney in New Orleans at the time of President John F. Kennedy's assassination. Intrigued by the links between assassin Lee Harvey Oswald and certain shadowy figures in New Orleans, Garrison began an investigation of his own into the background of the crime. The result was a pair of indictments, of figures Garrison said were tied to the CIA. One of the suspects died under mysterious circumstances before he could be brought to trial, and the second was acquitted. Garrison continued to maintain his belief that the CIA was behind the President's death, and to allege that the charges against himself of bribery and income tax evasion were instigated as a way to keep him quiet. (In trials, he was acquitted of both charges.) In 1988, Garrison, now retired, published a book, *On The Trial of the Assassins*, that detailed his version of the CIA conspiracy theory.

Charles de Gaulle

General Charles de Gaulle was president of France during the years that John F. Kennedy was President. President and Mrs. Kennedy visited France in early June 1961, the occasion on which the President described himself as "the man who accompanied Jacqueline Kennedy to France." Jacqueline's beauty, style, and ability to speak their language captivated the French, and their leader, de Gaulle. In private meetings with the President, de Gaulle was almost fatherly, advising the President not to pay too much attention to his advisors and not to feel bound by the policies he had inherited. The relationship between Kennedy and de Gaulle remained cordial and supportive, and de Gaulle was one of the most conspicuous of the world leaders who attended President Kennedy's funeral on November 25, 1963.

George Washington University

In 1951, Jacqueline Bouvier got her college degree from George Washington University, which she attended during her senior year, after her return from her junior year abroad.

Georgetown University

Georgetown University, in Washington, D.C., was the college attended by Maria Shriver in her junior and senior years. She graduated in 1977.

Roswell Leavitt Gilpatric

Roswell Leavitt Gilpatric served as under secretary of defense, hired by Robert S. McNamara, in the Kennedy administration. Born in Brooklyn in 1906, Gilpatric attended Yale University, where he received both his B.A. degree and his law degree. After practicing law in New York and lecturing at Yale, Gilpatric served as under secretary of the Air Force during the Truman Administration and then returned to the practice of law in New York when the Republicans won the White House. Appointed under secretary in 1961, Gilpatric resigned from the Defense Department in the summer of 1963 to return to New York to practice law. In 1967, Gilpatric accompanied Jacqueline Kennedy on a trip to Mexico, sparking rumors of a romance between the President's widow and the sixty-one-year-old attorney. In 1970, many of Jacqueline's letters to Gilpatric, whom she called "Roz," appeared in an auction catalog, and the following day his wife filed for divorce. Gilpatric sued for, and won, the return of the letters, but their affectionate contents had already been made public. It was later rumored that Aristotle Onassis bitterly resented the letter his bride had written to "Dearest Roz" from the *Christina* on the night of their wedding, and that it was the beginning of the breakdown of their marriage.

Glen Cove

When Robert F. Kennedy decided to run for the New York Senate seat in 1964, he had to establish a residence in the state in order to qualify. His brother-in-law Stephen Smith found a twenty-five-room house on Long Island, at Glen Cove, which he leased for two years in Bobby's name. The three-story farmhouse had a private beach on Long Island Sound, as well as an Olympic-size swimming pool.

Glen Ora

Glen Ora was the estate in the horse country of Virginia that President John F. Kennedy and his wife rented when he entered the White House, as a weekend getaway for himself and his family. The Kennedys redecorated at a cost of ten thousand dollars, putting in new rugs, curtains, and wallpaper. They also turned part of the pasture into a small golf course where the President could discreetly practice his swing and his putting. The owners of Glen Ora were not pleased by the changes, and insisted that the estate be returned to its original condition when the least expired.

Glens Falls

The town of Glens Falls, New York, was a special place for Robert F. Kennedy. During his 1964 campaign for the U.S. Senate, he had an appearance scheduled for the upstate New York town. That afternoon he was already tired from heavy campaigning in Buffalo, and he was running five hours behind schedule. As the campaign plane, the *Caroline*, approached Glens Falls, Bob asked staffers dejectedly, "Do you think anybody will still be there?" In fact, there were five hundred people waiting at the airport, and five thousand more gathered in the center of town. Touched by the warmth of his welcome in a traditional Republican stronghold, Kennedy announced, "I'd like to make my very first commitment of the campaign. Win or lose, the day after the election, I'm coming back to Glens Falls." On election night, RFK learned of his victory around midnight. He celebrated with a party at a posh hotel, made a quick stop at New York City's Fulton Fish Market, the spot where he had made his first appearance of his campaign—and then boarded a plane for Glens Falls, to keep his promise to the people of that town.

Arthur Joseph Goldberg

Arthur Joseph Goldberg was the first secretary of labor in the Kennedy administration. Goldberg was born in Chicago in 1908 and received both his B.A. and his law degree from Northwestern University. Goldberg specialized in the practice of labor law, and he met both Kennedy brothers when he worked as a lawyer on the Senate Racketeering Committee; he had also been counsel for the Steelworkers Union of the AFL-CIO. Goldberg served in the Cabinet for a year and a half. In the summer of 1962, President Kennedy appointed Arthur Goldberg to fill a vacancy on the Supreme Court. (Goldberg was succeeded in the Labor Department by W. Willard Wirtz.) Three years later, Goldberg agreed to President Lyndon Johnson's request to leave the bench in order to serve as the U.S. Ambassador to the United Nations from 1965 to 1968. Goldberg thereafter returned to the practice of law, as well as teaching and writing books. President Carter appointed him ambassador-at-large from 1977 to 1979. Goldberg died in 1986.

Dr. Frederick L. Good

Dr. Frederick L. Good was the Boston obstetrician who delivered all nine of Rose Kennedy's children. Rose was so devoted to Dr. Good that even after the Kennedy family moved to New York, she returned to Boston for the birth of her last two children, Jean and Edward.

G

Doris Kearns Goodwin

Doris Kearns Goodwin is the author of the carefully researched book, *The Fitzgeralds and the Kennedys*, published in 1987. Her husband, Richard Goodwin, was a Kennedy insider, and thus she had unusual access to people and papers that helped flesh out the story. A former professor of government at Harvard, Doris Kearns Goodwin also wrote a highly respected study of the politics and power of Lyndon B. Johnson, *Lyndon Johnson and the American Dream*.

Doris Kearns Goodwin. (Photo by Sigrid Estrada, courtesy of St. Martin's Press)

Richard Goodwin

Richard Goodwin was one of the men who helped shape the New Frontier. Goodwin, a graduate of Harvard Law School, had been a law clerk for Justice Felix Frankfurter. He joined the staff of Senator John F. Kennedy and then worked for the 1960 presidential campaign. The intellectual Goodwin followed Kennedy to the White House, helping to draft speeches and policy papers; Arthur Schlesinger called him a "supreme generalist." After what appeared to be a power struggle with Ted Sorensen, Goodwin left the White House and worked for a time at the State Department for Dean Rusk before he went over to the Peace Corps to write speeches for Sargent Shriver. He later joined the RFK team until Robert Kennedy's assassination in 1968. As advisor to Robert's son Joseph P. Kennedy II, he helped plan the Citizens Energy Corporation, of which Joe became president. Goodwin is married to teacher and historian Doris Kearns Goodwin, author of *The Fitzgeralds and the Kennedys*.

Grand Cross of Leopold II

The Grand Cross of Leopold is the highest honor the country of Belgium can bestow. It was bestowed on Joseph P. Kennedy in 1959 by King Baudouin I in gratitude for a pamphlet Kennedy had written in collaboration with James Landis that defended the decision of King Leopold II. Baudouin's father, to surrender to the Germans in May 1940.

Granny O

At the time that Jacqueline Bouvier Kennedy married Aristotle Onassis, she acquired the nickname in the press of "Jackie O." After the birth of her first grandchild, Caroline's daughter Rose, the press immediately dubbed her "Granny O."

Grey Gardens

Grey Gardens was the name of the seaside house in East Hampton that was the residence of Edith Bouvier Beale and her daughter Edie. Mrs. Beale was the sister of Jack Bouvier, and the aunt of Jacqueline Kennedy Onassis. In 1971, the Suffolk County Health Department announced that the two women—nicknamed Big Edie and Little Edie—would have to be evicted because Grey Gardens was unfit for human habitation. The house had no heat or running water, and was inhabited by eighteen cats and a pack of raccoons. The story made headlines, and the press delighted in contrasting the two Edies' life at Grey Gardens with that of Mrs. Onassis in her New York penthouse. Aristotle Onassis rescued his wife's aunt and cousin by spending the more than fifty thousand dollars needed to fix the house up, and the headlines faded away. Later, there was a documentary film made by the Maysles brothers about the two women, called *Grey Gardens*.

Guests at President Kennedy's Funeral

Among the guests at the funeral ceremonies for President John F. Kennedy were:

President and Mrs. Lyndon B. Johnson
President Charles de Gaulle of France
Emperor Haile Selassie of Ethiopia
King Baudouin of Belgium
Queen Frederika of Greece
Prince Jean, Hereditary Grand Duke of Luxembourg
Crown Princess Beatrix of the Netherlands
Crown Prince Harald of Norway
Prince Norodom of Cambodia
Prince Philip of Great Britain
Prime Minister Sir Alec Douglas-Home of Great Britain
President Eamon de Valera of Ireland
First Deputy Premier Anastas Mikoyan of the U.S.S.R.
Ambassador Anatoly Dobrynin of the U.S.S.R.
Prime Minister Lester B. Pearson of Canada
Chancellor Ludwig Erhard of West Germany

G

President Heinrich Lubke of West Germany

Prime Minister Hayato Ikeda of Japan

Foreign Minister Golda Meir of Israel

President Chung Hee Park of South Korea

Foreign Minister Ali Bhutto of Pakistan

Olaf Palme, Cabinet Minister of Sweden

U Thant, Secretary-General of the United Nations

Harold Wilson, leader of the Labour party in Great Britain

Governor and Mrs. Nelson Rockefeller of New York

President Harry S. Truman and his daughter Margaret Daniel

President and Mrs. Dwight D. Eisenhower

Mr. and Mrs. Richard M. Nixon

Senator Barry Goldwater of Arizona

Mayor Richard Daley of Chicago

Governor George Wallace of Alabama

The Reverend Billy Graham

Henry Ford II

Dr. Martin Luther King, Jr.

John Glenn

The HPTs

The HPTs, or Hyannis Port Terrors, was a club organized for summertime fun at the compound by some of RFK's sons in the late 1960s. Bobby and David, with their cousins Bobby Shriver and Chris Lawford, were the ringleaders; other members were friends from neighboring houses by the ocean. The boys would sneak out at night and play pranks, such as untying dinghies to drift down the shore or throwing cherry bombs from their bikes. According to Kennedy biographers Collier and Horowitz, as the HPTs grew older, their activities took on darker overtones of experiments with drugs and overt defiance of the law.

Najeeb Halaby

One of President Kennedy's appointments was to make Najeeb Halaby the administrator of the Federal Aviation Agency. Halaby had served in the Defense Department in a Republican administration, but he became part of the Kennedy circle. One of Halaby's daughters was a bridesmaid for Maria Shriver at her wedding to Arnold Schwarzenegger; another Halaby daughter married King Hussein and became Queen Noor of Jordan.

Pete Hamill

Journalist Pete Hamill was a frequent escort of Jacqueline Kennedy Onassis after the death of her second husband. Hamill was then a columnist for the *New York Daily News*; to his later embarrassment, he had once written a piece attacking Jacqueline Kennedy for her marriage to Aristotle Onassis. She graciously forgave the unflattering remarks he had made before he met her. Hamill, who had previously been involved with actress Shirley MacLaine, was a good friend to Jackie and her two children, and even after the romance ended, he continued to be a part of the Kennedy family circle.

Hammersmith Farm

Hammersmith Farm was the three-hundred-acre oceanfront estate in Newport, Rhode Island, that was owned by Hugh Auchincloss, Jacqueline Bouvier's stepfather. It was at Hammersmith Farm that Jackie's wedding reception was held after her marriage on September 12, 1953, to John F. Kennedy. The house itself was a typical Victorian mansion, with broad porches that faced the sea, and the pastoral quality of its setting was emphasized by its carefully raked pastures and the wandering herd of Black Angus cattle. There were twenty-eight rooms, many with magnificent views of Narragansett Bay, and an elevator, for the times when having fun left the residents too tired to climb the stairs. Hammersmith Farm was sold in the 1970s, but Jacqueline's mother retained a twelve-room "cottage" on the property for her use during her lifetime.

Happy Birthday, Dear Mr. President

On May 19, 1962, a forty-fifth birthday party was held for President John F. Kennedy at Madison Square Garden, organized by Frank Sinatra. The one unforgettable moment of the evening came when Marilyn Monroe, wearing a skin-tight beaded dress that outlined every curve, sang—or breathed—"Happy Birthday, Mr. President" to a bedazzled John F. Kennedy and millions of riveted television viewers. The President then told the audience, "I can now retire from politics after having had 'Happy Birthday' sung to me in such a sweet, wholesome way."

Averell Harriman

Elder statesman Averell Harriman played an important role as advisor to the Kennedy administration. Born in 1891, Harriman was the son of railroad magnate E. H. Harriman. He graduated from Yale in 1913 and worked for a time on Wall Street. In the 1930s, he switched from the Republican to the Democratic party. Under Roosevelt, Harriman served as administrator of the National Recovery Act, wartime Ambassador to Great Britain and then Russia. He served as secretary of commerce in the Truman administration and was the governor of New York from 1955 to 1959.

Initially, no one in the Kennedy administration, composed mostly of young men from a new generation of leaders, personally knew the sixty-nine-year-old Harriman, but he was brought into the Kennedy camp by Arthur Schlesinger, and his pragmatic advice won them over. A diplomat who had attended summit meetings with President Roosevelt, Harriman cheerfully accepted appointments first as roving ambassador and then as assistant secretary for the Far East. Kennedy trusted Harriman, used him for delicate negotiations, and relied on his judgment about handling the problems at "Foggy Bottom," as the State Department was nicknamed. After the death of the President, Harriman lent Mrs. Kennedy his three-story colonial-style house at 3030 N Street in Georgetown as a place to go when she left the White House. Harriman's last wife was Pamela Churchill Hayward, once Winston Churchill's daughter-in-law and a friend of the young Jack and Kathleen Kennedy. Harriman died in 1986.

Pamela Digby Churchill Hayward Harriman

In 1939, Pamela Digby had just become the daughter-in-law of Winston and Clementine Churchill, marrying their son Randolph after a brief acquaintance. At about the time of her marriage, Pamela met Kathleen Kennedy. The two young women were about the same age, and although Pamela was already married and the mother of young Winston Churchill II, she continued to attend the same parties as all the other postdebs. Pamela and Kathleen became fast friends, a friendship that continued for the rest of Kathleen's life and later extended to her brothers and sisters. When the war ended, Pamela divorced her husband; in 1959, she married Hollywood agent Leland Hayward. After his death, she married American elder statesman Averell Harriman, who had worked in the government during the Kennedy administration and remained a member of the Kennedy circle. At the 1971 wedding, Ethel Kennedy served as their witness. Harriman died in 1986, and Pamela chose to remain in the United States, still working actively to support the Democratic party and Kennedy political figures.

Lou Harris

Lou Harris was well known as a pollster when he joined Jack Kennedy's campaign for the presidency late in 1959. Throughout the campaign period, his sampling of public opinion helped fine-tune the candidate's choices of places to campaign and positions to support. The success of his work for Kennedy has made the use of pollsters common practice for all politicians.

Harvard

There has been a long association between Harvard University, one of the premier educational institutions in the country, and the Kennedy family. President Kennedy's grandfather, John F. Fitzgerald, was the first of the family to attend Harvard, spending a year in Harvard's Medical School before the death of his father forced him to drop out. Joseph P. Kennedy attended Harvard and graduated with the class of 1912, also obtaining his letter in baseball. In the next generation, Joseph P. Kennedy, Jr. arrived at Harvard in the fall of 1934 and graduated cum laude in the class of 1938. His younger brother Jack followed two years behind him, graduating in the class of 1940 with a bachelor's degree in political science. Thanks to his thesis on the European policy of appeasement on the eve of World War II (which was later published as the book *Why England Slept*), Jack also graduated cum laude. Robert F. Kennedy enrolled for his freshman year at Harvard in the fall of 1944, but left to enlist in the Navy as an able-bodied seaman. He returned when he was discharged in mid-1946 and graduated in June 1948. Edward M. Kennedy entered Harvard in 1951 but was asked to leave before the year was over because he had arranged to have another student take a Spanish test for him. Ted was permitted to return two years later and graduated in the class of 1954. All of the Kennedys of that generation lived in the same house when they were at Harvard: Winthrop House, which had a reputation as a residence for the jocks on campus.

Among the next generation, Harvard alumni include RFK's daughter Kathleen, who graduated with honors (from Radcliffe, a college of Harvard) in 1974; his son Robert, Jr., who earned a history degree in 1977; his son Michael in 1980; and his son Max. Jean Kennedy Smith's son, Stephen E. Smith, Jr., was in the Harvard class of 1979. Caroline Kennedy graduated from Radcliffe/Harvard in the class of 1981.

Harvard Law School

In the fall of 1940, Joseph P. Kennedy, Jr., enrolled as a student in Harvard Law School. He stayed for only two years before leaving to join the Navy six months prior to the entry of the United States into World War II.

Harvard-Yale Game of 1937

Joseph P. Kennedy, Jr., was a senior at Harvard in the fall of 1937, and a member of the college football squad. He of course hoped to win his football letter, which was by tradition awarded only to those players who participated in the annual game against Yale, held that year on November 20. But the contest proved to be a very close one, and the coach decided it was more important to win the game, using his strongest players, than to give young men on the bench a chance to get their crimson "H"s. Like other second-string players who were never sent into the game, Joe Junior was bitterly disappointed that he would not win his football letter. But his disappointment was nothing compared to that of his father, who was so angry about the episode that he vowed he would never give Harvard another cent.

Hayden, Stone and Company

Hayden, Stone and Company was the Boston brokerage house where Joseph P. Kennedy worked from 1919 to 1923, starting at a salary of ten thousand dollars—less than half of what he had been making at Bethlehem Steel during the war. But his new job had other benefits. Under the valuable tutelage of founder Galen Stone, Joe learned many of the financial skills that were to enable him within a few years to make a fortune in the stock market.

William Randolph Hearst

William Randolph Hearst was the newspaper magnate who was one of the richest men in America, model for the character played by Orson Welles in the move *Citizen Kane*. In 1937, Hearst hired Joseph P. Kennedy as a financial consultant, to help him solve the problems of his nearly bankrupt organization. Kennedy briskly advised the elderly Hearst to sell not only some of his vast collection of antiques and his real estate, but also some of the weaker newspapers as quickly as possible, to put an end to the cash drain they created. Hearst knew he was getting good advice from Kennedy, and at one point it was rumored that Kennedy would step in as general manager of the entire Hearst empire. But the decisions involved in liquidation were so painful to Hearst that it took years for him to act on Kennedy's advice. The two men remained on good terms, and Hearst often did favors for various members of the Kennedy family.

"Heart of My Heart"

One of the few times that John F. Kennedy indulged in a traditional campaign promise was during his run for the Massachusetts Senate in 1952. Kennedy had promised his volunteer workers that if he was the victor on Election Night, he would sing "Heart of my Heart" for them, and—in a flat tuneless voice—he kept his promise. Just for good measure, his brother Bob was the next to perform the song, in an equally nonmusical fashion.

Walter Heller

Walter Heller was one of the chief architects of the economic policy of the Kennedy administration. In December 1960, President-elect Kennedy announced the appointment of the University of Minnesota professor as chairman of his Council of Economic Advisors. Heller's liberal policies were thought to be responsible for the prolonged period of inflation-free economic growth the country enjoyed in the first half of the 1960s. He advocated tax cuts to help the economy reach its peak performance, and deficit spending in the interim. After the death of President Kennedy, Heller stayed on for a time to advise President Johnson, then returned to academic life. He died in 1987.

Hepatitis

In early 1933, while he was still a student at Choate, John F. Kennedy came down with an illness that the doctors could not diagnose at the time, but which was almost surely hepatitis.

He had to leave school, and his recovery proceeded slowly. Jack had another hepatitis attack late in 1935, which forced him to withdraw from Princeton and spend the rest of the year recuperating in Arizona, where the climate helped him regain his strength, so that he was able to enroll at Harvard for the fall semester.

Hickory Hill

Hickory Hill is a historic old house in Virginia that was the Union General McClellan's headquarters for a time during the Civil War. It was purchased for $125,000 by Senator John F. Kennedy and his wife, Jacqueline, in 1955, in the hope of raising a family there. Jackie redecorated the 140-year-old white brick house to her exacting taste, and in 1956 she spent happy months planning a nursery for the baby she was expecting later that year. When the baby was stillborn after premature labor, Jackie found herself unable to bear the emptiness of the big old house on its six-and-a-half acres. So it was sold for the original purchase price to Jack's brother Robert and his wife, Ethel, as they obviously needed more room for their family, already consisting of five children.

During the Kennedy presidency, Hickory Hill—official address, 4700 Chain Bridge Road—was a favorite gathering place of White House insiders, who enjoyed the rambunctious atmosphere of Ethel's household. There were two swimming pools (one with a jukebox beside it), and newspaper reports made it appear that someone was continually being thrown in one or the other. Bobby and Ethel added more bedrooms to the house, and also built a huge pool house that doubled as a private movie theater. Pets, including ponies, iguanas, a seal, and for a short time even a coati, roamed the grounds.

After the death of Robert F. Kennedy, Ethel continued to make Hickory Hill her primary residence and to raise their children there. The house is currently decorated in Laura Ashley prints, most of them a pretty and feminine pink.

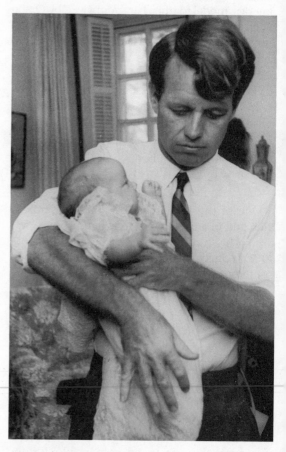

A tender moment at Hickory Hill. (Steve Schapiro, Black Star)

H

Hiding in the Sheets

When John F. Kennedy was President, he sometimes spent a few days at the family compound at Hyannis Port to decompress from the pressures and burdens of his office. He liked to play with the children there, both his own and his many nieces and nephews. Whatever game they played, the President was always a wholehearted competitor; in the Kennedy family, even children had to earn their victories. JFK's niece Kathleen remembers the time he played a game called "Chase One, Chase All" with the assembled children. The only person not yet caught by the end of the game, the President was running away from a pack of children when he spotted a laundry truck in the driveway of his parents' home and jumped into the back. "Let's go," he ordered. The driver could scarcely believe that the passenger hiding in the pile of dirty sheets was the President of the United States.

President Kennedy in the summer of 1963 with the Kennedy kids. (Courtesy of the Kennedy Library)

H

Historic Restoration of the White House

When John F. Kennedy became President, his wife, Jacqueline, decided that one of her special projects would be the historic restoration of the White House. She had been depressed by her first sight of her new home when she toured it with her predecessor, Mamie Eisenhower. In the private family quarters, the furniture was shabby and uncomfortable. In the public rooms, the general shabbiness was even more marked. Mrs. Kennedy was also troubled by the fact that many pieces of furniture and objects of art brought to the White House by previous Presidents had been sold and scattered.

To help her with the major project of restoring the President's home, Mrs. Kennedy brought together under the chairmanship of Henry F. DuPont a prestigious committee of philanthropists and people active in the arts, such as friends Mrs. Paul Mellon and Mrs. Charles Wrightsman, and began a thorough redecoration. Scholars provided information about the way various rooms had looked in the past, and they also set to work tracing the lost furniture. It turned out that some of it had merely been mislaid, and was found in disrepair in basement storerooms; one valuable pier table from the days of James Madison was discovered covered with silver radiator paint! Many original furnishings that were traced to private owners were donated to the White House, and others were purchased with funds raised by the committee. The restoration included American art, silver, china, wallpaper, and upholstery fabrics of the best quality, authentic to the period.

The result of months of work was presented to the nation in a televised tour, conducted by Mrs. Kennedy, in 1962. The great state rooms of the White House glowed in strong colors, historical associations with past Presidents were emphasized, and the mansion at last really looked fit to be the home of American Presidents.

James Hoffa

James Hoffa was vice-president of the Teamsters Union in 1957, when the McClellan Committee began its investigation into the union. Initially, Hoffa adopted a cooperative attitude toward the investigation, which he hoped to use for his own purposes, to oust union president Dave Beck and take over control of the union himself. As the investigation proceeded, he discovered that he too was being investigated by the McClellan Committee and its tenacious chief counsel, Robert F. Kennedy, and he became alarmed for his own well-being. The hearings turned into a fight between Kennedy and Hoffa, with Kennedy hoping to put Hoffa behind bars and Hoffa reportedly threatening Kennedy's life. The hearings ended in a stalemate, tarnishing Hoffa's reputation but failing to bring any indictments against him. They were, however, just the beginning of Hoffa's own problems, with the law, the unions, and the underworld. Those problems culminated in his disappearance in 1975, presumably a victim of underworld retribution.

"Honey Fitz"

During his days as the mayor of Boston in the early years of the century, John F. Fitzgerald was nicknamed "Honey Fitz," in an affectionate reference to the sweet effect of his speeches on the public.

The Honey Fitz

During President's Kennedy's administration, the presidential yacht, formerly called the *Sequoia*, was renamed. President Kennedy called it the *Honey Fitz*, in honor of his grandfather, Boston Mayor John F. Fitzgerald.

Honeymoon: Rose and Joe Kennedy

Rose and Joe Kennedy honeymooned for three idyllic weeks in Room 145 of the Greenbrier Hotel in White Sulphur Springs, West Virginia. They took long walks in the mountains, dined and played cards in the evenings—and conceived their first child, Joseph P. Kennedy, Jr., born nine months later.

Honeymoon: Kathleen and Billy Hartington

Kathleen and Billy Hartington were married during wartime, only weeks before Billy's military unit was scheduled to participate in the June 1944 Allied invasion of Normandy, so their honeymoon was necessarily brief. After the wedding reception in London's posh Eaton Place, Kathleen changed into a pink-and-white print dress and a white hat decorated with gardenias and the couple boarded a crowded train for the trip to Eastbourne, where the Duke of Devonshire owned a house called Compton Place. They walked from the station to the house. Shortly thereafter, Billy was sent to the front. He was killed in action on September 9.

Honeymoon: Ethel and Robert Kennedy

Ethel and Robert Kennedy spent their honeymoon in Hawaii, then moved into a modest rented house near the campus of the University of Virginia, where Bobby began his last year of law school.

Honeymoon: Jacqueline and Jack Kennedy

Jacqueline and Jack left their wedding reception at Merrywood and boarded a private plane for New York. The bride was wearing a gray Chanel suit, the diamond bracelet that was a gift from the groom, and a diamond pin given to her by her new father-in-law. They spent two nights in the honeymoon suite at the Waldorf-Astoria and then flew to Acapulco, a destination that was

H

largely the choice of the bride. They stayed in an oceanfront villa lent them by the President of Mexico. Jack found the quiet days on the beach too dull for his tastes, so the couple left Mexico several days ahead of schedule and flew to California to visit Jack's old Navy buddy Red Fay and his wife, Anita.

Honeymoon: Maria and Arnold Schwarzenegger

Maria and Arnold Schwarzenegger spent their honeymoon in a very private and posh resort, the St. James Club, on the Caribbean island of Antigua. According to some reports, their postnuptial activities included lessons for Maria from Arnold in the fine art of pumping iron.

Honeymoon: Caroline and Ed Schlossberg

The Schlossbergs' honeymoon began when they slipped out of the reception at the Kennedy compound and rode in a limo to Boston, where they stayed at the Ritz-Carlton Hotel. The following day, they boarded a plane for Hawaii.

Hoover Commission on Reorganization of the Executive Branch

Following World War II, former President Herbert Hoover headed a Presidential Commission on Reorganization of the Executive Branch that worked for many years to make formal recommendations for change. Joseph P. Kennedy was appointed to the commission in 1947 by President Harry S. Truman, and reappointed by President Eisenhower in 1953. For a few months of that year, Robert F. Kennedy served as his father's executive assistant on the commission.

House on Rodeo Drive

In 1928, Joseph P. Kennedy rented a house on Rodeo Drive so he could be near his RKO offices—and Gloria Swanson, with whom he was romantically involved, whose home was only five minutes away. Rose and the children stayed at home in Bronxville, New York, during Joe's frequent and lengthy visits to the Coast. At that time, the area was primarily residential, except for the Beverly Wilshire Hotel and the Brown Derby restaurant; the luxurious shops for which the area is now renowned came later. The lease on the Rodeo Drive house was allowed to lapse after Joe Kennedy sold out of the movie business in 1929.

How to Announce Bobby's Appointment

When incoming President John F. Kennedy was forming his cabinet, he knew that he wanted his brother, Robert F. Kennedy, to accept the post of attorney general. "I want the best men around," he said, "and they don't come any better than Bobby." But he also knew that Bobby's appointment would be seen by critics as nepotism, for which both he and his brother would be attacked. Jack jokingly discussed with a friend the way the controversial appointment should be announced: "I think I'll open the front door of the Georgetown house some morning about 2 A.M., look up and down the street, and if there's no one there, I'll whisper, 'It's Bobby.'"

How to Become a Hero

When John F. Kennedy entered national politics, his war record—and especially his heroism in the South Pacific—was one of his greatest assets. At a press conference, a reporter asked Kennedy how he had become a hero. "It was easy," Kennedy replied. "They cut my boat in half."

How to Sell More Copies of a Book

In 1958, Joseph P. Kennedy reflected on the popularity of his son Jack, then considered a strong contender for the presidential nomination of his party. "I'll tell you how to sell more copies of a book," Joe explained. "Put his picture on the cover. Why is it that when his picture is on the cover of *Life* or *Redbook* they sell a record number of copies? ... He has more universal appeal." Publishers seem to have learned the truth of Joe Kennedy's statement, for even today, a magazine or book with a picture of a Kennedy on the cover can be counted on to do well.

Father Oscar L. Huber

Father Oscar L. Huber was the seventy-year-old pastor of Holy Trinity Church in Dallas who gave President Kennedy the last rites of the Roman Catholic Church. Parkland Hospital was in Father Huber's parish, and when he heard the news of the shooting on the radio, he got his purple stole, rituals book, and holy oil, and drove to the hospital. After the doctors abandoned their hopeless effort to revive the President, Father Huber stepped forward and performed the last rites, telling Mrs. Kennedy, "I'm sorry. You have my deepest sympathy." Afterward she thanked him, and he replied, "I am convinced that his soul had not left his body. This was a valid last sacrament."

Page Huidekoper

Page Huidekoper was hired as personal assistant to Joseph P. Kennedy when he took the post as Ambassador to the Court of St. James. Page had been recommended for the job by her friend Jimmy Roosevelt, the son of the President. She later became a close friend of the Ambassador's daughter Kathleen. After she left London, she worked in Washington on the staff of the Washington *Times-Herald*, where Kathleen was employed as a reporter.

"The Human Postage Stamp"

Political rivals of Mayor John F. Fitzgerald in Boston used to call his brother Joe "the human postage stamp," in reference to the fact that Joe was paid an annual salary of eleven hundred dollars to deliver a traffic report from the Warren Avenue Bridge to City Hall. For all other bridges, the report was mailed in and cost only one penny in postage.

The Humor of JFK

Political commentator James Reston once said about John F. Kennedy that "he disarms you with a smile and a wisecrack." Both in private and in public, Kennedy was the master of the sly witticism, and it *was* a particularly effective way to disarm his critics.

Like all Presidents in modern times, President Kennedy utilized the services of others to write some of his comic material. During the time he was campaigning for the presidency, Kennedy retained two writers, John Bartlow Martin and Joseph Kraft, to provide humorous contributions to his speeches. Professional comic Mort Sahl also wrote some material for the Kennedy campaign, although Sahl later commented, "Jack Kennedy needed less help with humor than anybody alive!" Much the same attitude is maintained by Ted Sorensen, who, as Kennedy's chief speech writer, was also responsible for some of those Kennedy wisecracks.

It is, in fact, obvious that Jack Kennedy had his own keen sense of humor. Many of his funniest remarks were off-the-cuff responses to the way a reporter happened to phrase a question. For example, a reporter once introduced a question about the troubled relationship between President Kennedy and big business by saying, "Big business is forcing you to come to terms. Businessmen seem to have the attitude, 'Now we have you where we want you.'" JFK shot back, "I can't believe I'm where big business wants me."

Jack Kennedy rarely told jokes, or used prefabricated punchlines. His sense of humor was highly verbal, strongly ironic, and always related to the context of his remarks. Although President Kennedy dealt seriously with serious matters, he always retained a readiness to see the funny side of any issue. Said Ted Sorensen about his boss, "The ability to laugh at himself and avoid pomposity was a quality that was central to his success in politics and in the White House." It is also one of the reasons he is still remembered with such warmth and affection by the Americans who were able to share his humorous vision.

John G. W. Husted, Jr.

In early 1952, Mr. and Mrs. Hugh D. Auchincloss announced that their daughter Jacqueline Lee Bouvier was engaged to a man named John G. W. Husted, Jr. An engagement party was held at Merrywood, the Auchincloss estate in Virginia, and the tall, handsome, and urbane Husted gave Jackie an engagement ring that had been his mother's, a sapphire flanked by two diamonds. Son of a socially prominent New York banker, John Husted had attended St. Paul's preparatory school and Yale, and had sisters who attended Miss Porter's School in Farmington, Connecticut, which Jackie had also attended. John was a stockbroker working in New York, but Jackie took a job with the Washington *Times-Herald*, which meant they saw one another infrequently. He later told an interviewer he knew his days were numbered when he began to receive letters from Jackie telling him not to pay any attention "to the drivel you hear about me and Jack Kennedy." That spring, a quiet announcement appeared in the papers that the engagement had been broken off by mutual consent. In 1954, Husted married Mrs. Ann Hogerly Brittain, stepdaughter of the *New Yorker* publisher.

Hyannis Port

It was the summer of 1925 when Joseph P. Kennedy first took his family to Hyannis Port, Massachusetts, a small village of vacation houses on Cape Cod's southern shore. He initially rented a large white house that fronted on Nantucket Sound, and the family liked Hyannis Port so well that he bought the fifteen-room house from the owner in November 1928 for just twenty-five thousand dollars. The Kennedy residence in Hyannis Port, on a two-and-a-half acre site, is reached by a circular driveway at the side of the house, leaving the front facade to face the ocean; a large lawn separates the wide porch that runs around the length of the house from the sandy shore.

Built around the turn of the century in the style that was called a "cottage," the six-bedroom house has low ceilings, cheery rooms, and wonderful views of the Atlantic. Rose Kennedy initially furnished it as a summer house, with sturdy chairs and comfortable sofas that could withstand the heavy use of the nine little Kennedys and their friends, and the upstairs bedrooms were always crowded with young people. Later a tennis court and then an indoor pool were added. Today the house remains comfortable and welcoming. The living room, with its chintz curtains, is filled with photos of the family, and a painting of the U.S.S. *Joseph P. Kennedy, Jr.* occupies the place of honor over the mantel. In recent years, Edward Kennedy has made his mother's house his headquarters in Hyannis Port.

The house next door to the Joseph Kennedy residence came on the market soon after Robert and Ethel Kennedy had started to raise their own family, and they purchased it for their lively brood. A few years after Bobby and Ethel bought their house, the one behind it came on the market and was purchased by John F. and Jacqueline Kennedy, thus creating the so-called compound. The house owned by the President faced the street and the Kennedys had to erect a tall fence in front of it to preserve their privacy. Later Eunice and Sargent Shriver bought a house less than a mile away, and Edward and Joan then built a new house about a mile down the road from the Shrivers, at Squaw Point. Pat and Peter Lawford often rented a house in Hyannis Port for the summer, to be with the family.

Hyannis Port became the one constant in the

lives of all Joe and Rose's children, with the long summer vacations there bringing them together again even after they reached adulthood and started to have children of their own. Throughout the 1960s and 1970s, it remained a gathering point for the entire Kennedy clan, a place for cousins from Washington and California to meet and get to know one another, and the place where everyone went to unwind from the stress of political campaigns and assorted daily problems. The highlight of the summer was the big birthday party given every year on July 22 for matriarch Rose Kennedy, and the season was closed out every year with another birthday bash, one for Bobby Kennedy's oldest son, young Joe.

Today, the summers at Hyannis Port are quieter. Rose Kennedy lives the life of an elderly invalid, and her son shares her house when he can get away for a Cape Cod vacation. The white gambrel-roofed house next door is still home to Ethel and her children and grandchildren during the summers. Jacqueline Kennedy Onassis still owns the third house in the "compound," but she rarely goes there since she built her oceanfront house on the nearby island of Martha's Vineyard. Joan has kept the house at Squaw Point, and the Shrivers still own their house down the road. The next generation—the great-grandchildren of Joe and Rose Kennedy—are already beginning to experience the pleasures of Hyannis Port summers.

The Kennedy boys, Jack, Bobby, and Teddy, at Hyannis Port. (Courtesy of the Kennedy Library)

H

I

"Ich Bin Ein Berliner"

One of the most emotional speeches ever made by President John F. Kennedy came on June 23, 1963, when he addressed a huge crowd gathered on the West German side of the Berlin Wall. In a gesture of solidarity with victims of oppression all over the world, the President declared that he too was a citizen of the divided city of Berlin: "All free men, wherever they may live, are citizens of Berlin, and therefore, as a free man, I take pride in the words, 'Ich bin ein Berliner.'" One amusing sidelight on this famous speech is the fact that in Europe, "berliner" is the name given to a jelly-filled doughnut.

An Ill-Timed Sailing Trip

After the strain of the 1956 Democratic Convention, when Senator John F. Kennedy had unexpectedly found himself in the middle of an unsuccessful bid for the vice-presidential nomination, he decided to unwind by going on a sailing trip with his brother Teddy and a good friend George Smathers, the senator from Florida. While Jack was at sea somewhere in the Mediterranean and completely beyond the reach of communication, his wife Jacqueline, in the final months of a pregnancy, was rushed to the hospital for an emergency cesarean operation. The surgery came too late to save the stillborn baby girl. It was not until a number of days had passed that Jack learned the news and returned to be with his wife. The couple's sorrow over losing the baby, coupled with the fact that they were not together at the time, made this one of the low points in their relationship. Meanwhile, Jackie was comforted by her brother-in-law Robert Kennedy, who also quietly arranged for the burial of the unnamed baby. Years later, the tiny coffin of "Baby Kennedy" was reinterred at Arlington Cemetery near the grave of President Kennedy.

I'm for Roosevelt

In 1936, when President Franklin Delano Roosevelt decided to run for a second term, Joseph P. Kennedy offered to write a book defending Roosevelt's controversial economic policies. Kennedy had supported Roosevelt in the previous election, and had felt slightly disappointed that his only reward was a brief stint organizing the new Securities and Exchange Commission. Yet he still sincerely believed that Roosevelt's policies were the ones that would help the country pull through the Depression without a major social upheaval, so he remained firmly in the Roosevelt camp.

An outline of the proposed book was submitted to the White House for approval, and then Joe Kennedy hired his friend, respected journalist Arthur Krock, to help him do the actual writing. The 149-page book was published by Reynal and Hitchcock in August, just a few months before the election. Joe Kennedy used it as a forum to endorse the New Deal wholeheartedly, and that endorsement carried considerable weight with the conservative financial community and helped Roosevelt win reelection. A grateful FDR sent the book's author a note: "I'm for Kennedy. The book is grand."

"The Impossible Dream"

In January 1968, Senator Robert F. Kennedy was trying to make a decision about whether to run for the Presidency, and he summoned a group of his closest advisors to his home at Hickory Hill. The debate over the question was heated, revolving around the question of how good Bob's chances really were to win. The one light moment of the weekend came when several of his children turned the stereo on full blast and serenaded the amused advisors with the hit song from *Man of La Mancha*: "The Impossible Dream."

Inaugural Address

The Inaugural Address of President John F. Kennedy remains one of the most moving pieces of Presidential rhetoric ever delivered. It was written with the help of aide Theodore Sorensen, who was instructed to study Lincoln's Gettysburg Address as a model for directness and clarity. Many listeners felt that Kennedy's speech was destined for the same immortality. Here are some of the most memorable words:

We observe today not a victory of party but a celebration of freedom, symbolizing an end as well as a beginning, signifying renewal as well as change. For I have sworn before you and Almighty God the same solemn oath our forebears prescribed nearly a century and three-quarters ago ... Let the word go forth from this time and place, to friend and foe alike, that the torch has been passed to a new generation of Americans, born in this century, tempered by war, disciplined by a hard and bitter peace, proud of our ancient heritage, and unwilling to witness or permit the slow undoing of those human rights to which this nation has always been committed, and to which we are committed today at home and around the world. Let every nation know, whether it wishes us well or ill, that we shall pay any price, bear any burden, meet any hardship, support any friend, oppose any foe to assure the survival and the success of liberty ... To those peoples in the huts and villages of half the globe struggling to break the bonds of mass misery, we pledge our best efforts to help them help themselves ... If a free society cannot help the many who are poor, it cannot save the few who are rich ...

So let us begin anew, remembering on both sides that civility is not a sign of weakness and sincerity is always subject to proof. Let us never negotiate out of fear, but let us never fear to negotiate. Let both sides, for the first time, formulate serious and precise proposals for the inspection and control of arms ... Let both sides seek to invoke the wonders of science instead of its terrors. Together let us explore the stars, conquer the deserts, eradicate disease, tap the ocean depths and encourage the arts and commerce ...

All this will not be finished in the first one hundred days. Nor will it be finished in the first one thousand days, nor in the life of this Administration, nor even perhaps in our lifetime on this planet. But let us begin ...

Now the trumpet summons us again—not as a call to bear arms, though arms we need; not as a call to battle, though embattled we are; but a call to bear the burden of a long twilight struggle, year in and year out, "rejoicing in hope, patient in tribulation," a struggle against the common enemies of man: tyranny, poverty, disease and war itself ...

And so, my fellow Americans, ask not what your country can do for you; ask what you can do for your country.

My fellow citizens of the world, ask not what America will do for you, but what together we can do for the freedom of man.

Finally, whether you are citizens of America or citizens of the world, ask of us here the same high standards of strength and sacrifice which we ask of you. With a good conscience our only sure reward, with history the final judge of our deeds, let us go forth to lead the land we love, asking His blessing and His help, but knowing that here on earth God's work must truly be our own.

Inaugural Concert

The Inaugural Concert was the first of the celebratory events held on the eve of about-to-be-President Kennedy's Inauguration. It was organized by Frank Sinatra, and featured performances by scores of famous musicians, including Harry Belafonte, Ella Fitzgerald, and Ethel Merman. Despite the heavy snowstorm that evening, the concert was packed. Jackie wore a simple but elegant gown of heavy ribbed silk designed by Oleg Cassini.

Inaugural Gala at the National Guard Armory

The Inaugural Gala celebrating John F. Kennedy's inauguration as President actually took place the night before the Inauguration, right after the Inaugural Concert. It was a terrible, snowy night, and many of the guests had to struggle to the Armory, where the gala was held, on foot after their cars became stuck. Observers agreed it was probably the occasion on which the incoming President most enjoyed himself, sitting in a box seat and puffing a big cigar as his family, friends, and supporters danced and celebrated.

Inaugural Gown

From the official press release, here is the description of Mrs. Kennedy's gown, purchased from Bergdorf-Goodman, for the Inaugural Ball: The dress is a full-length sheath of white silk peau d'ange veiled with white silk chiffon. The hip length bodice is richly embroidered in silver and brilliants.

I

It is covered by a transparent overblouse of white silk-chiffon.... The floor-length cape is made of the same while silk peau d'ange and completely veiled in silk triple chiffon. Under the ring collar, the cape is fastened with twin embroidered buttons. The shape of the cape is an arch from shoulder to hem with soft waves in back....

With the ensemble Mrs. Kennedy will wear 20-button white glacé kid gloves and carry a matching white silk peau d'ange tailored clutch purse. Mrs. Kennedy's shoes will be matching white silk opera pumps with medium high heels.

The gown is now in the collection of the Smithsonian Institution.

Inauguration

John Fitzgerald Kennedy was inaugurated the thirty-fifth President of the United States on January 20, 1961. Although it had snowed heavily (eight inches) the evening before, Inauguration Day dawned sunny and bright. The incoming President wore an Oxford gray cutaway, a black overcoat, and a black silk top hat. Mrs. Kennedy wore a simple beige cloth coat, designed by Oleg Cassini, with four big buttons down the front and a matching pillbox hat. She carried a sable muff and wore a sable circlet at the neck of her coat. As tradition dictated, the Kennedys drove to the White House to meet outgoing President Eisenhower and his wife, and the two couples traveled together to the stands erected in front of the Capitol building.

The ceremony began with an invocation by Richard Cardinal Cushing (which caused a moment of excitement when a short-circuit in the lectern wiring produced a cloud of blue smoke) and then featured a poem of dedication from Robert Frost. The glare of the winter sun was so strong that the elderly poet could not read the poem in front of him but had to recite another one, "The Gift Outright," from memory. Contralto Marian Anderson sang the national anthem. With family, friends, and supporters looking on, John F. Kennedy took the oath of office at 12:51 P.M., on the Fitzgerald family Bible. At that very moment, bonfires were lighted in the Irish town of New Ross, the home of Kennedy's forefathers. Afterward, the President delivered his Inaugural Address to the crowd and the millions watching the event on television at home.

Inscription over the Mantel

After the widowed Jacqueline Kennedy moved out of the White House, it was discovered that she had arranged to have an inscription carved in the marble mantelpiece of the bedroom she and President Kennedy had occupied there. The inscription read, "In this room lived John Fitzgerald Kennedy with his wife, Jacqueline, during the two years, ten months, and two days he was President of the United States, January 20, 1961—November 22, 1963."

"Irish Mafia"

When Senator John F. Kennedy came to national prominence during his 1960 campaign for the presidency, journalists nicknamed some of his staff members "the Irish mafia." Kenny

O'Donnell, Larry O'Brien, and Dave Powers were the most visible of the Irish mafia, men who had been on the Kennedy staff for a number of years, who shared jokes with him during relaxed moments and fought his battles for him without hesitation, and loyally did whatever was needed to help their candidate win. As it happened, most members of the Irish mafia were with President Kennedy on that fateful trip to Dallas on November 22, 1963, and they formed a sort of honor guard that kept watch over his coffin on the flight back to Washington—one last service for their friend and leader. Mrs. Kennedy said to them during the long flight of Air Force One, "You were with him in the beginning, and you're with him now. That's as it should be."

Iver-Johnson Model 55 Sa

The gun used to shoot Senator Robert F. Kennedy was a snub-nosed eight-shot revolver, manufactured by Iver-Johnson, their model 55 Sa. The gun, priced at $32.95, was the way Los Angeles police managed to identify Kennedy's assassin, who was in custody but refused to give his name. They learned that the gun had been purchased by Albert L. Hertz as protection during the Watts riots in 1965. Hertz later gave it to his daughter, Mrs. Robert Westlake, who became concerned about having a gun in the house with young children and gave it to eighteen-year-old George Erhart, who then sold it to Munir (Joe) Sirhan. Joe Sirhan confirmed that he had given the gun to his brother Sirhan.

J Six Ranch

The J Six Ranch in Arizona was the location of John F. Kennedy's 1936 convalescence after his serious illness during his freshman year at Princeton. The forty-thousand-acre ranch belonged to a friend of journalist Arthur Krock, at that time a member of the Kennedy inner circle, and Krock arranged for Jack to spend some time there. The fresh air and outdoor exercise put the young man in such good condition he was able to return to Boston and enroll at Harvard for the fall semester.

JFK: The Man and the Myth

In 1967, Victor Lasky published a book entitled *JFK: The Man and the Myth*. The book was the first after the President's assassination to attempt to debunk the Kennedy legend, and it hit the number one position on the best-seller lists. Among the adjectives Lasky applied to the slain President were: passionless, opportunistic, vain, glib, mealy-mouthed, slick, shifty-eyed, snobbish, immature, shallow, calculating, and that old favorite, pusillanimous. Apparently the long list of adulatory biographies previously published by Kennedy insiders had created a public appetite for a look at the other side of the coin. Subsequently, biographers began to look more objectively at Kennedy's human mix of virtues and shortcomings.

JFK'S Cigars

President John F. Kennedy was known to relish the occasional cigar, although he usually attempted to do his smoking away from the lenses of photographers. His personal favorites were supplied by the august firm of Dunhill, whose temperature- and humidity-controlled humidors stored cigars for the President, as well as Nelson Rockefeller, Winston Churchill, and John Wayne.

JFK's Favorite Books

Samuel Flagg Bemis, *John Quincy Adams*
John Buchan, *Pilgrim's Way*
Eugene Burdick, *The Ninth Wave*
David Cecil, *Melbourne*
Winston Churchill, *Marlborough*

Marquis James, *The Raven*
Norman Mailer, *The Deer Park*
Allan Nevins, *The Emergence of Lincoln*
Stendahl, *The Red and the Black*

JFK's Serial Number

In the Navy, Lieutenant John F. Kennedy's serial number was 116071/1109. After his death, his Navy dog tags bearing the number were given to Cardinal Cushing, who had presided over his funeral.

JFK's Views on Agriculture

According to Kennedy insider John Kenneth Galbraith, John F. Kennedy had scant interest in and less knowledge about agricultural matters. "Where I grew up," Kennedy explained, "we were taken out on a bus to see a cow." During his 1960 campaign, Kennedy told Galbraith, who was acting as his advisor on agricultural issues, "I don't want to hear about agriculture from anyone but you, Ken. And I don't much want to hear about it from you either."

"Jackie, How Could You?"

In the fall of 1968, when Jacqueline Bouvier Kennedy announced that she would wed Greek shipping magnate Aristotle Onassis, public reaction all over the world was strongly negative. One newspaper headline summed up the popular sentiment: "Jackie, How Could You?" The public would probably have resented any second marriage for the widow of President Kennedy, especially at a time when memories of his assassination had just been reawakened by the death of his brother, Robert, that June. The choice of the short and swarthy Onassis, with his history of womanizing and occasionally falling afoul of the laws governing commerce, seemed especially disappointing to those who treasured the days of Camelot. At the time, it was difficult for people to sympathize with the desire for peace, privacy, and security that caused Jacqueline, newly grieved by the murder of her brother-in-law Robert, to choose to marry Aristotle Onassis.

The Jackie Look

When Jacqueline Bouvier Kennedy became First Lady, she immediately exerted an influence on fashion all over the world. Everyone from duchesses to dime-store clerks tried to imitate her personal style. The "Jackie Look," as it came to be known, was based on an A-line shape that skimmed the body rather than hugging it. Clothes were made of sumptuous fabrics, with pared-down detailing that focused on a single element, such as the buttons on a coat.

Colors were clear, often bright, such as lemon yellow, pistachio green, or clean, crisp white. The small pillbox hat was an integral part of the Jackie look, as were comfortable, low-heeled shoes, good leather handbags, a youthfully unrestrained coiffure, natural-looking makeup, and only the simplest of jewelry. Style was achieved through restraint and simplicity, and by a conscious decision to sacrifice some degree of variety to gain a single strong image.

The Jackie Look on Inauguration Day. (Bill Ray, Black Star)

J

Jacqueline Kennedy Thanks the Nation

Six weeks after the death of President Kennedy, his widow went on television to make a brief public statement, thanking all those who had sent messages of sympathy and grief. Wearing a black suit and no jewelry except her gold wedding band, Mrs. Kennedy sat in a chair in Attorney General Robert F. Kennedy's office, accompanied by the attorney general and Senator Edward M. Kennedy. She fought to maintain her composure as she delivered her brief message:

The knowledge of the affection in which my husband was held by all of you has sustained me, and the warmth of these tributes is something I shall never forget. Whenever I can bear to, I read them.

All his bright light gone from the world ... All of you who have written to me know how much we all loved him, and that he returned that love in full measure. It is my greatest wish that every one of the letters be acknowledged. It will take a long time to do so, but I know you will understand. Each and every message is to be treasured, not only for my children, but so that future generations will know how much our country and people in other nations thought of him. Your letters will be placed with his papers in the library to be erected in his memory on the Charles River in Boston, Massachusetts. I hope you and your children will be able to visit the Kennedy library.

Jacqueline's Wedding Ring

After President John F. Kennedy was pronounced dead in Parkland Hospital in Dallas, his widow Jacqueline stayed with him for a quiet moment of good-bye. Then she slipped her wedding ring off her finger and placed it on his, kissed him on the lips, and left the room. Immediately she began to worry over whether she should have parted with her ring, but aide Kenny O'Donnell assured her it had been the right thing to do. At ceremonies held in the Capitol Rotunda on the day before the President's funeral, Senator Mike Mansfield from Montana repeated that touching detail several times ... "and so she took a ring from her finger and placed it in his hands ..." In fact, O'Donnell had decided she ought to have the ring back, and had privately gone into the room in Bethesda Naval Hospital where the President lay and retrieved the ring for Mrs. Kennedy.

Henry M. Jackson

Henry M. Jackson was the young congressman from Washington State who was a friend of John F. Kennedy when they both served in Congress in the late 1940s. Like Kennedy, Jackson later became a senator and was once considered a possible candidate for the presidency.

Jaundice

In the fall of 1935, John F. Kennedy suffered an attack of jaundice while he was studying with Harold Laski at the University of London School of Economics. The young man was forced to withdraw from the school and return to the United States to regain his health.

J

Jeep Accident

In the summer of 1973, young Joseph P. Kennedy II, the oldest son of Robert F. and Ethel Kennedy, was vacationing on the island of Nantucket with his brother David and David's friend Pam Kelley. On the afternoon of August 13, Joe borrowed a friend's Jeep for a drive to the beach. He had six passengers: his brother David, Pam Kelley, Pam's sister Kim, and three other young women. Joe started to cut across a highway without noticing an oncoming station wagon. When he accelerated and swerved at the last minute to avoid hitting the station wagon, the Jeep flipped and rolled. Joe was unhurt, but David suffered fractured vertebrae and Pam was even more seriously injured, with resulting permanent paralysis of her legs. Joe was charged with "operating negligently so that the lives and safety of the public might be endangered." He appeared in court a week later, accompanied by his mother and his uncle, Senator Edward M. Kennedy. Although he pleaded not guilty, he was convicted of negligent driving. Joe's license was suspended for six months and he was fined one hundred dollars; he was later quoted as saying that the hardest punishment was the knowledge of the harm that had befallen his brother and his friend.

Joe Kennedy Stricken by Stroke

On December 19, 1961, Joseph P. Kennedy was hit by a massive stroke after playing fifteen holes of golf at the Palm Beach Golf Club, just a few blocks from his Florida winter home. He was rushed to St. Mary's Hospital, where he lay near death for several days. His son John, the President of the United States, immediately traveled to Palm Beach to see his father and to pray for him in the hospital chapel. Joe Kennedy survived the initial trauma of the severe stroke, but he was never able to overcome its debilitating effects. Despite treatment at the Rusk Institute in New York and the Institute for the Achievement of Human Potential in Pennsylvania, he was able to walk only a few steps at best and never regained the ability to speak clearly. He communicated by saying the word "no" with so many different intonations that family and friends were able to understand clearly what he wanted.

John F. Kennedy Center for the Performing Arts

In January 1964, Congress passed the John F. Kennedy Center Act, which named the planned cultural center in Washington after the late President, in recognition of his enthusiastic support for the arts. The ground-breaking ceremony for the Center was held in December of that year, with President Johnson lifting the first shovel of dirt. Kennedy family members in attendance included Robert and Ethel Kennedy, Edward and Joan Kennedy, and Jean Smith. The actual opening of the Center came on September 8, 1971, with the world premiere of Leonard Bernstein's *Mass*. Among the guests were Rose Kennedy and Edward and Joan Kennedy.

J

John F. Kennedy Library

The John F. Kennedy Library was opened on October 21, 1979, with a touching ceremony attended by many members of the Kennedy family. Senator Edward M. Kennedy and Joseph P. Kennedy II both spoke movingly, and then the Boston Pops Orchestra played Aaron Copeland's' "Fanfare for the Common Man."

President Kennedy had originally intended to house his papers in a library to be built on the Charles River, near the campus of his alma mater, Harvard. In 1965, a deed was signed by the Kennedy family to turn all the President's pa-pers over to the planned library. Shortly thereafter, his widow selected another site for the building, south of Boston on a windy point of land north of Cape Cod that was called Columbia Point Peninsula. The distinctive building was designed by world-renowned architect I. M. Pei. Before construction actually began, Senator Robert F. Kennedy was assassinated, and it was decided that the planned library would also serve as a memorial to the President's brother. The library itself is a dramatic structure of glass and concrete. It houses presidential papers, as well

President Jimmy Carter dedicates the Kennedy Library. Guests include left to right: John F. Kennedy, Jr., Jacqueline Kennedy Onassis, Lady Bird Johnson, Tip O'Neill, Senator and Mrs. Edward M. Kennedy, and Rosalynn Carter. (Courtesy of the Kennedy Library)

J

as oral histories from Kennedy insiders, and family memorabilia ranging from the dress Jackie wore to the Inaugural Concert to the millions of letters that poured in to the family after the deaths of the two Kennedy brothers. Nearly two and a half million people have visited the library since its opening. The current director is Charles U. Daly, a Yale graduate who formerly served as a staff assistant to President John F. Kennedy for congressional liaison.

Breaking ground for the Kennedy Library, left to right: *Jean Kennedy Smith, John F. Kennedy, Jr., Caroline Kennedy, Jacqueline Kennedy Onassis, and Pat Kennedy Lawford. (Courtesy of the Kennedy Library)*

The John Fitzgerald Kennedy Library, designed by I. M. Pei. (Courtesy of the Kennedy Library)

John Fitzgerald Kennedy School of Government

In the fall of 1966, a ceremony at Harvard University marked the renaming of its Graduate School of Public Administration as the John Fitzgerald Kennedy School of Government. The late President's brother, Senator Robert F. Kennedy, was the featured speaker.

John F. Kennedy Space Center

On November 29, 1963, just days after President John F. Kennedy was assassinated, President Lyndon B. Johnson responded to a suggestion from Mrs. Kennedy and formally signed an executive order that changed the name of the nation's space center in Florida from Cape Canaveral to Cape Kennedy. The new name was a commemoration of President Kennedy's interest in and support of America's space program. In 1974, the old name of Canaveral was reinstated, since, despite President Johnson's gesture, most employees continued to use the original name.

John-John

When John F. Kennedy, Jr., was a baby, the press learned that his parents sometimes called him by the affectionate diminutive John-John. For years, that was the standard journalistic way of referring to the President's son, and even today, it is possible to see the nickname used for the man who is approaching thirty. In grade school, boys who called him "John-John" were apt to end up with bloody noses, and Kennedy insiders say that calling him John-John to his face is even today one of the most reliable methods of making the young man angry.

Joseph P. Kennedy, Jr., Convalescent Home

In 1946, the Joseph P. Kennedy, Jr. Foundation gave a gift to the Archdiocese of Boston of six hundred thousand dollars to start construction of a convalescent home for poor children in the working-class Boston suburb of Brighton. The Foundation had been Joseph Kennedy's memorial gesture for his oldest son, who had been killed two years earlier flying a hazardous mission in World War II. Perhaps it was no coincidence that John F. Kennedy, who was then fighting his first battle for election, seeking the congressional seat for the Eleventh District in Massachusetts, was the family representative who handed over the generous check to Cardinal Cushing in front of a group of reporters and photographers. Joseph Kennedy thus managed to accomplish two kinds of good with a single check.

Joseph P. Kennedy, Jr., Foundation

The Kennedy family's most lasting memorial to oldest son Joseph P. Kennedy, Jr., after he was killed on a dangerous mission during World War II was the establishment of the Joseph P. Kennedy, Jr., Foundation. According to Rose Kennedy's account, it was originally funded by Joseph Kennedy with more than four hundred million dollars. It built two homes for children, named after Joe Junior, and has to date donated at least five hundred million dollars to other charitable causes. The foundation has also used its own funds to raise additional money, from other sources, for the causes it supports. The Joseph P. Kennedy, Jr., Foundation, of which Eunice Kennedy Shriver is now the head, concentrates much of its philanthropy in the field of mental retardation, an interest sparked decades ago by the problems of Eunice's older sister Rosemary.

"Joy She Gave"

The epitaph of Kathleen Kennedy, the Marchioness of Hartington, was selected by her mother-in-law, the Duchess of Devonshire. Kathleen's in-laws had asked to have her buried at the Devonshire family home, Chatsworth, after she was killed in an air crash in 1948. The line the Duchess chose was "Joy she gave, Joy she has found."

Judge Frank M. Johnson, Jr.

Judge Frank M. Johnson, Jr.: A Biography was a book written by Robert F. Kennedy, Jr. It was originally developed as his senior thesis at Harvard. The project was a study of a liberal southern United States District Judge, appointed by the Republican administration to the bench in 1955, who had nevertheless been sensitive to the civil rights ideals of Bobby's father, the attorney general, and his uncle, the President. Young Bobby and another Harvard student, Peter Kaplan, had gone to Montgomery, Alabama, to conduct their initial research, and Bobby stayed there for nearly a year, interviewing friends and colleagues of the judge and immersing himself in a new point of view. After the work was submitted to Harvard, contacts of the family arranged for the book's publication by G. P. Putnam's Sons in 1978. The book had modest sales.

Keeping the Winning Ball

A story often told about Joseph P. Kennedy's college days concerns the afternoon of June 23, 1911, when he won his varsity "H" in baseball at Harvard and then outraged the entire team with his unexpected behavior. It was the day of the big game with Yale, and only those who played in it were entitled to wear the coveted letter. Joe Kennedy sat on the bench until the final play of the ninth inning. With Harvard in the lead by three runs, the coach decided to risk sending in three substitutes at that last moment, to give them the chance to win their letters. Kennedy went in at first base, and made the final play, catching the throw from the shortstop that forced the runner out and ended the game. Then, to the disbelief of the captain of the team, whose hitting and pitching for nine innings had been the decisive factor in the game, Joe walked off the field with the game-winning ball—and refused to give it up.

Keith-Albee-Orpheum (KAO)

Keith-Albee-Orpheum was a chain of more than three hundred movie theaters (many of them old vaudeville houses) in which Joseph P. Kennedy bought a controlling interest in 1928. After forcing president Edward Albee to resign, Joe Kennedy took over the management of the theater chain and brought about a sharp increase in both sales and profits. KAO also owned one of the major Hollywood studios, Pathé, famous for its lavishly produced Cecil B. deMille epics. Within a year of the purchase, in Joe Kennedy's biggest deal to that date, KAO and Pathé, along with Kennedy's previous purchase of FBO, and David Sarnoff's RCA, were merged to create one giant holding company with enormous clout in the movie industry—Radio-Keith-Orpheum, or RKO.

Kenlaw Production Company

After Pat Kennedy married Peter Lawford, they formed a business called Kenlaw Production Company. It created two hit television series: one, starring Peter Lawford, called *Dear Phoebe*, and the other, based on the popular series of movies, called *The Thin Man*.

Bridget Murphy Kennedy

Bridget Murphy, born in 1821, was an Irish immigrant to Boston who arrived on the same ship as Patrick Kennedy; he was two years younger than she. They were married on September 26, 1849, and had four children: Mary, Margaret, Johanna, and Patrick Joseph. Patrick died on November 22, 1858, at the young age of thirty-five, leaving Bridget to raise their four children alone. She worked in a small notions shop, of which she eventually became co-owner, and later was a hairdresser at Boston's fashionable department store, Jordan Marsh. Bridget Murphy Kennedy died of a cerebral hemorrhage on December 20, 1888, shortly after the birth of her grandson, Joseph Patrick Kennedy, the father of the President.

Christopher George Kennedy

Christopher George Kennedy is the eighth child of Ethel Skakel and Robert F. Kennedy, born on Independence Day in 1963, a birthday he shares with his older sister Kathleen. Christopher was christened at St. Francis Xavier Church in Hyannis amid a spotlight of publicity, since his uncle Jack was then in the White House. In his childhood, Christopher impressed friends of the family as exceptionally good-natured and thoughtful, and he also seemed to be one of the few members of his generation interested in business. As a teenager, he organized a boat-rental business on Cape Cod, which provided summer employment for other members of his generation. Chris graduated from Boston College in 1986 and then worked for Archer-Daniels-Midland, an international conglomerate. In August 1987, he was married to Sheila Sinclair Berner, a law student who also graduated from Boston College. Christopher Kennedy currently works as leasing agent for the Kennedy-owned Merchandise Mart in Chicago and devotes part-time efforts to fund-raising for a variety of public causes, including setting up a program to feed the homeless.

David Anthony Kennedy

David Anthony Kennedy was the fourth child of Robert F. and Ethel Skakel Kennedy, born on June 15, 1955. A picture of David as a boy standing on the White House lawn hung on the wall at Hickory Hill with the joking caption, "A future President inspects his property," but David's life seemed darkly shadowed by the assassination of his uncle and father and the subsequent family difficulties. He was in Los Angeles with his family on June 5, 1968, and was sitting up in bed in his hotel room watching television when he saw the news stories about his father's shooting by Sirhan Sirhan; it was several hours before anyone realized the horrified boy was awake and went to comfort him.

After some troubled years in and out of various boarding schools, David was admitted to Harvard. But he seemed restless, unable to find his niche in the Kennedy family and unable to choose a direction for his life. He was arrested for a drug buy in New York City and received a suspended sentence; at the urging of family members, he had enrolled in several different treatment programs, but no one seemed to be able to find the key to helping David. On April 25, 1984, while the twenty-eight-year-old David was visiting his grandmother Rose Kennedy at Palm Beach during spring vacation, he died of a drug overdose in his room at the Brazilian Court Hotel. Police found 1.3 grams of cocaine in his wallet, and the autopsy also showed he had taken Demerol and Mellaril. Authorities later arrested two bellhops at the hotel in connection with the sale of the drug. David was buried in the family plot in Brookline, Massachusetts.

Douglas Harriman Kennedy

Douglas Harriman Kennedy is the tenth child of Robert F. and Ethel Skakel Kennedy, born on March 24, 1967. He was named after two important figures of the Kennedy administration: Douglas Dillon, the former secretary of the treasury, and former New York Governor Averell Harriman. Doug attended Georgetown Prep before entering Boston College. He later transferred to Brown University.

Edward Moore Kennedy

Edward Moore Kennedy is the ninth and last child of Joseph P. and Rose Fitzgerald Kennedy. He was born in Boston's St. Margaret's Hospital on February 22, 1932. His older brother Jack, also his godfather (his godmother was his older sister Rosemary) had suggested the baby should be named George Washington Kennedy, after the President whose birthday he shared, but his parents chose instead to name him after Kennedy's long-time aide, Eddie Moore. Teddy, as he was known in the family, attended a variety of schools before graduating from Milton Academy, in Massachusetts. Following family tradition, he enrolled in Harvard but was asked to leave near the end of his freshman year when another student took a Spanish test for him. After two years in the Army, Ted was reaccepted by Harvard, graduating in 1956. He went on to law school at the University of Virginia.

Edward Kennedy married the former Virginia Joan Bennett in 1958. The couple had three children: Kara Anne, born in 1960; Edward Moore, Jr., born in 1961; and Patrick Joseph, born in 1967. After graduating from law school, Kennedy became an assistant district attorney in Boston and a year later, in 1962, won the Massachusetts election to fill the Senate seat left vacant when Senator John F. Kennedy became President. He was reelected in 1964, 1970, 1976 and 1982. In 1988, he was reelected by a landslide 66 percent of the votes, his biggest margin ever; he says he attributes his margin of victory to the work of his children Kara and Ted Jr., who served as co-chairmen of his campaign. He is currently fifth in seniority in the hundred-member Senate.

After the deaths of older brothers John F. Kennedy and Robert F. Kennedy, the role of leadership was handed to Edward Kennedy. He was spoken of as a presidential candidate as early as 1968, but the tragedy of Chappaquiddick raised questions in the minds of the voters, and the Kennedy family made clear their reluctance to see the last Kennedy expose himself to the physical risks of a campaign and a presidency. It was not until 1980 that Ted made a concerted run for the nomination. His bid failed. Shortly thereafter, the senator and his wife officially separated, and they were divorced two years later. The only remaining male of his generation, Ted Kennedy has become the unofficial head of the Kennedy clan.

Official portrait of Massachusetts Senator Edward M. Kennedy. (Courtesy of the office of Senator Edward M. Kennedy)

K

Edward Moore Kennedy, Jr.

Edward Moore Kennedy, Jr., is the second child and older son of Edward M. and Joan Bennett Kennedy, born September 25, 1961. He attended St. Alban's Preparatory School and graduated from Wesleyan College in 1984. In November 1973, when Ted was just thirteen, it was discovered that he had a rare form of cancer that necessitated the amputation of his right leg. Since then, young T.K., as the family calls him, has learned to use an artificial leg to ski, play tennis and football, and dance—in other words, to participate in a full life. The founder of the nonprofit organization Facing the Challenge, Ted often acts as a spokesperson for causes related to the disabled and has been responsible for his father's great sensitivity to the needs of handicapped Americans. T.K. says, "I reject the term disabled. I reject the term handicapped, because that sets restrictions on people's minds, and one of the things we're trying to do isn't just break down the physical barriers which prevent people from realizing their full potential in life, but break down the attitudinal barriers." Rumor has it that T.K. is another Kennedy considering a political career in the future.

Edward M. Kennedy, Jr. (Courtesy of Committee to Re-Elect Senator Kennedy)

Ethel Skakel Kennedy

Ethel Skakel was born on April 11, 1928, the daughter of George and Ann Brannack Skakel of Chicago. Her father was a classic American entrepreneur (and conservative Republican), whose small Chicago-based company eventually became the huge multinational Great Lakes Carbon Corporation, of which he was CEO. In 1955, both George and Ann Skakel were killed in the crash of their private plane. Ethel's brother George died in a similar crash eleven years later, and his widow choked to death at the dinner table that same year.

Ethel, the sixth of seven children, moved with her family to Greenwich, Connecticut, when she was nine. She later attended Manhattanville College, run by the Sisters of the Sacred Heart, where her roommate was Jean Kennedy. She was introduced to Jean's brother Bob on a skiing trip to Canada in 1944. At the time, Bob was more interested in Ethel's older sister Pat, and it was not until Pat married and moved to Ireland that Bob began to call Ethel. They were married on June 17, 1950, immediately after Ethel's college graduation. The couple had eleven children: Kathleen (1951), Joseph P. II (1952), Robert, Jr. (1954), David (1955), Courtney (1956), Michael (1958), Kerry (1959), Christopher (1963), Max (1965), Douglas (1967), and Rory (1968).

Ethel was a tireless helpmate to her husband throughout his career, as well as his biggest booster and best friend. His death in 1968, at the hands of assassin Sirhan Sirhan, left her with a large family to bring up alone—including youngest child Rory, who was not born until six months after her father died. In recent years, Ethel has devoted much of her time to the Robert F. Kennedy Memorial, a foundation that tries to carry on her husband's work. And with grandchildren arriving regularly, she remains an anchor of Kennedy family life.

Robert and Ethel with their children at Hickory Hill, left to right: *Max, Christopher, Kerry, Courtney, Kathleen, Ethel, Douglas, Bob, Joe, Bobbie, David, and Michael. (Courtesy of the Kennedy Library)*

John Fitzgerald Kennedy

John Fitzgerald Kennedy was the second child born to Joseph P. and Rose Fitzgerald Kennedy. The birth took place in the master bedroom of the couple's modest house in Brookline, Massachusetts, on the afternoon of May 29, 1917. Always called Jack by the family, the little boy's childhood was marked by illness. He nearly died from a serious case of scarlet fever when he was two, and had to spend three months in the hospital. After his recovery, his health remained so precarious that he promptly caught first whooping cough and then the mumps. His first schooling was at the nearby public school in Brookline, but then he was sent to Canterbury Preparatory School and later to join his older brother, Joe Junior, at Choate. Jack's record at Choate was not so illustrious as that of his brother, yet even though he was ranked sixty-fourth in a class of 112, his fellow students voted Jack "most likely to succeed." Perhaps it was to avoid the constant comparison with his older brother that Jack decided to enroll at Princeton in the fall of 1935 rather than Harvard, where Joe was starting his junior year. But ill health forced Jack to withdraw midway through the year. When he was able to go back to school the following fall, he chose Harvard.

As he was graduating cum laude from Harvard in June 1940, John F. Kennedy was also receiving congratulations on publishing his first book. *Why England Slept*, an elaboration of his senior thesis, focuses on the question of why England had been so unprepared to enter World War II. The author then spent a year auditing classes at Stanford University and traveling extensively. In October 1941 he entered the Navy and worked in the Office of Naval Intelligence in Washington. He was posted to the South Pacific in 1942, as the commander of a PT boat. When his boat, PT-109, was rammed by a Japanese destroyer in August 1943, his heroic actions saved all the crew members who survived the collision. He was awarded the Navy and Marine Corps Medal for valor.

In 1946, John F. Kennedy ran for and won the Congressional seat in Massachusetts's Eleventh District. After serving six years as a representative, he ran for the Senate in 1952, defeating the incumbent Henry Cabot Lodge II. The young

Senator Kennedy was considered one of the most eligible bachelors in Washington, but in the summer of 1953, it was announced that he would marry Jacqueline Bouvier. The wedding took place in Newport, Rhode Island, on September 12. The couple had two children who survived infancy. Caroline Bouvier Kennedy was born on November 27, 1957, and John Fitzgerald Kennedy, Jr., was born on November 25, 1960. A third child, Patrick Bouvier Kennedy, died two days after his birth on August 7, 1963.

While recuperating from back surgery in 1954–55, Kennedy authored his second book, *Profiles in Courage*, studies of political leadership. It won the Pulitzer Prize for biography in 1955. The acclaim stood him in good stead at the Democratic Convention in 1956, when he

A formal portrait of President Kennedy. (A&E Cable Network)

K

proved to be a surprisingly strong candidate for the vice-presidential nomination, which was finally won by Senator Estes Kefauver of Tennessee. Shortly thereafter, Kennedy made the decision to run for the presidency in 1960. After a tough fight in the primaries, John F. Kennedy won his party's nomination for the presidential candidacy in 1960 and, in a very close vote, defeated Richard Nixon to become the thirty-fifth President of the United States. At the age of forty-three, he was the youngest man ever to be elected to that office.

The Kennedy presidency was marked by a number of challenges, among them the Bay of Pigs invasion, the division of Berlin by the Wall, and the Cuban missile crisis. Today, the administration of John F. Kennedy is probably best remembered for its expressions of the best of American idealism, its grace and culture, and its belief that public service is one of the highest callings open to people of education and talent.

On November 22, 1963, President Kennedy was assassinated as he rode in a motorcade through downtown Dallas, Texas. The nation and the Kennedy family said their final farewells three days later. After lying in state in the White House and the Capitol Rotunda, the President's body was taken to St. Matthew's Cathedral, followed by mourners on foot. He was buried at the foot of the Custis-Lee mansion in Arlington National Cemetery, overlooking the city of Washington.

Dallas police arrested Lee Oswald for the murder of the President, only to see him killed by a bullet fired by Dallas nightclub operator Jack Ruby as he was being transferred from one jail to another. President Johnson appointed the Warren Commission to investigate the assassination, and their report concluded that Oswald had acted alone. A subsequent Senate investigation in 1979 concluded, however, that Oswald was likely part of a conspiracy that may have included members of organized crime, although no concrete evidence proved the assertion incontrovertibly.

John Fitzgerald Kennedy, Jr.

John Fitzgerald Kennedy, Jr., the son of President-elect John F. Kennedy and his wife Jacqueline Bouvier Kennedy, was born at Georgetown University Hospital in Washington on November 25, 1960, only a few weeks after his father's triumph at the polls. Just three years old when President Kennedy was killed, John says he has no memory of his early White House years. After the family moved to New York City, John attended first a parochial school, St. David's, and then the Collegiate School, a prestigious private school on the city's West Side. He went to boarding school at Phillips Academy in Andover, Massachusetts, and to college at Brown University, graduating in 1983.

After graduating from Brown John worked as a staff member for the New York City Office of Economic Development, responsible for job-promotion and job-retention strategies. An interest in acting led to a role in *Winners*, a play by Brian Friel. His costar was fellow Brown grad Christina Haag, also his steady girlfriend of the last few years. John graduated from law school at New York University in May 1989. He has had summer jobs clerking in the civil rights group at the Justice Department and in the prestigious Los Angeles law firm of Marratt, Phelps, Rothenberg and Phillips. It has been announced that he will join the Manhattan district attorney's office, in a $29,000-a-year job doing legal research and legwork. His new boss, Robert Morgenthau, was appointed to the post as U.S. attorney by President Kennedy in 1961.

Young John Kennedy. (Adam Scull, Black Star)

Joseph Patrick Kennedy

Joseph Patrick Kennedy was born on September 6, 1888, the first child of saloon-owner Patrick Joseph Kennedy and his wife, Mary Augusta Hickey. Joe attended prestigious Boston Latin School and then Harvard University, graduating in 1912. His first job after he left Harvard was at the Columbia Trust Company, a small bank of which his father was a founder. When a larger bank tried to take it over, Joe was the one to organize the successful defense of Columbia Trust; he was afterward given the post of president, making him one of the youngest bank presidents in the country. He stayed at the bank until the U.S. entered World War I, when he went to Bethlehem Steel to supervise its Massachusetts shipyard.

When the war was over, Joe Kennedy joined the Boston brokerage firm of Hayden, Stone and Company, and thereafter went out on his own to wheel and deal in the financial world. In the late 1920s, he became involved with the movie business (and movie star Gloria Swanson) but sold out his holdings in Hollywood, as well as most of his other stocks, by the time of the crash in 1929. Through the early 1930s, Kennedy continued to make money in the stock market by selling short, and he also profited from the end of Prohibition, when his Somerset Company had warehouses full of good imported scotch to sell Americans as soon as they were able to drink legally again. In 1934, President Roosevelt appointed him a member of the Securities and Exchange Commission, of which he was then elected head. Later he served as chairman of the Maritime Commission, and in 1937, after Roosevelt was elected to a second term as President, Joseph Kennedy was appointed Ambassador to the Court of St. James. He resigned that post in February 1941, and thereafter confined his attention to his family and his own fortune.

Joseph P. Kennedy married Rose Elizabeth Fitzgerald in 1914, and the couple had nine children: Joseph Patrick, Jr. (1915), John Fitzgerald (1917), Rosemary (1918), Kathleen (1920), Eunice Mary (1921), Patricia (1924), Robert Francis (1925), Jean Ann (1928), and Edward Moore (1932). After the eldest son was killed in World War II and daughter Kathleen in a plane crash a few years later, Joe Kennedy retired from public life and concentrated his efforts on helping his children, especially his son Jack, whose political ambitions he encouraged. Although he kept a low profile during Jack's campaigns for the House, the Senate, and finally the presidency, insiders say that Joe Kennedy was always consulted on important matters, and it was the Kennedy money that financed the bids for public office. In the first year of John F. Kennedy's presidency, his father suffered a serious stroke and never recovered the ability to move without help or to speak. The twin tragedies of the deaths of his sons Jack and Bobby depressed him further, and he died at home at Hyannis Port on November 18, 1969. A funeral mass was conducted at St. Francis Xavier's church in Hyannis by Richard Cardinal Cushing, with burial in the Kennedy family plot in Holyrood Cemetery in Brookline. Honorary pallbearers were his grandchildren Joseph P. Kennedy II, Christopher Lawford, Robert Shriver, Stephen Smith Jr., John F. Kennedy Jr., and Edward M. Kennedy, Jr. The eulogy was delivered by Kennedy's only living son, Senator Edward M. Kennedy.

Joseph Patrick Kennedy, Jr.

Joseph Patrick Kennedy, Jr., was the oldest child of Joseph P. and Rose Fitzgerald Kennedy. Joe Junior, as he was usually called in the family, was born on the morning of July 25, 1915, at a house his parents had rented for the summer near the oceanfront town of Hull, Massachusetts. Although Joe Junior attended public schools in his early years, he went as a ninth-grader to boarding school at prestigious Choate, where he achieved an excellent record both as an athlete and a student. His college years were spent at Harvard, from which he graduated cum laude in 1938. During his undergraduate career, he spent one semester studying with leftist philosopher Harold Laski at the London School of Economics. After months of traveling in Europe and observing the course of the civil war in Spain, Joe Junior enrolled in Harvard Law School in 1939. He said he was preparing himself for a career in politics, and his father supported his ambition wholeheartedly. Joe Junior was groomed for success, and all the Kennedys expected him to achieve it. He was an aggressive and determined young man, whose desire to win at all costs was softened by his warmth, his enthusiasm, and his good-natured grin.

Joe Junior spent two years in law school before he left to join the Navy. He became a cadet in the Naval Aviation Reserve on October 15, 1941, underwent flight training at the naval base in Jacksonville, Florida, and was commissioned as an ensign in April 1942. After promotion to Lieutenant (j.g.), he was posted to a bombing squad in England in July 1943. In the summer of 1944, after the Allied invasion of Normandy, Joe (by then a full lieutenant) volunteered for a hazardous flying mission. He was to pilot a plane loaded with explosives toward its target, a German base that launched the V-1 rockets that were causing high casualty rates among London's civilian population. The plan called for Kennedy to set the plane on its course and then bail out, but something went wrong during the mission. On the night of August 12, 1944, the plane exploded in midair, ten minutes from its target, killing Kennedy and his copilot instantly. Kennedy was posthumously awarded the Navy Cross for valor. The loss of their eldest son and seemingly brightest hope for the future was a heavy blow to Rose and Joe Kennedy.

Joseph Patrick Kennedy II

Joseph Patrick Kennedy was the second child and first son of Robert F. and Ethel Skakel Kennedy. He was born on September 24, 1952, in the midst of John F. Kennedy's campaign for the Massachusetts Senate; his mother made a speech on behalf of her brother-in-law the night before he was born. The baby's christening by Archbishop Cushing just before Election Day was thought to be the stimulus for additional votes for his uncle Jack. The baby was named after his grandfather and always called "young Joe" by the Kennedy family. He attended Our Lady of Victory School, then Georgetown Prep, Milton Academy, and the University of Massachusetts. On February 3, 1979, he married socially prominent Sheila Brewster Rauch of Philadelphia, whom he had known for ten years. On October 4, 1980, they became the parents of twin sons, Joseph and Matthew. The family lived in an old farmhouse on Massachusetts's South Shore, in suburban Boston.

As the eldest male of his generation, Joe was expected to carry on the Kennedy traditions, a point made explicit in a letter his father wrote him on the day of President Kennedy's funeral: "You are the oldest of all the male grandchildren. You have a special and particular responsibility now which I know you will fulfill. Remember all the things that Jack started—be kind to others that are less fortunate than we—and love our country." Joe had to begin shouldering that heavy responsibility five years later when his father was assassinated. Young Joe, who left his boarding school and flew out to Los Angeles right after the shooting, was the one who had to break the news of their father's death to his younger brothers and sisters. A few days later, he traveled on the funeral train from New York to Washington and impressed those who saw him by his poise and his ability to put others at their ease during those dreadful hours. Wearing one of his father's suits, fifteen-year-old Joe walked up and down the aisles, shaking hands and saying, "I'm Joe Kennedy, thank you for coming."

Joe took another step toward fulfilling his inherited responsibility in 1976, when he graduated from the University of Massachusetts in

Boston and then managed his Uncle Ted's successful campaign for reelection to the Senate. A few years later, with the help of a plan devised by Kennedy intimate Richard Goodwin, he founded the Citizens Energy Corporation, a non-profit organization that made shrewd business deals in oil and used the profits to provide home heating oil to the poor at low prices. In 1986, Joe followed his father and uncles into government service. He ran for the retiring "Tip" O'Neill's congressional seat from Massachusetts and won by a respectable margin. The young man who was once dubbed "The Reluctant Prince" is the first of his generation to win public office. In 1988, he was easily re-elected to his Congressional seat.

In March 1989, Joe Kennedy announced that he and his wife were separating. "This has been a very painful day for me and my family. As a father, my principal obligation and deepest personal desire is to assist my children through the most difficult time in their lives." At the same time, he announced that he would not run for governor in 1990, when Michael Dukakis retires.

Joseph P. Kennedy II campaigns for the Congressional seat his uncle Jack once held. (Rick Friedman, Black Star)

K

Joseph Patrick Kennedy III

Joseph Patrick Kennedy III is one of the twin sons of Joseph Patrick Kennedy II and his wife Sheila Rauch, born on November 3, 1980; his twin's name is Matthew Rauch Kennedy.

Kara Anne Kennedy

Kara Anne Kennedy is the oldest child of Edward M. and Joan Bennett Kennedy, born on February 27, 1960. Kara graduated from Boston's Tufts University in 1983 and subsequently took a job in the news department of Metromedia Television in New York. In 1988, she served as co-chairman (with brother Ted Jr.) of her father's re-election committee.

Kathleen Kennedy, Lady Hartington

Kathleen Kennedy was the fourth child of Joseph P. and Rose Fitzgerald Kennedy. She was born at the family home in Brookline on February 20, 1920. Kathleen was educated at various Sacred Heart schools in the United States and France, graduating from Noroton in 1938. She made her debut in London in the summer of 1938 and spent two years, 1939–41, at secular Finch College in New York, studying art and design. In November 1941, she took a job at the Washington *Times-Herald*, writing a column called "Did You Happen To See?" Hoping to return to England and her friends there, Kathleen finally managed to get into a Red Cross unit posted to London during the war, arriving there in July 1943.

Always a popular young woman, Kathleen (appropriately nicknamed "Kick") seemed to feel most at home in England, where she had lived while her father served as Ambassador to Great Britain. There she fell in love with William Cavendish, the Marquess of Hartington and heir to the Duke of Devonshire. Although religious differences made her decision to marry Billy a difficult one, they were wed in 1944. Hartington was killed in action three months later. She returned to her family in the United States, but after the war had ended, Kathleen decided to remain a resident of England, and bought a town house of her own in London. In 1946, Kathleen met and began an affair with Lord Peter Fitzwilliam, a Protestant not yet divorced from his wife.

When Kathleen made the decision to marry Peter, she told her parents; Rose Kennedy replied that if Kathleen chose to marry a divorced Protestant, she would no longer be regarded as a member of the Kennedy family. Despite that threat, Kathleen opted to pursue her own happiness, and succeeded in persuading her father to meet Peter in Paris in May 1948.

While Kathleen and Peter were waiting for Joe Kennedy to arrive, they decided to fly to Cannes for a few days of sun on the Riviera. Their small private plane was caught in a thunderstorm, and both Kathleen and Peter (along with the pilot and copilot) were killed on May 13, 1948. Her body lay in state in Paris at the Church of St. Philippe du Roule and then was escorted by her father to London for a funeral on May 20, at the Immaculate Conception Church. Among the hundreds of mourners were Anthony Eden, Randolph Churchill, Lady Astor, and U.S. Ambassador Lewis Douglas. That afternoon, Kathleen was buried in her husband's family plot at Chatsworth, the beautiful country home of the Devonshires.

K

Kathleen Alexandra Kennedy

Kathleen Alexandra Kennedy is the second child of Robert F. Kennedy, Jr., and his wife Emily Black Kennedy. The baby, named after her father's older sister, was born April 13, 1988, in Mount Kisco, New York.

Kyle Frances Kennedy

Kyle Frances Kennedy is the second child and first daughter of Michael and Victoria Gifford Kennedy, born on July 6, 1984.

Mary Augusta Hickey Kennedy

Mary Augusta Hickey was born on December 6, 1857, the daughter of a successful Boston businessman who had achieved far more than most Irish immigrants. One of her brothers was a policeman, another a doctor, a third the mayor of nearby Brockton. On November 23, 1887, she married Patrick Joseph Kennedy at Boston's Church of the Sacred Heart. The couple had four children, the oldest of whom was Joseph P. Kennedy, the father of the President. One of Mary's unusual talents was the ability to spell with great accuracy; her son Joe used to bring home his school friends and dare them to stump her with a word, but they never succeeded. Quick-witted and full of imagination, Mary Kennedy was the center of her family's life until her death from stomach cancer on May 20, 1923.

Mary Kerry Kennedy

Mary Kerry Kennedy is the seventh child of Robert F. and Ethel Skakel Kennedy, born on September 8, 1959. Kerry attended the Potomac School, the Putney School, and the Convent of the Sacred Heart in Bethesda, Maryland. She received her college degree from Brown University in 1982, and her law degree from Boston College. She is currently the executive director of the RFK Memorial Center for Human Rights, which supports the work of political activists all over the world.

Matthew Maxwell Taylor Kennedy

Matthew Maxwell Taylor Kennedy is the ninth child of Robert F. and Ethel Skakel Kennedy, born on January 11, 1965. Max was named after General Maxwell Taylor, chairman of the Joint Chiefs of Staff in the Kennedy Administration. He attended the Moses Brown School in Providence, Rhode Island, and majored in American history at Harvard.

Matthew Rauch Kennedy

Matthew Rauch Kennedy is one of the sons of Joseph Patrick Kennedy II and his wife Sheila Rauch, born on November 3, 1980. His twin's name is Joseph Patrick III.

Michael Lemoyne Kennedy

Michael LeMoyne Kennedy is the sixth child of Robert F. and Ethel Skakel Kennedy, born on February 27, 1958, and named after close family friend LeMoyne Billings. Michael graduated from Harvard in 1980, and, like his father, earned a law degree from the University of Virginia (1984). On March 14, 1981, he married Victoria Gifford, the daughter of sports figure Frank Gifford. Michael and Vicki have three children: Michael, Jr., born in 1983; Kyle, born in 1985; and Rory, born in 1987.

Michael began working for the Citizens Energy Corporation after he finished law school, and when older brother Joe won the congressional election in 1986, Michael took his place as president of the organization. He says about his work, "You can't sit back and enjoy the life that we in the United States, and my family in particular, have been born into, that is wealth, and any power that goes along with it. You have to go out and help others. You have to add something positive."

Patrick Kennedy

The first Kennedy to come to America was Patrick Kennedy, the President's great-grandfather. He was the youngest of three sons, the eldest of whom fought and was killed in the battle of Vinegar Hill, an uprising of Irish farmers against the British Army; Patrick also had a sister named Mary. Patrick was born in 1823 to a family that farmed a small holding, about twenty-five acres, in southeast Ireland. Growers of beef and barley, the Kennedys fared relatively well in the economic hard times of the potato famine, but a desire to improve the family fortunes led Patrick to decide to try his chances in America in 1848, traveling over on the *Washington Irving*.

On his arrival in the New World, Patrick Kennedy worked as a cooper on Noddle's Island, the small strip of land that was the main docking area for cargo ships bound for Boston. On September 26, 1849, at Boston's Cathedral of the Holy Cross, Patrick married Bridget Murphy, who had been a passenger on the same ship from Ireland. The couple had four children: Mary, Johanna, Margaret, and Patrick Joseph. Patrick Kennedy died of cholera on November 22, 1858, at the age of thirty-five, leaving his widow to raise their four children, the youngest of whom was less than a year old.

Patrick Bouvier Kennedy

Patrick Bouvier Kennedy was the son born to President and Mrs. John F. Kennedy on August 7, 1963. The premature birth took place at the Otis Air Force Base Hospital on Cape Cod, nearly six weeks before the due date. The Kennedy infant showed immediate signs of breathing difficulties and was flown to Children's Medical Center in Boston, where the President, accompanied by his brother Robert, kept vigil throughout the attempts to save his infant son. The baby succumbed in the early morning hours on August 9. The following day Cardinal Cushing conducted the Mass of the Angels in his private chapel for Patrick Kennedy. Jacqueline Kennedy was too ill to attend the service. Cardinal Cushing later remembered the President's obvious sorrow: "He wouldn't take his hands off of that little coffin. I was afraid he'd carry it right out with him." As it was, the Cardinal had to coax the President to leave the chapel, saying, "Come on, Jack, let's go. God is good." The baby was buried in the family plot in Brookline, and later reinterred with President Kennedy at Arlington National Cemetery.

Patrick Joseph Kennedy

Patrick Joseph Kennedy, known as P.J., was the father of Joseph P. Kennedy and the grandfather of the President. P.J. was born in Boston on January 8, 1858, the son of Irish immigrant Patrick Kennedy and his wife, Bridget Murphy. P.J.'s father died while he was less than one year old, and the family was held together by his mother, who clerked in and later became co-owner of a tiny notions shop. P.J. briefly attended a parochial school run by the Sisters of Notre Dame, but dropped out because of financial necessity and went to work on the docks. He somehow managed to save enough of his earnings to buy a tavern in Boston's Haymarket Square, from which he plowed the profits into two additional, more profitable, saloons. In 1887, on Thanksgiving Day, he married Mary Augusta Hickey, and they had four children: Joseph Patrick (1888); Francis (1891), who died in infancy; Loretta (1892); and Margaret (1898).

The earnings of the saloons brought comfortable circumstances, and P.J. went into politics in search of more power and influence. He was elected to the state house of representatives in 1885 and won annual reelection until 1891, when he ran for and won a seat in the state senate. Kennedy was also three times a delegate to the Democratic conventions to select a Presidential candidate. He served Boston as fire commissioner and as commissioner of wires. But his real preference was for operating behind the scenes, so he became a district boss of Boston's powerful Democratic machine, meeting regularly in Room 8 of the old Quincy House. Kennedy exercised power by running what amounted to a little welfare state in his neighborhood. He was a small real estate speculator, and in 1895 he helped organize the Columbia Trust Company, the bank of which he was to become president (as was his son Joe). After the death of his wife in 1923, Patrick J. Kennedy lived with his daughter Margaret and her husband, Charles Burke. P.J. Kennedy died of a liver disease on May 18, 1929, while his only son was in California making a film with Gloria Swanson. It was his grandson, Joseph P. Kennedy, Jr., who attended the funeral in Joe's place, along with honorary pallbearer, in-law John F. Fitzgerald. Years later, in 1951, Joseph P. Kennedy memorialized his father by giving the city of Boston a donation to establish the Patrick J. Kennedy Medal of Honor for firemen who display heroism in the line of duty.

K

Patrick Joseph Kennedy

Patrick Joseph Kennedy is the third child of Edward M. and Joan Bennett Kennedy, born on July 14, 1967. Like his father, Patrick attended the Fessenden School; his preparatory school was Phillips Academy in Andover. He graduated from Providence College as a philosophy major with the class of 1989. A childhood history of asthma failed to dim Patrick's Kennedy competitive spirit, as did recent surgery to remove a benign tumor on a spinal nerve near the neck.

In 1988, Patrick ran for and won his first elective office while still a student at Providence. In the primary he defeated the incumbent Democratic state representative, John Skeffington, a veteran of five terms in the Rhode Island State House, and then ran unopposed in the November election. He will serve in the part-time, three-hundred-dollar-a-year post.

Patrick Kennedy and Senator John Pastore (R.I.) converse with the Prime Minister of Italy at a reception at the Kennedy Library. (Courtesy of the Kennedy Library)

Robert Francis Kennedy

Robert Francis Kennedy was the seventh child of Joseph P. and Rose Fitzgerald Kennedy. Like his older brothers and sisters, Bobby was born at home, in Brookline, Massachusetts. His date of birth was November 20, 1925. As a child, he was considered by the family to be the sweetest and most generous of his generation. Bobby attended school at Portsmouth Priory for two years, the only one of the Kennedy sons to stay in a Catholic school for more than a single term. He graduated from Milton Academy and began his studies at Harvard before they were interrupted by his World War II enlistment in the navy. After his discharge, Bob Kennedy returned to Harvard, where he had to struggle to keep his grades up. He did manage to accomplish a goal that had eluded his older brothers however; despite his small size, Bobby won his letter in football. He graduated from Harvard in March 1948 and enrolled in the University of Virginia Law School, from which he received his degree in 1951. On June 17, 1950, Robert Kennedy married Ethel Skakel, a college roommate of his sister Jean, at Greenwich, Connecticut. The couple had eleven children.

Robert Kennedy's first job, in 1952, was working for the Justice Department in New York City, investigating cases against former members of the Truman administration. At about the same time, he experienced his first in-depth involvement with politics, when he agreed to manage his brother Jack's successful campaign to become a senator. When Jack went to Washington, Bobby did too, working as counsel for several different Senate subcommittees. His involvement with the Senate Investigating Committee, which he joined at the invitation of Senator Joseph McCarthy, a Kennedy family friend, led to his involvement in the Army-McCarthy hearings as counsel for the minority of Democratic senators on the committee. Later, he worked tirelessly for the subcommittee that was investigating labor racketeering, a position that brought him into conflict with teamster boss Jimmy Hoffa.

After managing John F. Kennedy's successful campaign for the presidency in 1960, Robert agreed to accept the Cabinet post of Attorney General, and for the duration of his brother's administration, Robert Kennedy served as the President's closest advisor. Shattered by the President's death in 1963, Kennedy decided to seek elective office himself, running for the Senate seat from New York in 1964, and winning. As a politician in his own right, Robert Kennedy showed a special concern for the problems of the poor, the minorities, the disadvantaged Americans who were unable to share in the nation's prosperity. Energetic and idealistic, he seemed to be finding his voice and his platform as he campaigned for the Presidency in 1968, as a discouraged Lyndon Johnson withdrew from the race.

On the night of June 5, 1968, Robert F. Kennedy was celebrating his victory in the California presidential primary with friends and campaign workers at the Ambassador Hotel in Los Angeles. As he walked from one room to another, he was shot by Sirhan Sirhan, and died without regaining consciousness on June 7. His funeral was held at St. Patrick's Cathedral in New York, with burial at Arlington National Cemetery, beside his brother, the President.

Robert Francis Kennedy, Jr.

Robert Francis Kennedy, Jr., is the third child of Robert F. and Ethel Skakel Kennedy, born January 17, 1954. Bobby did his undergraduate work at Harvard in history, graduating in 1977. He then followed in the footsteps of his uncles and studied for a term at the University of London School of Economics. As a child, Bobby was especially interested in unusual animals, and kept Hickory Hill full of such creatures as lizards and iguanas; he also kept and trained falcons. Bright and mischievous in his youth, Bobby was usually the ringleader of the Kennedy family pranks.

Like his father, Bobby received a law degree from the University of Virginia (1982). He married fellow attorney Emily Ruth Black in Bloomington, Indiana, on April 3, 1982, and they are the parents of two children: Robert Francis Kennedy III, born in 1985, and Kathleen Alexandra Kennedy, born in 1988. Like some other members of his generation, Bobby has weathered some difficult times. He made headlines early in his marriage when he failed his bar exam and Emily passed. Shortly thereafter, he was arrested for possession of heroin. He received a suspended sentence in return for enrolling in a drug rehabilitation center and doing community service work, and that seems to have marked an important turning point in his life. In 1985, the American Bar Association approved the resumption of his law career. Robert F. Kennedy, Jr., currently teaches environmental law at Pace University in New York and serves as staff counsel for the Natural Resources Defense Council and the Hudson River Fishermen's Association. He and his family live in suburban New York.

Robert Francis Kennedy III

Robert Francis Kennedy III is the first child of Robert F. Kennedy, Jr., and his wife, Emily Black Kennedy. The grandson of Robert and Ethel Kennedy was born on September 2, 1985.

Rory Katherine Elizabeth Kennedy

Rory Katherine Elizabeth Kennedy was the last child of Robert F. and Ethel Skakel Kennedy, born on December 12, 1968, six months after her father was assassinated in Los Angeles. She was christened by Archbishop Terence Cooke; her godparents are her older siblings Kerry and Michael. Rory attended the Potomac School in Virginia, the Madeira School, and is currently a student at Brown University. Carrying on the family tradition of political activism, Rory, along with her brother Douglas, was arrested in 1985 for protesting apartheid is front of the South African embassy in Washington.

Rose Elizabeth Fitzgerald Kennedy

Rose Elizabeth Fitzgerald, the oldest of the six children of John F. and Josie Hannon Fitzgerald, was born on July 22, 1890, in the Boston home of her parents, just up the street from the Paul Revere house. The baby was named after her father's mother, Rosanna Cox. The family moved from Boston to the peaceful country town of Concord when Rose was seven, and she attended public school there. She later switched to Dorchester High School when the family moved back to Boston, occupying a comfortably large house in that area. She graduated from Dorchester High School, after taking an extra, "thirteenth" year there, in 1907.

Although Rose had hoped to go to college at Wellesley, her father decided to send her instead to Boston's Convent of the Sacred Heart. The following year, after her father lost the 1907 mayoral election and found himself under investigation by a grand jury for corruption during his administration, Rose and her younger sister Agnes were enrolled for a year's study at the Blumenthal Sacred Heart Convent in Vale, Holland. She finished her education at the Sacred Heart Convent in Manhattanville, in the Morningside Heights area of New York City (later to become Manhattanville College), graduating in 1910. The following year, she studied piano at the New England Conservatory of Music.

In October 1914 Rose married longtime suitor Joseph P. Kennedy. The Kennedys had nine children: Joseph (1915), John (1917), Rosemary (1918), Kathleen (1920), Eunice (1921), Patricia (1924), Robert (1925), Jean (1928), and Edward (1932). While her husband was away for long stretches at a time, working in the government and pursuing opportunities for making money,

Rose stayed out of the public eye, at home raising the children. She accompanied her husband to England when he was appointed Ambassador to the Court of St. James, and threw herself into the role of Ambassador's wife. When her son Jack first ran for public office after the war, she helped him campaign, and thereafter she was one of Jack Kennedy's secret weapons for winning votes—a role she later performed for her other sons, Robert and Edward, as well as for son-in-law Sargent Shriver. After the joys of the White House years, when she occasionally acted as official hostess for her son, and the sorrows of the two assassinations and the death of her husband, Rose Kennedy retired into a quiet life in her houses at Hyannis Port and Palm Beach, going to Mass every morning, taking daily swims and long walks, and acting as matriarch to her family of twenty-eight grandchildren, with another generation beginning to arrive. A series of strokes have left her in precarious health, but she was able to celebrate her ninety-eighth birthday at Hyannis Port in 1988, with many members of the family present to sing "Sweet Adeline," attend a special mass at the house, and help her blow out the candles on her cake.

Rosemary Kennedy

Rosemary Kennedy was the third child and first daughter of Joseph P. and Rose Fitzgerald Kennedy. She was born in the family home at Brookline on September 13, 1918. It became evident when Rosemary was still a pretty and good-natured toddler that her development was retarded. Throughout the 1920s, her parents took her to a variety of specialists, hoping to find an answer to her problems as well as help in teaching and training her. They received little encouragement; most authorities in that day considered mental retardation hopeless and could only recommend institutional care.

The Kennedys decided to do all they could to provide a normal life for Rosemary. They engaged special tutors to work with her and insisted that her brothers and sisters include her in their own social lives. During the family's stay in England, Rosemary was enrolled in a Montessori school that brought about her most significant progress. Despite her handicap, Rosemary struggled valiantly to learn to read and write, and to take her place in the active and accomplished Kennedy family. But as she matured, her mood swings became increasingly difficult for the family to handle at home, and they worried about the attractive young woman with the mind of a child. In 1941, without consulting his wife, Joe Kennedy authorized a specialist to perform a lobotomy in the hope of ameliorating Rosemary's behavior. The surgery was a disaster that left Rosemary profoundly retarded and slightly paralyzed on the left side. Her father immediately made arrangements for her to enter an excellent Catholic home for the mentally retarded in Wisconsin, St. Coletta's, where she has remained ever since. Rosemary is regularly visited by her sister Eunice, and she has occasionally been taken by the nuns for visits to her mother. In 1983, the Kennedy family donated one million dollars to St. Coletta's in honor of Rose Kennedy's ninety-third birthday.

Virginia Joan Bennett Kennedy

Virginia Joan Bennett was born in Riverdale, New York, at the Mother Cabrini Hospital, on September 9, 1936, the daughter of Henry Wiggin Bennett, a New York advertising executive, and Virginia Joan Stead. The Bennetts, with Joan and her younger sister Candace, moved to Bronxville about the time the Kennedys left there to go to England when Joseph P. Kennedy became the Ambassador. Joan graduated from Bronxville High School and then went to Manhattanville College, in Purchase, New York, graduating in 1957. She made her debut at the New York Debutante Cotillion and did a little modeling while she was still a college student.

It was at Manhattanville that she met Edward M. Kennedy, when he and the rest of the family attended the dedication of a gymnasium that was a gift to the school from the Joseph P. Kennedy, Jr., Foundation and named in memory of Ted's older sister Kathleen, who had also been a student there. Joan and Ted were married on November 30, 1958 at St. Joseph's Roman Catholic Church in Bronxville, New York, by Francis Cardinal Spellman. The couple have three children: Kara, born in 1960; Edward, Jr., born in 1961, and Patrick, born in 1967. Joan and Ted separated after his failed bid for the Presidency in 1980 and quietly divorced two years later. According to newspaper reports, the divorce settlement gave Joan about $5 million plus an annual alimony of $175,000, as well as the Cape Cod house on Squaw Island. Joan has been courageously outspoken about her battle with alcoholism, at the same time that she has fought to become a person in her own right. An accomplished musician, she received a master's degree in education from Lesley College in 1982 and is active in promoting cultural events in the Boston area, where she still resides.

Kennedy Arms

For years, the New York cops used the ironic name the "Kennedy Arms" for the drug supermarket in an abandoned building at Eighth Avenue and 116th Street, where in 1979 David Kennedy was mugged when he tried to make a drug buy. In 1988 the "Kennedy Arms" was torn down by the city to make room for a shelter for the homeless.

Kennedy Family Flag

In the 1950s, Ambassador Joseph P. Kennedy asked heraldry experts to design a Kennedy family flag. The result featured three gold helmets on a black background, a device that could be traced back to early forebears in Ireland. The Kennedy family flag sometimes flew from the flagpole at the ambassador's house in the Hyannis Port compound. Senator Robert F. Kennedy carried a Kennedy family flag during his ascent of Mount Kennedy and planted it on the summit.

Kennedy Half-Dollar

On December 30, 1963, Congress passed a directive ordering the U.S. Mint to begin manufacturing the new John F. Kennedy fifty-cent piece. The Kennedy half-dollar replaced the Franklin coin, which was discontinued. The new coins began to appear the following March, and initially they were so highly prized as remembrances of the late President that almost none were in general circulation for many years. Kennedy half-dollars are still being minted today.

Kennedy Postage Stamp

In May 1964, the United States Postal Service issued a stamp honoring the late President John F. Kennedy. The design for the stamp, personally selected by Mrs. Kennedy, featured a portrait of the President, a drawing of the Eternal Flame, and a quote from the Inaugural Address: "And the glow from the fire can truly light the world."

"Kennedys Don't Cry"

The children of Joseph P. Kennedy said the family motto was "Kennedys don't cry." That came from the lectures their father gave them on how to get ahead in the world. "I don't want any sourpusses around here," he told them. "We don't want any crying in this house." The meaning of this comment was not that Kennedys don't have emotions, but that they are not losers who weep for their sad fates.

The Kennedys on Videocassette

Thank You, Mr. President. The best moments from JFK's press conference.

Kennedys Don't Cry. Behind the scenes look at triumphs and tragedies.

The Killing of President Kennedy. Examination of facts and theories surrounding the assassination of JFK.

K

Robert F. Kennedy's First Campaign Speech

In 1952, attorney Robert F. Kennedy left his job with the Justice Department to help his brother Jack campaign for election as Massachusetts senator against incumbent Senator Henry Cabot Lodge. Bob's forte was behind-the-scenes organization, but on one occasion, a Kennedy appearance had been promised and neither the candidate nor any other member of the family was available to make it, so Bobby reluctantly stepped before an audience and made a brief speech, which someone luckily recorded for posterity:

My brother Jack couldn't be here. My mother couldn't be here. My sister Eunice couldn't be here. My sister Pat couldn't be here. My sister Jean couldn't be here. But if my brother Jack were here, he'd tell you Lodge has a very bad voting record. Thank you.

Arthur Krock

Arthur Krock was a longtime journalist, probably best known for his column in *The New York Times*. Krock met Joseph P. Kennedy in 1932, when they were both helping Roosevelt campaign for his first term as President. Krock and Kennedy became good friends, and Krock helped Kennedy write his 1936 book, *I'm For Roosevelt*. The friendship eventually ended, and afterward Krock became a very harsh critic of all politicians named Kennedy.

Krock was also a close friend of Hugh Auchincloss, and Krock was the one who found a job at the Washington *Times-Herald* for Hugh's stepdaughter, Jacqueline Bouvier.

L

Lace

"Lace" was the Secret Service code name for Jacqueline Kennedy.

Bernard Lamotte

Bernard Lamotte was the French artist commissioned by Joseph P. Kennedy to paint murals on the walls of the basement swimming pool in the White House. The pool had been installed by President Franklin D. Roosevelt for his physical therapy, and President Kennedy decided a daily swim would be good therapy for his own back problems. To make the dreary, long-neglected basement more cheerful for his son, Joe Kennedy asked Lamotte to paint scenes of the harbor at St. Croix, in the American Virgin Islands. Lamotte added a few personal touches to the scene, including the President's sailboat, the *Victura*, riding at anchor in the harbor, and the name "Kennedy" spelled out by signal flags on one ship's mast.

Lancer

Lancer was the Secret Service code name for President John F. Kennedy.

James M. Landis

James M. Landis was a member of the circle of advisors assembled by Joseph P. Kennedy in the course of his own government career. Landis, a young lawyer who was formerly a teacher at Harvard Law School and a member of the Federal Trade Commission, was appointed by President Roosevelt to be a member of the Securities and Exchange Commission when it was first established in 1933. A missionary's son who was born in Japan, Landis was deeply committed to the ideals of the New Deal. He and Chairman Joseph P. Kennedy worked together well, and they kept in touch after Kennedy left the commission and Landis replaced him as chairman. Landis left Washington in 1937 to take the prestigious position of dean of the Harvard Law School and then went back into government service during World War II. In 1948, Joe Kennedy invited him to join his legal staff. Thereafter, Landis began to advise not only Joe Kennedy but also his son Jack, who had recently embarked on his own political career. Landis remained within the Kennedy circle until his death.

Harold Laski

Harold Laski was a professor at the University of London School of Economics who was sometimes described as the greatest teacher who ever lived. A man with a strong leftist bent in politics, he taught his students primarily by talking with them, usually outside the classroom, as for example at his Sunday teas. At the suggestion of Justice Felix Frankfurter, Joseph P. Kennedy decided to send his two oldest sons, Joe Junior in 1933–34 and then Jack in 1935–36, to study for a year with Laski. Laski's political sentiments were poles apart from Kennedy's, but both men had the strong conviction that their own beliefs would prevail in open argument. The two Kennedy boys left Laski with their beliefs in their father's brand of conservatism basically intact, but they also absorbed from their teacher in London an increased sympathy for the common man and his problems.

Last Words of Robert F. Kennedy

According to testimony given during the investigation into the assassination of Senator Robert F. Kennedy, someone standing near him as he lay in a pool of blood on the floor of the kitchen of the Ambassador Hotel heard him ask, "Is Paul [aide Paul Schrade, who had been grazed by one of the bullets] okay? Is everyone all right?"

Christopher Lawford

Christopher Lawford is the first child of Peter and Pat Kennedy Lawford, born on March 29, 1955. Christopher attended Tufts and Georgetown Universities, and went to Boston College Law School, graduating in 1983. In the late 1970s and early 1980s, a drug problem put Christopher in a clinic for a time, but he was able to straighten out his life and continue with his education. While living in the Boston area, he set up a program at the North Charles Mental Health clinic to treat opiate dependency. He warns young people, "There's a price to pay, whether it's a hangover the next morning or alcoholism five years later or a drug habit five years later. There's always a price to pay." Chris served as a lecturer in psychiatry for Harvard Medical School. He married Jeanne Olssen in December 1984; Jeanne ran SHAPES fitness center in Boston, where she has pioneered a fitness program for the physically handicapped. Christopher returned to his native California in 1988 to pursue an acting career.

Patricia Kennedy Lawford

Patricia Kennedy was the sixth child of Joseph P. and Rose Fitzgerald Kennedy, born at home on May 6, 1924, in Brookline, Massachusetts, while her father was away in New York, working to save the Yellow Cab Company. Pat attended Sacred Heart convent schools in the

Patricia Kennedy Lawford and her mother, Rose Kennedy, attend a ball. (Walter Fischer, Black Star)

United States and England, graduating from the Maplehurst Convent of the Sacred Heart in New York City in 1941. That fall, she enrolled in Rosemont College, a small liberal arts school in Pennsylvania, from which she graduated in 1945.

Pat Kennedy married actor Peter Lawford on April 24, 1954, in a wedding that required police barricades to restrain the crowd. The Lawfords lived in California, where Peter worked in movies and television, and had four children: Christopher (1955), Sydney (1956), Victoria (1958), and Robin (1961). According to rumors, the Lawford marriage was in a shaky state by 1963, but President Kennedy asked his sister to take no action until after the 1964 election. In the aftermath of the shock of the President's assassination, Pat and the children moved back to the East Coast, occupying a large apartment on Manhattan's East Side. The Lawfords were divorced on February 1, 1966, with Pat charging "mental cruelty." She was granted full custody of the four children. Pat later moved to Paris and worked briefly with couture designer Jean-Louis Scherrer. Currently, she lives in New York City and summers at an estate on Long Island.

Peter Lawford

English actor Peter Lawford was the husband of Pat Kennedy. He was the only child of Sir Sydney and Lady May Lawford, born on September 7, 1923, in London. His father was an English general, later knighted for his services to Great Britain. Young Peter began his acting career at the tender age of eight. Later he went to Hollywood, where he was signed by M-G-M and starred in several classic musicals, including *Good News* with June Allyson, *Royal Wedding* with Jane Powell, and *Easter Parade* with Judy Garland. His good looks and debonair charm made him a natural leading man.

Peter Lawford married Patricia Kennedy on April 24, 1954, and the couple had four children: Christopher, born in 1955; Sydney, 1956; Victoria, 1958; and Robin, 1961. The Lawfords separated after the assassination of President Kennedy, when Pat and the children moved to the East Coast, and they were divorced in February 1966, with Pat being granted full custody of their four children. Lawford stayed in Hollywood. On October 30, 1971, Lawford married Mary Rowan, the twenty-one-year-old daughter of comedian Dan Rowan, in Puerta Vallarta. That marriage ended in divorce in 1975. Lawford's third wife was the former Deborah Gould, whom he married in a judge's chambers in Arlington, Virginia, in June 1976; that marriage, too, ended in divorce. His fourth and last wife was Patricia Seaton. In 1988, she published a book about Lawford, *The Peter Lawford Story: Life with the Kennedys, Monroe and the Rat Pack*, in which she described his infidelities and drug addictions.

Five months after his last marriage, Lawford died of cardiac failure and complications of cirrhosis on December 24, 1984. Four years later, his widow removed his ashes from a crypt in Westwood Village, Los Angeles, and scattered them in the ocean, a move she said she was forced to because his children would not pay the ten thousand dollars worth of funeral costs outstanding. A spokesperson for the four children of Pat and Peter Lawford released a statement saying, "The children only recently learned of the existence of financial problems in connection with their father's funeral expenses and they have taken care of all such obligations."

Robin Lawford

Robin Lawford is the fourth child of Peter and Pat Kennedy Lawford, born on July 2, 1961; her godfather was Robert F. Kennedy. She attended the United Nations International School in New York and graduated from Marymount Manhattan College in 1984. Robin works as a stage manager of off-Broadway productions in New York.

Laying a Wreath on the President's Grave

Every year for twenty-five years since President John F. Kennedy was assassinated, the Green Berets laid a wreath on his grave at Arlington National Cemetery on the anniversary of his death. At the urging of the Kennedy family, the practice ended in 1988. Thereafter, the commemorative ceremony is to take place on the former President's birthday, May 29.

Lucien Lelong

Lucien Lelong was one of the foremost couturiers in Paris during the 1920s. On one of Joseph and Rose Kennedy's trips to Europe in that decade, Joe (then in the movie business) dispatched his wife, Rose, to visit Lelong's salon—in the company of the movie star who was his mistress, Gloria Swanson. According to Rose Kennedy's own account of this curious event, being with Gloria "magnified the experience" of shopping at one of the great couture houses. "She was the great celebrity. I, by comparison, was a nobody, just the wife of a producer. But it was fun being with her and sharing in the excitement she generated." This introduction to the world of the couturier by Gloria was the beginning of serious clothes shopping for Rose, and her Paris shopping trips (continued well into her eighties), eventually landed her on the Best-Dressed List. Joseph Kennedy was always proud of his wife's stylish appearance.

Le Pavillon

Le Pavillon was an elegant Manhattan restaurant known for its haute cuisine. It was run by Henri Soulé, and one of Soulé's financial backers was Joseph P. Kennedy.

Lesley College

Lesley College is the Boston educational institution from which Joan Bennett Kennedy received her master's degree in music education in 1982.

Libra

In 1988, author Don DeLillo published a novel entitled *Libra*, a fictional attempt to pull together many of the conspiracy theories surrounding the assassination of President John F. Kennedy. *Libra* is just one more contemporary indication of the hold those conspiracy theories have on the American imagination.

Lieutenant Joseph P. Kennedy, Jr., Home for Children

The Lieutenant Joseph P. Kennedy, Jr., Home for Children was the second of the buildings constructed with money from the Joseph P. Kennedy Jr. Foundation and named after the Kennedy son who was killed during World War II. Located on Stillwell Avenue in the Bronx, New York City, the home was set up to care for three hundred neglected and dependent children of all faiths, ranging in age from six to eighteen. It was built with a $2.5 million donation from the Joseph P. Kennedy, Jr., Foundation and opened in 1950. Inside the home is the small St. Rose Chapel, named after Rose Kennedy's patron saint and dedicated by Francis Cardinal Spellman.

The Limited Test Ban Treaty

One of the most significant accomplishments of the Kennedy administration was negotiating a limited test ban treaty, covering the testing of nuclear weapons, with Russia in 1963. Kennedy's commitment to the treaty was spurred by the events of the Cuban missile crisis in 1962, which dramatized the threat posed by nuclear weapons. The President told the nation, "Negotiations were concluded in Moscow on a treaty to ban all nuclear tests in the atmosphere, in outer space, and under water. For the first time, an agreement has been reached on bringing the forces of nuclear destruction under control."

Evelyn Lincoln

Evelyn Lincoln was President John F. Kennedy's personal secretary. Mrs. Lincoln started to work for JFK when he was in the Senate, and she followed him to the White House and continued to handle correspondence that came in after his death. Evelyn Lincoln was widely known for her efficiency and her enormous devotion to her boss. She later wrote a book about her association with him, entitled *My Twelve Years with John F. Kennedy*.

The Lincoln and Kennedy Funerals

When President Kennedy's widow, Jacqueline, made her decisions about the details of the slain leader's funeral, she consciously modeled some of them after the funeral of another assassinated president, Abraham Lincoln. She had asked Chief of Protocol Angier Biddle Duke to gather information about the way Lincoln had been buried, and she chose to incorporate certain of the details in the nation's last rites for President Kennedy. Like Lincoln, Kennedy lay in state first in the candle-lit East Room of the White House and then in the Rotunda of the Capitol, there resting on the very same catafalque that had held Lincoln's coffin. In the funeral procession itself, Kennedy's coffin was placed on a gun caisson and drawn by a set of matched gray horses, just as in the Lincoln funeral procession. (The caisson also happened to be the same one that had borne the body of President Franklin D. Roosevelt.) The final echo of that earlier funeral was the inclusion of the riderless horse, with boots reversed in the stirrups, that followed the coffin as a military symbol of a fallen warrior.

Sir Thomas Lipton

Sir Thomas Lipton, the Irish tea magnate and well-known yachtsman, was a friend of Boston Mayor John F. Fitzgerald, and John's daughter Rose frequently visited Lipton and traveled with him aboard his magnificent yacht, the *Erin*. At one time, there was even gossip that Rose might marry the elderly Irishman and become Lady Lipton—a rumor with no foundation in fact.

"Little Brother Is Watching"

As attorney general, Robert F. Kennedy frequently wandered the corridors of various Justice Department offices all around the country, popping in to introduce himself and ask employees what they were working on. The joke around the Department was "Little Brother is watching."

Little John's Salute

One memorable image of the funeral of President John F. Kennedy that the world will always remember is the salute given by the President's son, John, Jr. The funeral took place on young John's third birthday, and he looked terribly small and vulnerable in his light blue coat amidst the sea of black-clad adults. As John stood with his mother and sister at the foot of the cathedral steps, watching the honor guard carry his father's coffin down to the waiting caisson for the procession to Arlington Cemetery, Mrs. Kennedy bent down and whispered to her son. He handed her his prayer book, and then his right hand went up in a salute to his father, the President.

Athina Mary Livanos

Athina Mary Livanos, always called Tina, was the daughter of wealthy Greek shipping magnate Stavros Livanos. She married Aristotle Onassis in 1946, and the couple had two children: Alexander, born in 1948, and Christina, born in 1950. They were divorced in 1960, when her husband's "friendship" with Maria Callas became too much for her to ignore. The following year, Tina married the Marquess of Blandford, heir to one of England's oldest dukedoms. That marriage also ended in divorce. In 1971, she married her sister Eugenie's ex-husband Stavros Niarchos, arch-rival of Onassis (who was by then married to Jacqueline Bouvier Kennedy). Tina died in 1974.

Lobotomy

In 1941, Rosemary Kennedy underwent an operation called a prefrontal lobotomy, hailed at that time as a great advance in the treatment of the agitation and confusion that some retarded individuals experience. For more than a year before the operation, Rosemary had been in an increasingly angry and hostile mood, and it became extremely difficult for her family to supervise her adequately. Without consulting his wife, who was away from home traveling at the time, Joseph P. Kennedy decided to have their daughter lobotomized, in the hope of calming her down so she could continue to live at home.

Unfortunately, something went quite wrong during the procedure, and Rosemary was left in a state of profound retardation, along with weakness and near-paralysis on her left side. Joe Kennedy immediately arranged to have Rosemary institutionalized, still telling his wife nothing about the surgery but only that their daughter could no longer live at home. It was not until twenty years later that Rose Kennedy finally saw her daughter again, during a visit to St. Coletta's, and learned the whole story of the operation that failed.

Henry Cabot Lodge II

Henry Cabot Lodge II was a Massachusetts politician from a wealthy upper-class New England family with a tradition of public service. Lodge was an incumbent senator from the state in 1952, when Congressman John F. Kennedy decided to run against him. A Harvard graduate and war hero, Lodge had first won the Senate seat in 1934, campaigning against another dominant name in Massachusetts state politics, James Michael Curley, who was surprised to see the opponent he scornfully called "Little Boy Blue" win the race. Lodge won again in 1940 but resigned during his second term to join the military. He was then reelected in 1946 by a large majority. Many people considered the well-financed Lodge an unquestionable winner again in 1952, but John F. Kennedy triumphed by a narrow margin. By an interesting coincidence, Lodge was the grandson of the man who had defeated Kennedy's grandfather, John F. Fitzgerald, in a Senate race thirty-six years earlier.

L

M

Torbert MacDonald

Torbert MacDonald was one of John F. Kennedy's lifelong friends. A football hero at Harvard when Jack was at school there, "Torby" remained close to Jack after they had graduated. During the war, Torby joined Jack at the training school for PT-boat officers in Melville, Rhode Island. Afterward, he took a position as assistant football coach at the Medford (Massachusetts) high school. In 1956, MacDonald ran for and won a seat in Congress as a representative from the Eighth Congressional District in Massachusetts.

Senator Joseph R. McCarthy

Joseph R. McCarthy was a senator from Wisconsin first elected in 1946 and reelected in 1952. From the beginning of his political career, McCarthy had devoted much of his energies to a crusade against communism, and particularly against the presence of Communists in the government of the United States. That crusade had, in fact, been responsible for much of his political success. In 1953, he was made chairman of the Senate Subcommittee on Investigations, a body of the Committee on Government Operations, and he decided to use the position to pursue his anti-Communist activities. McCarthy was at that time a good friend of the Kennedy family and frequent visitor to Palm Beach and Hyannis Port. He had formerly dated Pat Kennedy, and Joseph P. Kennedy had contributed generously to his political campaigns. When Kennedy asked McCarthy to give his son Bobby a job with the subcommittee, McCarthy obliged. Bobby stayed just seven months, then resigned for unknown reasons.

The following year, the Army brought charges that McCarthy and his chief counsel, Roy Cohn, had acted improperly in trying to arrange preferential treatment for a former employee and friend, G. David Schine, who had entered the Army as a private. McCarthy's own subcommittee held hearings on the charges, and Robert F. Kennedy served as counsel to the Democratic minority. The official result of the hearings was predictable: Fellow Republicans held that McCarthy was not guilty of impropriety, whereas Democrats charged him with inexcusable actions. The unofficial result was that McCarthy's power in Washington was ended. He died on May 2, 1957. Former employee Robert F. Kennedy, who never lost his respect for McCarthy despite serving on the side of his opposition, attended both his Washington funeral and the subsequent burial in Appleton, Wisconsin. The Kennedys' refusal to repudiate McCarthy was for a long time held against them by the liberal wing of the Democratic party.

Senator John S. McClellan

Senator John S. McClellan of Arkansas was the chairman of the Senate Select Committee on Improper Activities in the Labor and Management Field. His chief counsel was attorney Robert F. Kennedy.

Charlotte McDonnell

Charlotte McDonnell was the daughter of a rich Irish Catholic family on Long Island. Rose Kennedy had hoped to make friends with the McDonnell family, attracted by their social prominence, but the family had repeatedly snubbed her. It was left for the next generation to forge the friendship she desired. Charlotte McDonnell was a student at Noroton when Kathleen Kennedy was there, and the two girls became fast friends. Charlotte briefly dated Jack Kennedy, but no real romance ever blossomed. Charlotte's sister Anne would later marry Henry Ford II, and their daughter Charlotte would marry Stavros Niarchos, whose previous spouse was the ex-wife of his arch-rival of Aristotle Onassis, who would marry the widow of Jack Kennedy.

Sydney Maleia Kennedy Lawford McKelvey

Sydney Maleia Kennedy Lawford is the second child of Peter and Pat Kennedy Lawford, born on August 25, 1956. Named after her paternal grandfather, Sir Sydney Lawford, she attended the Foxcroft School in Virginia and Franklin College in Switzerland, then studied at the Tobé-Coburn School in New York to prepare for a fashion career. On September 17, 1983, she married James Peter McKelvy, an editor at a Boston TV station, who is now the producer of "USA Today: The Television Show." Sydney and Peter have two children, Peter (1985) and Christopher (1987).

President William McKinley

William McKinley was President of the United States while John F. Fitzgerald was a congressman, and the two men were genial acquaintances. When Fitzgerald was traveling through Washington one winter with his family on his way to a vacation in Palm Beach, he stopped off to introduce his two daughters, Rose and Agnes, to the President. Rose always liked to tell the story of how he called Agnes the "prettiest girl ever to visit the White House," until the day her son Jack responded by asking innocently, "Why didn't he say it to you, Mother?" That was the end of the story about President McKinley.

McLean Hospital

McLean Hospital, located just outside Boston, is a well-known treatment center for addiction to drugs and alcohol. There is an outpatient program, as well as a residential program at the hospital's Appleton House. David Kennedy, Christopher Lawford, and Joan Kennedy are among members of the Kennedy family who have sought help there.

Patrick "Pappy" McMahon

Patrick McMahon, nicknamed "Pappy" because he was older than most of the other crew members, was the engineer of PT-109, the boat commanded by Lieutenant John F. Kennedy in the Solomon Islands in 1943. On the night of August 1, when the PT-109 was rammed by a Japanese destroyer, McMahon was in the engine room and was severely burned at the moment of the collision. Since McMahon was too badly injured to be able to swim, Kennedy towed him to safety, first to the floating remnants of the PT-109, later to several different islands. Kennedy saved McMahon's life, but his own indelible impression was of McMahon's own courage in enduring the pain of his burns without complaint and in making every effort asked of him. Kennedy later drew a moral from McMahon's courage: "I felt that his courage was the result of his loyalty to the men around him. Most of the courage shown in the war came from men's understanding of their interdependence on each other."

Robert Strange McNamara

Robert Strange McNamara was the secretary of defense in the Kennedy administration. At the time the forty-four-year-old McNamara was appointed, he had just been named president of Ford Motor Company, and he had to forfeit more than a million dollars in stock options to leave the company. McNamara, a Phi Beta Kappa graduate of the University of California, had been a Harvard Business School graduate and member of the faculty. He was brought to the Pentagon in World War II by Assistant Secretary of War Robert Lovett, who later recommended him to the Kennedy team. When the war was over, McNamara became one of the celebrated team of "Whiz Kids" that brought new vigor to Ford Motors. A respected intellectual, McNamara was known to read history and philosophy, and to insist on finding a correspondence between what was expedient and what was right. McNamara later became the head of the World Bank.

Macaroni

Macaroni was a pony given to Caroline Kennedy in March 1961 by Vice-President Lyndon B. Johnson. Macaroni usually stayed in the stables of the house the Kennedys had leased in the Virginia countryside, Glen Ora, for Caroline to ride on weekends. Occasionally, the pony was transported to the White House lawn, where Caroline and her brother, John, could go for a short ride. One winter, Macaroni was hitched up to a sleigh and whisked the children across the snow-covered White House grounds. Macaroni provided the press with a number of irresistible "photo opportunities," leading Mrs. Kennedy reportedly to exclaim one day, "I'm so sick of reading about Macaroni I could scream!"

Madonna

In the early summer of 1988, rumor connected handsome law student John F. Kennedy, Jr., with rock and stage star Madonna. He was seen attending the Broadway play in which Madonna was then starring, *Speed-the-Plow*, and photographers snapped him riding his bike alongside Madonna (and her bodyguard) as she jogged in Central Park. Kennedy denied that he and Madonna were more than just social friends.

Durie Malcolm

Durie Malcolm was the woman rumored to have been secretly married to John F. Kennedy. Durie, born in December 1916, frequently visited the Palm Beach home of her mother and stepfather, Isabel and George Malcolm, located near the Kennedy winter residence, after the end of World War II. In the winter season of 1946–47 Jack Kennedy dated the twice-divorced Durie, and they attended many Palm Beach social functions together. The romance seems not to have survived their separation in the spring, and later that year, in Fort Lee, New Jersey, Durie married Thomas Shevlin, a wealthy lumberman.

Ten years later, a privately published book called *Blauvelt Family Genealogy* listed Durie Malcolm as a descendant of that Dutch family. The book failed to mention her marriage to Shevlin but claimed instead that she had married John F. Kennedy in 1947. Somehow, that obscure volume surfaced when Kennedy became President, setting off rumors of a secret marriage and a quick annulment arranged by Joseph P. Kennedy to protect his son's political career. Despite the fact that Durie herself denied the rumors and that subsequent press investigation could find no trace of any evidence to support the claim, the rumors about the secret marriage circulated for years.

"The Man Who Accompanied Jacqueline Kennedy to Paris"

During a state visit to France in 1962, President and Mrs. John F. Kennedy attended a dinner given in their honor by General and Mrs. Charles de Gaulle at which the President was to make a brief speech. Referring to the never-ending and wildly enthusiastic coverage in the French press of every detail of his wife's clothes, jewels, and behavior, the President began his remarks by saying, "I do not think it altogether inappropriate to introduce myself to this audience. I am the man who accompanied Jacqueline Kennedy to Paris, and I have enjoyed it."

Manhattanville

Manhattanville College, in the Morningside Heights area of New York City, has played an important role in the history of the Kennedy family. Founded in 1845 as the Academy of the Sacred Heart, it was later renamed Manhattanville College, after the suburban village in which it was located. It was the institution where young Rose Fitzgerald received her education after her return from the Blumenthal Sacred Heart convent in Holland. In the next generation, Rose Kennedy sent her daughters Eunice (1939–41) and Jean there. Jean, the only one of the Kennedy girls actually to graduate from Manhattanville, roomed there with 1950 graduate Ethel Skakel, who married Jean's brother Robert. Jean met another Manhattanville student, Joan Bennett of the class of 1958, at an alumnae function and subsequently introduced Joan to her younger brother Ted, who married Joan several years later. The gymnasium at Manhattanville was a gift to the school from Joseph P. Kennedy and named in honor of his daughter Kathleen. The school moved to Purchase, New York, in 1950. In the next generation of the family, Maria Shriver attended Manhattanville from 1973 to 1975.

Mannlicher-Carcano

The rifle used by Lee Harvey Oswald to kill President John F. Kennedy was a 6.5 mm Mannlicher-Carcano. In March, Oswald had ordered it from Klein's, a Chicago mail-order house, for $19.95, using the name A. Hidell. Later he took it to a Dallas gunsmith to line up the telescopic sight. Then he took the gun to the Sportsdrome rifle range, in a suburb of Dallas called Grand Prairie, and practiced his marksmanship. One observer remembered noting that "he could shoot as tight a group as anyone there."

Maplehurst

Maplehurst was a convent school of the Sacred Heart in New York City, where two of the Kennedy girls attended classes as day students. Eunice was enrolled in the fall of 1935, Pat in 1936. Pat graduated from Maplehurst in June 1941, after the Kennedy family returned from London. In 1945, the school moved to Greenwich, Connecticut.

The Margin of Victory

The 1960 presidential election remains the most closely contested election of our national leader. The total number of votes cast was about 68,000,000. John F. Kennedy won by a margin of 118,500 votes.

Maria's Weight Loss

Since her marriage to Arnold Schwarzenegger, Maria Shriver says she has lost twenty-five pounds. She attributes the weight loss to a diet and exercise program that her husband worked out for her, as well as his encouragement in keeping her working at it.

Marilyn Monroe and Bobby Kennedy

For many years, persistent rumors have linked Robert F. Kennedy in a love affair with Marilyn Monroe. It is certain that Bobby was introduced to Marilyn by his brother-in-law Peter Lawford, who was a close friend of Marilyn, and that his first meeting with the glamorous movie star took place not long after his brother's election to the presidency. It is also established that Bobby and Marilyn occasionally met at dinner parties at the Lawfords' house in Santa Monica. All else is conjecture. There are claims that Marilyn frequently telephoned Bobby at the Justice Department, but the phone records that might prove or disprove such a claim have never been released. There are reports of eyewitness accounts that place Bobby at Marilyn's house on several occasions, including the night of her death on August 4, 1962. None of the witnesses has ever been questioned about the truth and accuracy of their identification.

Within the Kennedy family, there is great skepticism about the allegations, because it was obvious that Bobby remained very much in love with his wife. Rose Kennedy commented that she disbelieved the rumors about Bobby's affair with Marilyn because he was too much of a "prig" to do such a thing. Ethel was overheard to tease Bobby about the rumors, which suggested to onlookers that she dismissed them as silly. All the Kennedys regarded Bobby as an uxorious husband, and if he *did* have an affair with Marilyn Monroe, it did no damage to his deep love for Ethel.

Marilyn Monroe. (Movie Star News)

Marilyn Monroe and Jack Kennedy

Rumors concerning an affair between John F. Kennedy and Marilyn Monroe began even before the star's death in 1962 and continue to the present day. Gossip columnist Earl Wilson published a book in 1974 that made the rumors explicit. Wilson quoted a source close to Monroe as saying, "She was so proud to be the girl having an affair with the President of the United States, because that was important."

Senator John F. Kennedy was introduced to the blonde movie star in the late 1950s by his brother-in-law, actor Peter Lawford. They met occasionally in Hollywood before and during the 1960 presidential campaign, but no personal liaison has been incontrovertibly established. One spur to the rumors was the report by Peter Lawford of his telephone conversation with Marilyn just before she lost consciousness due to the overdose of pills that killed her. "Say good-bye to Pat, say good-bye to the President, and say good-bye to yourself because you're a nice guy," were Marilyn's last words according to Lawford.

According to C. David Heymann, in his 1989 biography *A Woman Named Jackie*, Peter Lawford told him that Marilyn once called Jackie at the White House and asked her to divorce Jack. The shrewd First Lady supposedly retorted that she would be happy to step aside if Marilyn would marry Jack and move into the White House. She knew, of course, that whatever her husband's feelings about the sexy star, divorce was the farthest thing from his mind.

Marking Twenty Years Since the RFK Assassination

On June 6, 1988, members of the Kennedy family marked the twentieth anniversary of the day that Senator Robert F. Kennedy was assassinated. An evening mass was held at the rose-decorated gravesite, conducted by Father Jerry Creedo, the priest who has officiated at the weddings of many of the next generation of the Kennedy family. RFK's eldest son, Congressman Joseph P. Kennedy II, delivered a remembrance of his father in the presence of his mother, his uncle, and all ten of his brothers and sisters, including young Rory Kennedy who never knew the father who was killed before she was born. Ten grandchildren of Robert Kennedy were also present. The Senator's nephew, John F. Kennedy, Jr., spoke briefly and recited the lines from Shakespeare that Robert Kennedy had quoted after the death of John's father: "When he shall die, take him and cut him out in little stars, and he will make the face of heaven so fine that all the world will be in love with night, and pay no worship to the garish sun." Other guests included Senator John Glenn, union leader Cesar Chavez, and Martin Luther King III, son of the civil rights leader who was also slain in 1968. Thousands of other mourners joined the Kennedy family and friends at the ceremony.

The Marlin

The *Marlin* was the power boat owned by Joseph P. Kennedy. He used it to go out deep sea fishing off Cape Cod, and to follow his children as they competed in sailboat races. Later, the boat was frequently used by JFK and his advisors as a quiet place to plan strategy and relax at the same time.

Marrying Out of the Faith

Rose and Joseph had put a great deal of effort into bringing up their family as good Catholics; for Rose especially, it was an important part of her mission in life. One of the possibilities they feared the most was that their children might marry outside the Catholic faith. At the slightest hint of a Kennedy's romance with a Protestant, Rose began to worry over the consequences, and she suffered many anxious moments over her children's youthful involvements.

For nearly a year, from the summer of 1943 until the summer of 1944, Mr. and Mrs. Kennedy fretted over the strength of daughter Kathleen's attachment to William Cavendish, the Marquess of Hartington. His aristocratic family had been members of the Church of England for generations, and it was unthinkable that Billy would agree to convert to Catholicism or agree to have his children raised in the Catholic faith. Kathleen struggled for many months to find a solution to her religious dilemma, but there was simply no way she could marry the man she loved within the Catholic faith. She talked frankly to her parents about the situation, and her father, distressed by his daughter's inner turmoil, told Kathleen she could count on his love and support no matter what she decided. But Kathleen's registry wedding to Billy in June 1944 was a serious blow to Rose Kennedy, undermining her own sense of accomplishment in regard to her children's upbringing. Interest-

ingly, in later years, Rose Kennedy corresponded frequently with her unwelcome son-in-law's mother, the Dowager Duchess of Devonshire, and seemed to derive real comfort and pleasure from the relationship.

A second trial awaited the Kennedy family a few years later. After Kathleen recovered from the shock and sorrow of Billy's death and was received back into the Church, she fell in love a second time, with Lord Peter Fitzwilliam. He was not only a staunch Protestant, he was also married at the time the two met in the summer of 1946. Early in 1948, Kathleen told her parents about her intention of marrying Peter as soon as he could obtain a divorce. It was a step Rose Kennedy could not countenance, and she made it clear that if Kathleen persisted in her plan, she would be cut out of the family. Joe Kennedy shared his wife's dismay, but he also wanted to see his daughter happy. So he agreed to meet with her and Peter in Paris in May to see what could be worked out. It was while the couple was waiting for Joseph Kennedy to arrive in France that they decided to fly to Cannes for a few days in the sun. They were killed in the crash of their small plane during a thunderstorm.

Martha's Vineyard

In 1981, Jacqueline Kennedy Onassis built a thirteen-room waterfront home on the island of Martha's Vineyard, off the Massachusetts coast. Three years earlier, she had purchased a 356–acre tract of undeveloped land for $1.5 million. The house itself is rumored to have cost $3 million to construct. Designed by Washington architect Hugh Newell Jacobsen, it is a glamorized New England saltbox cottage with a thirty-four-foot central chimney. Georgina Fairholme, an En-

glish interior designer, gave it the cozy, rosy look Jackie loves.

The Vineyard is where Jackie goes to relax, waterski, eat fresh seafood, and perfect her light tan. Although she still owns the house in Hyannis Port in the Kennedy compound where the family used to summer, she rarely goes there now, preferring the greater privacy and easier access to the ocean of her Vineyard home.

Marwood

During the period in the mid-1930s when Joe Kennedy worked in Washington as the chairman of the Securities and Exchange Commission, his residence was a lavish mansion he leased called Marwood, set on an estate large enough to have its own private bridle paths. Located in the beautiful Maryland countryside, Marwood was a thirty-three room house built in the French Renaissance style at the turn of the century by Samuel Martin of Chicago. It had all the amenities rich men of the day expected, right down to a hundred-seat movie theater in the basement, Kennedy lived there for more than a year, with aide Eddie Moore as the only other resident, although he entertained frequently for cocktails or dinner. President Roosevelt visited Marwood often enough for Kennedy to install a special elevator for the President's wheelchair, and the two men would watch new movies that Kennedy had flown in each week from Hollywood. Joe Kennedy gave up Marwood when he resigned from the SEC, but he was able to rent the estate again in 1936, during the period when he was back in Washington as head of the Maritime Commission. Joe nicknamed the place the "Hindenburg Palace."

Mayor's Cup

When John F. Fitzgerald was mayor of Boston in the early years of the century, he made it a habit to hand out trophies on all possible occasions, thus providing excellent "photo opportunities" and a chance to boost his beloved Boston. In 1907, he awarded the Mayor's Cup for batting in the city high school league to a young man with an unbelievable batting average of .667: Joseph P. Kennedy, who would later marry Mayor Fitzgerald's daughter.

Vaughn Meader

In November 1962, comic Vaughn Meader brought out a record called *The First Family* that satirized the foibles of the entire Kennedy family. It was an instant best-seller, staying on the charts for more than three months. President Kennedy, enjoying the fun, cracked, "I thought it sounded more like Teddy than it did me." The album sold more than five million copies, and Meader had just released a second album, called *The Kennedy Family, Volume Two*, at the time the President was assassinated. Meader quickly announced that he was withdrawing the album from sale, and that he would never again perform his imitations of the Kennedys.

Mrs. Paul Mellon

Mrs. Paul Mellon, known to her friends as Bunny, is a socialite who is also renowned as a superb gardener. A longtime friend of Jacqueline Kennedy's, Mrs. Mellon lent her assistance with a variety of White House projects, ranging from teaching the staff how to arrange flowers in low bowls so they would not obstruct the view of diners at the table to installing the beautiful Rose Garden outside the President's office.

The Merchandise Mart

In the summer of 1945, Joseph P. Kennedy bought the Merchandise Mart in Chicago. It was at that time the largest privately owned building in the country, exceeded in size only by the military's Pentagon in Washington. Joe was able to buy the fifteen-year-old Mart from its owner, Marshall Field, for the bargain price of $12.9 million, because it had been losing money for years and Field was afraid the government tenants would leave when they were hit with post-war budget cutbacks. Kennedy's first step was to obtain a $12.5 million mortgage from the Equitable Life Assurance Society. He then completely renovated the building and installed air condi-tioning, so he could raise the rents and push out the government tenants as fast as possible, substituting more lucrative corporate occupants. The Mart has been a money-maker for the Kennedy family ever since, and current annual rents are larger than the total purchase price. Joe sent R. Sargent Shriver, soon to marry Eunice Kennedy, to manage the Mart in the late 1940s, and later the overseeing of the Mart was entrusted to Stephen E. Smith, the husband of Jean Kennedy. Christopher Kennedy, a son of Ethel and Robert, currently works as a leasing agent for the Mart.

Merrywood

The forty-six acre estate owned by Hugh D. Auchincloss in Virginia was named Merrywood. After Janet Lee Bouvier divorced her first husband, John V. Bouvier and married Auchincloss, she and her daughters Jacqueline and Lee lived at Merrywood. (A previous occupant had been Gore Vidal, whose mother was Auchincloss's second wife. He used it as the setting for his 1967 novel, *Washington, D.C.*) Merrywood had eight bedrooms, two stables, an Olympic-sized pool, and an automatic car wash. Auchincloss later sold the estate to TV newscaster Nancy Dickerson.

The Message on a Coconut

After the sinking of PT-109 in the Pacific by a Japanese destroyer, on the night of August 1, 1943, commanding officer Lieutenant John F. Kennedy was determined to save the ten crew members who had survived the initial disaster and who were camped on an island without food or water. He swam in the nearby straits, trying to flag down passing ships, and he also swam to neighboring islands in search of friendly contact. On Nauru Island, Kennedy encountered native scouts for an Australian coast-watcher and gave them a coconut on which he had carved a message with his knife:

NATIVE KNOWS POSIT
HE CAN PILOT
11 ALIVE NEED
SMALL BOAT
KENNEDY

The coconut message led to the rescue of the crew within two days.

M

Migratory Grape Workers

Senator Robert F. Kennedy was a member of the Migratory Worker Subcommittee of the Senate Labor Committee, which held hearings on the 1966 strike of the migratory grape workers. In order to inform himself about the situation, Kennedy made a trip to Delano, California. There he met Cesar Chavez, the head of the striking union and organizer of La Causa, a nonviolent organization trying to improve conditions for all migrant workers. A strong bond developed between Kennedy and Chavez, with the result that Kennedy supported the grape workers' strike, and the union headed by Chavez later supported RFK's presidential candidacy. Even today, the friendship formed between the two men finds expression: In 1988, Cesar Chavez was among the thousands who attended a ceremony of remembrance at Kennedy's grave on the twentieth anniversary of his death.

Milton Academy

Milton Academy, in Milton, Massachusetts, just south of Boston, was the preparatory school to which young Robert Kennedy was sent in 1942 to complete his high school education; he graduated in June 1944. Bobby lived in the dorm room that had once been occupied by T. S. Eliot. Bobby made few friends in the predominately Protestant boarding school and had trouble with his studies in the academically rigorous environment, as well.

Bobby's younger brother Edward also attended Milton, arriving in 1946 and graduating in June 1950 in a ceremony in which his father delivered the commencement address. Other Milton alumni in the family include RFK's son Joe.

Miss Chapin's School

Jacqueline Bouvier, like her mother before her, attended Miss Chapin's School in New York City. Jackie was at Miss Chapin's from first grade until 1942, when her mother remarried and the family moved to Washington.

Miss Porter's School

Jacqueline Bouvier attended Miss Porter's School, a preparatory school for girls, in Farmington, Connecticut, from which she graduated in June, 1947. In the yearbook, she listed her ambition as "not to be a housewife."

Deborah Mitford, Duchess of Devonshire

Deborah Mitford was the youngest child of Lord and Lady Redesdale, and thus one of the fascinating Mitford children whose childhoods were chronicled by Deborah's sister Nancy in her novels. Deborah married Andrew Cavendish, who was the younger brother of William Cavendish, the husband of Kathleen Kennedy. After Billy was killed in Germany in the Allied offensive of 1944, Andrew became the heir to the dukedom of Devonshire and acquired Billy's title, the Marquess of Hartington. Deborah later became the Duchess of Devonshire when her father-in-law died.

Molyneux Dress

In 1938, when Rose Kennedy was to present her two oldest daughters, Rosemary and Kathleen, to King George VI and Queen Elizabeth of Great Britain, she flew to Paris to buy her own dress for the important occasion. Rose selected a design by leading couturier Molyneux, a dress with a silver lamé train that was covered with gold and silver embroidery and sparkling with paillettes. More than twenty years later, on January 20, 1961, she was able to wear the same dress to the Inaugural Ball on the night of the day her son John F. Kennedy was sworn in as President of the United States.

Edward E. Moore

Edward E. Moore, always known as Eddie, was Joseph P. Kennedy's most trusted aide and confidant. Moore had worked as secretary to Kennedy's father-in-law, Mayor John F. Fitzgerald, and then to the next two Democratic mayors as well. In 1920, Joe Kennedy offered him the post of "confidential advisor," a job Moore held until he was too old and ill to work. He went everywhere with Joe Kennedy: from Gloria Swanson's Hollywood mansion to the Court of St. James. Joe's youngest child, Edward Moore Kennedy, was named after this closest of associates. Eddie was also Rosemary Kennedy's godfather; in fact, all the Kennedy children spent as much or more time with Eddie and Mary Moore as they did with their parents. The Moores bought the house at 83 Beals Street in Brookline from Joe Kennedy when the Kennedys moved to a bigger house on Naples Road, so the two families were close neighbors for a number of years. Eddie Moore lived long enough to play a minor part in helping Jack Kennedy win the 1952 election as senator from Massachusetts. He died on August 16, 1953, just a few weeks before Jack's wedding to Jacqueline Bouvier. Eddie's wife, Mary, died in June 1964 of burns suffered in a fire at the Cape Cod nursing home where she lived.

Janet Lee Bouvier Auchincloss Morris

Janet Norton Lee was born in 1907, the second of three daughters of James T. Lee, chairman of the board of the New York Central Savings Bank, and his Irish-born wife, Margaret. Janet attended Miss Spence's School in Manhattan and spent her summers riding in East Hampton. In 1928, she married John Vernou Bouvier III. They had two daughters, Jacqueline Lee

(1929) and Caroline Lee (1933). Janet divorced her husband in 1940, and thereafter married wealthy stockbroker Hugh D. Auchincloss, with whom she had two more children: Janet (1945) and James (1947). She was an expert horse-woman, for many years the Junior Master of the Suffolk Fox Hounds, a clubwoman, and a perfectionist in the art of gracious living.

After Auchincloss's death in 1976, Janet lived quietly in a small cottage on Hammersmith Farm, although the rest of the estate had to be sold. In 1979, she married old family friend Bingham Morris, her third husband. In 1985, she was hard-hit by the death of her thirty-nine-year-old daughter, Janet (Jackie's half sister), from cancer. Rumor has it that she subsequently began to suffer from Alzheimer's Disease, and she was no longer seen in public. She died July 22, 1989, six days before her daughter Jackie's sixtieth birthday.

Francis X. Morrissey

Francis X. (Frank) Morrissey was a crony of Joseph P. Kennedy, and became a municipal judge through Kennedy's influence. He was an early political advisor to Jack Kennedy, and eventually something of a political embarrassment, since Morrissey represented the old machine politics of Massachusetts that Kennedy publicly decried.

Motto of P. J. Kennedy

P. J. Kennedy, the grandfather of the President, had commissioned the engraving of a plaque with the motto by which he tried to conduct his business as a political ward boss. Hanging above his desk, the plaque read, "I shall pass through this world but once. Any kindness I can do, or goodness show, let me do it now—for I shall not pass this way again."

Mount Kennedy

In late 1963, the Canadian government re-named the highest unclimbed peak in the Yukon Mountains in honor of the assassinated President, John F. Kennedy. The top of Mount Kennedy is 13,900 feet high. In March 1965, the President's brother, Senator Robert F. Kennedy, along with professional climbers Jim Whittaker and Barry Prather and five other men, made the ascent to the top of the uncharted mountain. Whittaker asked Kennedy, who had no mountain-climbing experience, what he was doing to prepare himself. "I'm running up and down the stairs, practicing hollering for help," he replied. (His mother lovingly waved him off on the expedition, saying, "Don't slip, dear.") When the party reached the summit, they left behind in the snow a Kennedy family flag, a Kennedy fifty-cent piece and a PT-109 tie clip. Those close to Bob thought the climb was a kind of catharsis for him, which put an end to his lengthy period of silently anguished mourning for his brother.

Movies and TV Shows about the Kennedys

Blood Feud. The story of the eleven-year war between Robert F. Kennedy (played by Cotter Smith) and Jimmy Hoffa (played by Robert Blake). Called "an excellent re-creation of recent history."

Call to Glory: JFK. A series episode about an Air Force colonel and his family at the time of the President's assassination.

Executive Action. A Burt Lancaster movie mixing fact and fiction about the assassination of President Kennedy.

JFK—The Childhood Years: A Memoir for Television by His Mother. Rose Kennedy reminisced about her son with Harry Reasoner in this half-hour special first aired in 1967.

Kennedy. A miniseries about JFK, starring Martin Sheen in the title role.

Jacqueline Bouvier Kennedy. An emotional look at the life of the President's wife (played by Jacqueline Smith), with James Franciscus playing JFK in the TV movie. It was a fan-magazine approach that was beautifully photographed.

Johnny, We Hardly Knew Ye. Starred Paul Rudd as JFK.

The Missiles of October. William Devane played JFK in this made-for-TV movie about the Cuban missile crisis.

Onassis: The Richest Man in the World. Raul Julia played Onassis, Francesca Annis his wife,

Anthony Quinn plays Aristotle Onassis and Jacqueline Bisset his wife Jackie in the film The Greek Tycoon. *(Universal Studios)*

M

Jacqueline. *The New York Times* review summed it up: "Why can't television leave these people alone?"

Rose Kennedy Remembers. A sixty-minute interview with the Kennedy matriarch.

The Teddy Kennedy Story. A made-for-TV movie about the courage of young Teddy Kennedy after he lost his right leg to cancer.

The Kennedys at Massachusetts. A six-hour series on ABC based on Doris Kearns Goodwin's book, with William Petersen playing Joe Kennedy and Annette O'Toole as Rose.

Muckers Club

While a student at Choate in the early 1930s, Jack Kennedy organized a club with eleven other boys. They called it the Muckers Club, in a joking reference to the term the headmaster often used to describe "bad elements" at the school. Jack even had the local jeweler make pins for the members, choosing as their insignia a shovel. When the headmaster got news of the existence of the Muckers Club, he denounced the members as "public enemies" of Choate, and that tickled Jack's sense of humor, a response that further infuriated the headmaster.

Joseph P. Kennedy was summoned to Choate to discuss whether his son should be expelled from the school for his offense, and Jack later admitted he was much more afraid of confronting his father than the headmaster. He was greatly relieved when his father whispered, "You sure didn't inherit your father's directness or his reputation for using bad language. If that crazy Muckers Club had been mine, you can be sure it wouldn't have started with an M." Perhaps at the urging of Joe Kennedy, the headmaster decided that the Muckers would not be asked to leave Choate. As punishment, they were required to spend a few holiday weekends at the school. Joe Kennedy then warned his son that he should not expect to get away with such authority-baiting again.

A Mystery to Lyndon Johnson

Lyndon Johnson, the Senate majority leader during the period that John F. Kennedy was a senator from Massachusetts, later revealed to an oral historian his unflattering impressions of the youthful Kennedy at that point in his career.

Here was a young whippersnapper, a malaria-ridden and yellah, sickly, sickly. He never said a word of importance in the Senate and he never did a thing. But somehow with his books and his Pulitzer Prizes he managed to create the image of himself as a shining intellectual, a youthful leader who would change the face of the country. Now, I will admit that he had a good sense of humor and that he looked awfully good on the goddamn television screen and through it all he was a pretty decent fellow, but his growing hold on the American people was simply a mystery to me.

N

Naval Reserve Officer Candidate

In October 1943, six weeks before he turned eighteen, Robert F. Kennedy enlisted in the navy, signing up for a naval reserve officer training program. The program specified a year of college before preflight training, which would then lead to a commission in the navy. In March, 1944 Kennedy reported to Harvard to begin his training. By late 1945, with the war over, Bobby was stationed at Lewiston, Maine, frustrated and bored with his training program. On February 1, 1946, without telling anyone in his family, he left the program to sign up as an apprentice seaman aboard the destroyer U.S.S. *Joseph P. Kennedy, Jr.,* named after his oldest brother, who had been killed in the war. Bobby's active duty was passed in scraping paint and scrubbing floors as the ship cruised the Caribbean off the island of Cuba. He received an honorable discharge on May 30, 1946, and returned to Harvard to finish his undergraduate studies.

Navy and Marine Corps Medal

On June 12, 1944, Lieutenant John F. Kennedy was awarded the Navy and Marine Corps Medal for his heroism in saving the crew of PT-109 when it sank on the previous August 1. The citation read as follows:

For extremely heroic conduct as commanding officer of Motor Torpedo Boat 109 following the collision and sinking of that vessel in the Pacific war area on August 1–2. Unmindful of personal danger, Lieutenant Kennedy unhesitatingly braved the difficulties and hazards of darkness to direct rescue operations, swimming many hours to secure aid and food after he had succeeded in getting his crew ashore. His outstanding courage, endurance and leadership contributed to the saving of several lives and were in keeping with the highest traditions of the United States Naval Service.

Shortly after, the Navy sent Lieutenant Kennedy home for medical attention.

Lt. John F. Kennedy receives the Navy and Marine Medal. (James Coyne, Black Star)

Navy Cross

Lieutenant Joseph P. Kennedy, Jr., was posthumously awarded the Navy Cross on June 27, 1945. The award was presented to his mother, Rose Kennedy, in a simple ceremony witnessed only by his father and four of his brothers and sisters: Pat, Bobby, Jean, and Teddy. The citation read:

For extraordinary heroism and courage in aerial flight as pilot of a United States Navy Liberator bomber on August 12, 1944. Well knowing the extreme dangers involved and totally unconcerned for his own safety, Lieutenant Kennedy unhesitatingly volunteered to conduct an exceptionally hazardous and special operational mission. Intrepid and daring in his tactics and with unwavering confidence in the vital importance of his task, he willingly risked his life in the supreme measure of service and, by his great personal valor and fortitude in carrying out a perilous undertaking, sustained and enhanced the finest traditions of the United States Naval Service.

Hugh Nawn

Hugh Nawn was one of Rose Fitzgerald's suitors when she was a young woman. Nawn was said to be the man her father wanted her to marry. He was the son of a wealthy Catholic contractor in Boston who was a friend and political crony of John Fitzgerald. Rose obediently went to dances and parties with Hugh, but she never swerved in her emotional commitment to Joe Kennedy, and eventually Hugh recognized the hopelessness of his position and withdrew from the triangle. It took longer for Rose's father to admit defeat and give his consent for his daughter's marriage to Joe Kennedy.

"A Needed Rest"

In 1920, worn out by the demands of a baby and three toddlers, two of whom were ill, and made lonely and isolated by the constant absences demanded by the fortune-founding activities of Joseph P. Kennedy, Rose Kennedy left her husband and returned to her father's home. Although Rose later described this period euphemistically as "a needed rest," it clearly marked a crisis point in the couple's marriage. According to Kennedy biographer Doris Kearns Goodwin, Rose's father, John Fitzgerald, let three weeks pass before he sat down and talked to his favorite daughter about her situation. "You've made your commitment, Rosie," he told her, "and you must honor it now. What is past is past. The old days are gone. Your children need you and your husband needs you. You *can* make things work out. I know you can. If you need more help in the household, then get it. If you need a bigger house, ask for it. If you need more private time for yourself, take it. There isn't anything you can't do once you set your mind on it. So go now, Rosie, go back where you belong." Rose took her father's advice and returned to her own home with a renewed commitment to making her marriage work—a commitment strong enough to last nearly fifty more years, ended only by the death of Joe Kennedy.

Jawaharlal Nehru

Although Jawaharlal Nehru was the prime minister of India throughout the whole of the Kennedy presidency, John F. Kennedy never got along well with him on a personal level. It seems that the problem dated back to their first meeting in 1951, when Kennedy was a congressional representative on a semiofficial trip to India whose primary purpose was to prepare himself for the Senate race the following year. Accompanied by various members of his family, Jack was able to arrange a meeting with Nehru. Then he was nonplussed to find that the prime minister's principal interest seemed to be not politics but Jack's sister Pat. According to Robert

N

F. Kennedy, who was also at the meeting, "He didn't pay the slightest attention to my brother but was just destroyed by my sister Pat. He wouldn't talk to Jack and directed everything to her. My brother always remembered that. It was very funny, you know, and we really laughed about it."

As President, Kennedy met with Nehru in Washington in 1961. Relations between the two men appeared strained, but Jackie walked arm in arm with Nehru, chatting happily. The following year, Mrs. Kennedy made her tremendously successful visit to India—without her husband.

Richard Neustadt

Richard Neustadt was a Columbia University historian whose 1960 book, *Presidential Power*, had a significant influence on the policies of President Kennedy and the entire Kennedy administration. Because of the book, Neustadt became a Kennedy advisor in the crucial period after the election and before the inauguration, when the administration was being formed.

Bertha Newey

Bertha Newey was the English nanny hired in 1929 by Janet and Jack Bouvier to look after their two daughters, Jacqueline and Lee. She stayed with the family until she was fired in 1937.

The New Frontier

The New Frontier, which came to be an identifying phrase for the Kennedy presidency, was first mentioned in John F. Kennedy's acceptance speech when he won the Democratic nomination at the convention in Los Angeles. On the night of July 15, 1960, he addressed the convention and said:

We stand today on the edge of a New Frontier—the frontier of the 1960s—a frontier of unknown opportunities and perils, a frontier of unfulfilled hopes and threats . . . The New Frontier of which I speak is not a set of promises—it is a set of challenges. It sums up, not what I intend to offer the American people, but what I intend to ask of them. It appeals to their pride, not their pocketbook; it holds out the promise of more sacrifice instead of more security.

The success of that speech at the convention convinced Kennedy to use the theme of the New Frontier as part of his campaign against Richard M. Nixon, and later as a label for his presidential administration.

"A New Generation"

From the very beginning of his career in politics, John F. Kennedy had emphasized the theme of leadership passing to a new generation. When he first ran for Congress in 1946,

Kennedy was just thirty years old, and looked even younger, but he billed himself as the representative of the new generation that had gone to war for America and come home to help the country in peacetime as they had in war. When Kennedy was first elected to the Senate, in 1952, he was only in his mid-thirties, and those who helped him in the election, such as his brother Bob, Larry O'Brien, Kenny O'Donnell, were his age or younger. His staff, too, was a young one, with such figures as Ted Sorensen and Richard Goodwin. John F. Kennedy was elected President in 1960 when he was forty-three years old. Many of his staffers were men in their thirties, and his brother Ted, who played such a prominent part in his campaign, was still in his twenties. The fact that Jack Kennedy had waited until he was in his thirties to marry, and that he and his wife didn't have their first child until he was almost forty, made the First Family seem especially youthful.

The Party's choice at the 1960 convention. (Gene Daniels, Black Star)

New Ross

The little market town of New Ross, on the Barrow River in Wexford County, was the port from which Patrick Kennedy, the first of the family to go to America, embarked in 1848; it was just six miles away from the Kennedy homestead at Dunganstown. One hundred years later, in the late 1940s, Jack Kennedy made his first trip to New Ross to look for traces of the ancestors who had moved to America, and the beauty of the country and warmth of the people made a great impression on him. He returned there as President in June 1963 and stopped to drink a cup of tea at the birthplace of his great-grandfather Patrick Kennedy with his third cousin, Mrs. Mary Ryan. He told the crowd there, "It took 115 years to make this trip, and three generations. When my great-grandfather left here to become a cooper in East Boston, he carried nothing with him except two things: a strong religious faith and a strong desire for liberty. I am glad to say that all of his great-grandchildren have valued that inheritance."

After the assassination of President Kennedy, the town of New Ross closed its shops and drew its shades in mourning. In 1968, a 460-acre park near the Kennedy homestead was dedicated by Ireland's president Eamon de Valera in memory of the slain President.

President Kennedy and his sisters Jean and Eunice enjoy a warm welcome in Ireland. (Courtesy of the Kennedy Library)

New York Hospital for Special Surgery

The New York Hospital for Special Surgery was where, in October 1954, Senator John F. Kennedy underwent a double fusion of his spinal discs, a surgical procedure it was hoped would end the years of severe back pain he had suffered. The operation was judged extremely risky because of the complication of Addison's disease, from which Kennedy also suffered; the disease hampers the ability of victims to fight any kind of infection. In Kennedy's case, the site of the surgery became badly infected and he went into a coma from which the doctors did not expect him to emerge. But he finally succeeded in conquering the infection and was released from the hospital by the end of the year. After a difficult period of convalescence in Palm Beach, it became obvious that the surgery had not been a success. The open wound would not heal, and pieces of bone were clearly visible. Therefore a second operation, to perform bone grafts and insert a metal plate, was performed in February 1955, again at the New York Hospital for Special Surgery. This time the result was good. Jack Kennedy returned to his duties in the Senate in May of that year, able to walk again without crutches.

New York's Municipal Art Society

New York's Municipal Art Society is a group that has dedicated itself to preserving the aesthetic environment of New York City. One of its most visible members is Jacqueline Kennedy Onassis. She has lent her time, her money, and her talents to the fight to preserve such landmarks as Grand Central Station and St. Bartholomew's Church, and to block the construction of giant towers at Columbus Circle that could obstruct the sunlight in Central Park.

No Short Pants for Joe

When Joseph P. Kennedy became the United States Ambassador to Great Britain, the press wondered aloud what he would choose to wear to present his credentials to King George V. The ceremony in which new ambassadors to Great Britain are received always takes place at Buckingham Palace and has many traditional elements handed down over the centuries. In the 1930s, one of those traditions was that the ambassadors wore the formal court dress of an earlier age, consisting of knee pants, silk stockings, and buckled shoes. Ambassador Kennedy refused to wear any such un-American outfit, and he applied for (and received) special permission from the court to make his appearance in a tailcoat and long trousers, suitable formal morning wear.

No Smoking, No Drinking

Joseph P. Kennedy didn't want his children to smoke or drink, and he took practical steps to try to see that they didn't. He offered each child a check for one thousand dollars on their twenty-first birthday if they could honestly state that they had not yet touched cigarettes or alcohol. Seven of the nine children claimed their checks; one of the two who didn't was Jack Kennedy, who admitted he had sampled beer while a student at Harvard.

Dr. Thomas T. Noguchi

Dr. Thomas T. Noguchi was the longtime coroner of Los Angeles who performed the official autopsy on the body of Senator Robert F. Kennedy. (He had also conducted the autopsy on Marilyn Monroe six years earlier.) Noguchi stated firmly in his testimony that the gunshot wound that killed Kennedy was fired at point-blank range, by a gun held no more than an inch or two behind the Senator's head. His evidence thus conflicted with the official account of the crime, which had Sirhan Sirhan standing in front of Kennedy to fire at him, and being at least three to four feet away. This discrepancy gave rise to the so-called second gun theory, which hypothesizes that another assassin was concealed behind Kennedy and that two men were firing at him simultaneously.

Noroton

Noroton was a boarding school run by a Sacred Heart convent in Noroton, Connecticut, to which Rose Kennedy, the parent in charge of educational decisions for the girls in the family, sent first her daughter Kathleen in 1933, and later her daughter Eunice as well. Kathleen graduated in June 1937; Eunice didn't graduate from Noroton but transferred to a Sacred Heart school in England when her father became U.S. ambassador to Great Britain and the family moved to London. Located on a lovely and comfortable old estate, Noroton had the same austere standards Rose Fitzgerald had experienced in the Blumenthal Sacred Heart convent in Holland. Pat Kennedy was scheduled to follow her older sisters to Noroton but didn't want to leave home to go to boarding school. Years later, she confessed to her mother how she had managed the situation: She purposely failed the exam for admittance. The youngest Kennedy daughter, Jean, attended Noroton for the last two years of high school, graduating in 1945.

"Not So Little"

According to a story told by a former aide, Robert F. Kennedy was often amused by the stories that circulated about his so-called ruthless personality. One time he heard that a certain Washingtonian had characterized him as "a vicious little monster." Bobby laughed and said, "Tell him I'm not so little!"

Angie Novello

Angie Novello was the longtime secretary of Robert F. Kennedy. She met him when she was a stenographer on the Investigations Subcommittee staff.

"Number One Uninvited Guest in America"

When John F. Fitzgerald was campaigning for the office of Mayor of Boston in the early years of the century, he made it a habit to drop in on every party, every wake, every meeting, to meet and greet the assembled guests. His indefatigability in attending such social events gave him the nickname of "Number One Uninvited Guest in America."

O'Brien Manual

The "O'Brien Manual" was the sixty-four-page political bible that laid out the master strategy of the John F. Kennedy presidential campaign in 1960. In essence, the manual decreed that the campaign should be run by a huge army of volunteers, each of whom would be made to feel a crucial part of the effort. The manual, carried by every member of the Kennedy political organization, was written by one of Jack's chief political strategists, Larry O'Brien: hence the name.

Lawrence Francis O'Brien

Lawrence Francis O'Brien, universally called Larry, was a Kennedy staffer often referred to jokingly as a member of the "Irish mafia." O'Brien had been a public relations man in Springfield, Massachusetts, where he was born in 1917. A graduate of Northeastern University, O'Brien had formerly worked for Massachusetts Governor Foster Furcolo, and he was hired by John F. Kennedy for the 1952 senatorial campaign. O'Brien remained on Kennedy's staff thereafter, organizing the political nuts and bolts of the 1956 vice-presidential bid and the 1960 presidential campaign. He continued to work for President Kennedy in the White House, and he was with him that day in Dallas when the dream was shattered. O'Brien, a New Deal liberal with a kindly sense of humor, continued as a special assistant for President Johnson until 1965, when he was appointed to the office of Postmaster General, serving until 1969. After a brief stint in investment banking, O'Brien became the commissioner of the National Basketball Association in 1975, leaving the post in 1984. Today he works in real estate and public relations.

Observing the Twenty-Fifth Anniversary of the President's Death

Although the Kennedy family has repeatedly requested that President John F. Kennedy be remembered on the day of his birth rather than his death, the public continues to observe the anniversary of the assassination. In 1988, on the occasion of the twenty-fifth anniversary, a number of public events took place to honor the President's memory. On November 21, five hundred former members of the Peace Corps gathered in the Capitol Rotunda to hold a twenty-four-hour vigil as they read aloud their recorded thoughts about the President who established the idealistic Corps. At 8:15 on the morning of November 22, members of the Kennedy White House Staff assembled for a memorial mass at Arlington and then placed forty-six red roses, one for each year of his life, on the President's grave. Chapel services were conducted at Arlington later in the day, and there were wreath layings by the Green Berets, by the class of the motor boat torpedo squadron with which young Lieutenant Jack Kennedy trained, by Phi Kappa Theta, his Harvard fraternity, and by the Old Hibernians, an Irish-American organization. At 1 P.M., a commemorative service was held in St. Matthew's Roman Catholic Cathedral, site of the President's funeral.

In Dallas, more than 400 people gathered at Dealey Plaza, the site of the assassination, and flowers were placed on the grass. In Runnymede, England, Senator Edward M. Kennedy laid a bouquet on the monument there dedicated to his brother. Ethel Kennedy and Eunice Kennedy Shriver knelt silently at the President's grave in Arlington. The President's widow and two children attended a private mass in New York City, at St. Thomas More Roman Catholic Church.

Kenneth O'Donnell

Kenneth O'Donnell, always called Kenny, was one of John F. Kennedy's close political aides. Kenny had been the captain of the Harvard football team when Bobby Kennedy was a lowly bench-warmer, and the two young men, both devout Irish Catholics, became good friends. During World War II Kenny served in the Eighth Air Force as a bombardier. In 1952, at Bobby's suggestion, Kenny quit his job with a paper company in New England and joined the Kennedy political organization to help Jack gain control of the Massachusetts Democratic Committee. He stayed with Jack Kennedy thereafter, functioning as his appointments secretary. O'Donnell was with President Kennedy in Dallas on November 22, 1963.

Three years later, O'Donnell entered the race for governor of Massachusetts but was defeated in the Democratic primaries by Edward J. McCormick. He later coauthored a book of reminiscences of JFK with Dave Powers, called *Johnny, We Hardly Knew Ye*, published in 1972. O'Donnell died of liver cancer in Beth Israel Hospital in Boston on September 9, 1977.

The Oil Business

In the late 1940s, Joseph P. Kennedy began to invest in the oil business. He first bought an exploration company named Arctic, then formed Kenoil to hold leases and royalties. With the establishment of a company called Mokeen, he got into drilling and development, and the purchase of Sutton Producing brought in more royalties. The Kennedy family still retains interest in these oil companies.

Old Orchard Beach

Old Orchard Beach, Maine, was a summer resort highly favored by Bostonians, and especially by Bostonians who were involved in politics. Both John F. Fitzgerald and P. J. Kennedy took their families to Old Orchard Beach many summers in the early years of the century, and thus it was the place where P. J.'s son Joe first met young Rose Fitzgerald, whom he would eventually marry. A picture of the two families together at Old Orchard Beach still exists to document the occasion.

Aristotle Onassis

Aristotle Socrates Onassis was the Greek shipping magnate who became the second husband of the widowed Jacqueline Bouvier Kennedy. Onassis was born in Smyrna, a Turkish port on the Aegean, and in 1923 boarded a freighter in the Greek port of Piraeus bound for Argentina.

Ari and Rose. (Black Star)

The young man was either sixteen or twenty-two at the time; his Argentinean passport gave his birth date as 1900, but he later said that was a falsification, designed to get around a prohibition of immigrants under the age of twenty-two, and that he was actually born in 1906. In Argentina, Onassis went into the business of importing Turkish tobacco and became a millionaire by 1930. He then began to pick up oil tankers at bargain prices during the Depression. Thereafter his personal wealth continued to grow until he became one of the richest men in the world.

Mrs. Kennedy was Onassis's second wife. His first, whom he married in 1946, was Athina Mary Livanos, daughter of another wealthy Greek shipping family. Tina and Aristotle Onassis had two children, Alexander, born in 1948, and Christina, born in 1950. The couple divorced in 1960. Thereafter, Onassis's name was publicly linked with that of opera star Maria Callas.

Jacqueline Kennedy had met Onassis through her sister, Lee, and he had thoughtfully extended the hospitality of his fabled yacht, the *Christina*, to the First Lady during her recuperation from the birth and death of the Kennedys' second son, Patrick, born prematurely and the victim of respiratory problems. The friendship between the Greek tycoon and the President's widow culminated in marriage on October 18, 1968, four months after the death of Robert Kennedy. Once married, the couple frequently went their separate ways, causing rumors of a separation. Onassis's health began to deteriorate in 1973, when it was discovered he was suffering from an incurable neurological ailment, myasthenia gravis. In February 1975, he was taken to Paris for an operation to remove his gall bladder, and he died there on March 15, 1975. Aristotle Onassis was buried on his private island, Skorpios, next to his beloved son, Alexander, who had been killed in a plane crash two years earlier. His will left his widow an annual allowance of $250,000, but Jacqueline Onassis later was said to have negotiated a settlement of $26 million in exchange for dropping all further claim to his estate, valued at about $500 million.

Christina Onassis

Christina Onassis was the daughter of Aristotle Onassis and his first wife, Athina Livanos. Born on December 11, 1950, Christina grew up surrounded by wealth. Her father called her "Chryso Mou," or "my golden one," and named his huge yacht in her honor. At the time that Aristotle Onassis married Jacqueline Kennedy, there were rumors that Christina and her older brother, Alexander, opposed the match. In 1970, Christina defied her father's wishes and married a Los Angeles real estate broker more than twice her age. Although she was divorced within the year, it took time for the rift to heal, but she and her father were brought closer together by her brother's death in 1973. When Aristotle Onassis died, his daughter was his primary heir. The relationship between Christina and her former stepmother, Jacqueline Onassis, became markedly less cordial, and Mrs. Onassis subsequently took legal steps to obtain a larger share of the estate. Christina eventually offered a $26-million settlement, in return for which Mrs. Onassis agreed to waive all future claims. Christina married three more times and had one child, Athina, apparently without yet finding the happiness she sought. On November 18, 1988, Christina died in Buenos Aires, Argentina, while visiting friends. The cause of her death, officially described as a heart attack, was privately attributed to misuse of diet pills. The entire Onassis fortune is now being held in trust for little Athina.

Jacqueline Bouvier Kennedy Onassis

Jacqueline Bouvier was born on July 28, 1929, in South Hampton, the daughter of stockbroker John Bouvier III and his wife, the former Janet Lee. She went to boarding school at the fashionable Miss Porter's School in Connecticut, then attended Vassar College, spent a year at the Sorbonne in Paris, and graduated from George Washington University. In 1951, Jacqueline was working in Washington for the *Times-Herald* when she met the bachelor congressman from Massachusetts, Jack Kennedy. They were married in Newport on September 12, 1953, and had three children: Caroline Kennedy, born in 1957, John F. Kennedy, Jr., born in 1960; and

Jackie in Paris. (Black Star)

O

Patrick Bouvier Kennedy, who died two days after his birth in 1963.

When John Kennedy was elected President in 1960, Jacqueline Kennedy became First Lady. Her personal style, her clothes, her impeccable taste, all enchanted the world. Enchantment turned to admiration as she endured the ordeal of her husband's death under the eyes of the entire world. She led the mourning for her husband with grace and gallantry.

In 1968, Jacqueline Bouvier Kennedy was married to Greek shipping magnate Aristotle Onassis, in a Greek Orthodox ceremony on his private island of Skorpios. She was widowed again when he died in a Paris hospital seven years later. In 1974, Mrs. Onassis took up a career as an editor, a commitment she has maintained for more than a decade. Her life today is filled with work, with family life, and with a variety of social and charitable events.

1026 North Beckley Road

1026 North Beckley Road was the address of the rooming house in Dallas in which Lee Harvey Oswald, going under the name O. H. Lee, lived at the time he assassinated President John F. Kennedy. His landlady, Mrs. Arthur C. Johnson, remembered him as a man who rarely went out and kept his room neat and clean.

"When he took a bath, he'd clean out the tub as clean as any woman you ever saw," she later told the press. Lee Harvey Oswald was only a few blocks away from the Beckley Road house when he shot and killed police officer, J. D. Tippett and then ducked into the Texas Theater, where police arrested him for that crime.

1040 Fifth Avenue

In 1964, Jacqueline Kennedy bought a co-op apartment at 1040 Fifth Avenue in New York City, as a primary residence for herself and her two children. The fourteen-room apartment, at the corner of Fifth Avenue and Eighty-fifth Street, cost $200,000 and had annual maintenance charges of about $14,000. Additionally, Mrs. Kennedy spent about $125,000 on refurbishing the apartment. The apartment, on the top floor of the building, was created by joining two apartments together. Windows looked out on a peaceful view of Central Park. Mrs. Kennedy moved to New York because she felt that she and her children could not lead private lives in Washington. The Fifth Avenue location had the advantage of being close to her sister, Princess Lee Radziwill, to her stepbrother, Yusha Auchincloss, and to her in-laws, Stephen and Jean Smith, and Patricia Lawford and her children. The Fifth Avenue apartment, with elegant decor that is primarily French, remains her chief residence today and is currently estimated to be worth about $4 million.

1095 North Ocean Boulevard, Palm Beach

In 1933, Joseph P. Kennedy purchased an oceanfront home in Palm Beach, Florida, located at 1095 North Ocean Boulevard. The house was built in 1923 for just under $50,000 by famed architect Addison Mizner, for client Rodman Wanamaker of Philadelphia, who called it La Guerida. Wanamaker sold it to Kennedy in the depths of the Depression for about $100,000, and Kennedy paid another $15,000 to get the lot next door, to protect the family's privacy. With a pool, tennis courts, an underground tunnel to the beach, and six large bedrooms, the house was an ideal winter getaway for the Kennedy family, and it remains the site of many Kennedys' winter vacations. John F. Kennedy stayed there during his convalescence from back surgery in 1954–55; as the newly elected President in late 1960, he made it his headquarters before the Inauguration. Joe Kennedy always loved to sit in the "Bull Pen," a white-fenced private enclosure near the swimming pool, where he could sunbathe nude and talk on the telephone. Rose Kennedy continued the tradition of wintering in the Palm Beach house until forced by age and illness to give it up. Currently in rather shabby condition, the house is still favored by Ted Kennedy for long winter weekends in the sun, and by various Kennedy grandchildren for the fun of Palm Beach's social whirl and the sun and sea air.

122 Bowdoin Street

In a modest apartment building at 122 Bowdoin Street, near Boston's State House, John F. Kennedy rented an apartment during his 1946 bid to be elected a congressional representative from Massachusetts. There were two bedrooms, a living room, and a kitchen, initially furnished with discards from previous tenants. After Rose Kennedy visited her son on Bowdoin Street, new furnishings arrived to make the small apartment more comfortable. Jack Kennedy retained the apartment for the rest of his life, and 122 Bowdoin remained his official voting residence. Later, his younger brother Edward M. Kennedy also used the apartment as a legal residence in Massachusetts.

131 Naples Road

In the summer of 1920, Joseph P. Kennedy recognized that his family—four children and another on the way—had outgrown the house on Beals Street in which he and his wife, Rose, had started their married life, so he sold it (to aide Edward Moore) and bought a larger one on nearby Naples Road, also in Brookline. The Naples Road house had twelve rooms and was a more formal and elegant dwelling, as befitted a man who was already beginning to prosper from his ventures in the stock market. Built in the popular shingle style, the house had a large veranda on which the children could play on rainy days. The price of the Naples Road house was seventeen thousand dollars.

1607 Twenty-Eighth Street

The five-bedroom brick house in Georgetown at 1607 Twenty-eighth Street was the home of Edward M. and Joan Kennedy in the early 1960s. Located on a quiet street, it had a lovely enclosed garden for Teddy and Kara to play in, and an air of peace and privacy.

O

One Special Summer

Jacqueline and Lee Bouvier spent the summer of 1951 traveling in Europe; the trip was a gift from Hugh and Janet Auchincloss to mark Jackie's graduation from George Washington University and Lee's from Miss Porter's preparatory school. As a gift for their mother, the two young women made a scrapbook they called *One Special Summer*, containing stories of the trip written by Lee and illustrated by Jackie. It was published in book form in 1974.

Only Women and Children

The press, long accustomed to coping with the amazing solidarity of the Kennedys, started to refer to them collectively as "the Kennedy family" when John F. Kennedy became a national political figure. The habit continued, even though the family itself changed. A sad commentary on the change was made by Joan Kennedy, who was asked by a reporter in 1970 if there was pressure on her husband from "the Kennedy family" to run for President in 1972. "What family?" said Joan sadly. "What's left of the Kennedys? Besides Ted, only women and children."

The Order of President Kennedy's Funeral March

District of Columbia police escort
Escort Commander Major General Philip C. Wehle
Commander of troops and staff Lieutenant Colonel Richard E. Cross
United States Marine Corps Band
A company of Military Academy cadets
A company of Naval Academy midshipmen
A company of Air Force Academy cadets
A company of Coast Guard Academy cadets
A company of the 1st Battalion, 3rd Infantry
A company of Marines
A company of Navy men
A squadron from the Air Force
A company from the Coast Guard
A company of women from the various armed services
The United States Navy Band
A company from the Army National Guard
A company from the Army Reserves
A company from the Marine Corps Reserves
A company from the Naval Reserves
A squadron from the Air National Guard
A squadron from the Air Force Reserves
A company from the Coast Guard Reserves
The United States Air Force Band
Representatives from national veterans' organizations
The cortege
The Special Honor Guard
A detachment from the Scottish Black Watch
A detachment from the U.S. Special Forces
A detachment of Marines
The Joint Chiefs of Staff
The National Colors
The clergy
The horse-drawn caisson
The President's personal flag
The riderless horse
Mrs. Kennedy, President Johnson, and Robert F. Kennedy
The Justices of the U.S. Supreme Court
The members of the Cabinet
The members of the Senate and House of Representatives
Other mourners

O

The funeral procession crosses the bridge to Arlington Cemetery. (Don McCoy, Black Star)

The Order of the Sacred Heart

The Order of the Sacred Heart is a Roman Catholic teaching order founded in France about 1800. The curriculum is the same in all Sacred Heart convent schools, making it easy for pupils to transfer from one to another. The goal of the Sacred Heart education is to turn out young women who combine a strong spiritual life with the ability to function well as wives and mothers and members of the community. The quality of a Sacred Heart education is so respected that socially prominent non-Catholics often send their daughters to Sacred Heart schools. Rose Fitzgerald went to Sacred Heart schools after she finished high school, and her daughters attended them for both high school and college.

O

David Ormsby-Gore

David Ormsby-Gore was an Englishman who became friendly with Kathleen Kennedy at the time that his cousin, the Marquess of Hartington, fell in love with her. Ormsby-Gore himself later married a member of Kathleen's circle in London, Sylvia Thomas (always called Sissy), and Kathleen was godmother to their first child. Through Kathleen, David met her brother Jack, and the two men became great friends. After Kennedy was elected to the presidency, he told Ormsby-Gore, then a minister in the British government, that he should come to Washington as ambassador from Great Britain. Harold Macmillan, to whom Ormsby-Gore was related by marriage, announced the appointment in October 1961. President Kennedy, who called Ormsby-Gore the most intelligent man he'd ever met, was delighted. The Ormsby-Gores were an integral part of the Washington social scene during the Kennedy administration. On the death of his father in 1964, Ormsby-Gore inherited the title of Lord Harlech. Lady Harlech was killed in a car crash in 1967, and thereafter Lord Harlech's name was romantically linked to Jacqueline Kennedy by the press—so much so that Mrs. Kennedy's secretary had to issue a denial of reports that the two would marry. Lord Harlech died in January 1985.

Lee Harvey Oswald

Lee Harvey Oswald, the man who assassinated President John F. Kennedy, was born on October 18, 1939, in New Orleans. His father, Robert E. Lee Oswald, died before he was born, and his mother, Marguerite Claverie, remarried when her son was six, giving young Lee a stepfather (Edwin A. Ekdahl) for three years before that marriage ended in divorce. The family moved to New York to be closer to Mrs. Oswald's son from her first marriage, and then returned to New Orleans when Lee was in high school. Through much of his childhood Oswald was a loner, and often a discipline problem. In October 1956, he joined the Marine Corps, where his personal isolation continued. After his discharge in 1959, he applied for admission to Albert Schweitzer College but instead of attending defected to Russia, where in 1961 he met and married pharmacist Marina Nicholaevna. Initially, he attempted to renounce his American citizenship, which led the Marine Corps to change his discharge to a dishonorable one. In 1962, he turned to the U.S. government to obtain a loan of $435.71 to enable him to return to America on June 13, 1962, with his wife and their four-month-old baby daughter, June Lee. They went to Texas, then New Orleans, where just months before the assassination, Oswald was arrested for distributing pro-Castro leaflets.

Through a recommendation by his wife's friend Ruth Paine, Oswald obtained a job at the Texas Book Depository on October 15, only a few weeks before the President's scheduled trip to Dallas. (The Oswalds' second child, a baby girl, was born five days later.) The fact that the official route of the President's motorcade would pass by the building was published November 19, and Oswald marked the route on a map of the city in his room. More than six witnesses placed Oswald in the building at the time of the assassination, and the police actually saw him there minutes later, but assumed that because he was a legitimate employee of the Book Depository, he couldn't be the assassin they were looking for.

After the shooting, Oswald took a cab back to

the rooming house where he lived (apart from his wife and daughter) under the name O. H. Lee. He changed his jacket and walked back outside. A few blocks away, Oswald encountered Patrolman J. D. Tippitt and killed him. Then he ducked into the Texas Theater, where the movie playing was *War Is Hell*. There, after a brief scuffle, the police arrested Oswald, who was armed with a .38 revolver, for the murder of Officer Tippett. Meanwhile, evidence began to accumulate implicating Oswald in the assassination of the President as well. On November 23, 1963, Oswald was arraigned for both murders. On the following morning, as the police attempted to move Oswald from the city to the county jail, he was shot before the eyes of police escorts as well as television viewers all over the world by nightclub operator Jack Rubenstein, who commonly used the name Jack Ruby. Oswald was taken to Parkland Hospital (the same hospital that had vainly attempted to treat President Kennedy), where he died at 1:03 P.M., almost exactly forty-eight hours after the President he had assassinated. He was buried on November 25, the same day as President Kennedy, in Rose Hill Cemetery in Fort Worth. The funeral, arranged by the Secret Service, was attended by his widow, who placed her wedding ring in the coffin, in a macabre echo of Jacqueline Kennedy.

Reverend Jerry Owen

The Reverend Jerry Owen was a preacher and horse breeder in Santa Ana, California, who may have been innocently involved in a plot to assassinate Senator Robert F. Kennedy. After Kennedy's death, Owen came forward to say he had picked up a hitchhiker whom he identified as Sirhan Sirhan. He said that Sirhan told him he was an exercise boy at a stable and wanted to buy a horse. Owen obligingly took Sirhan to look at horses in several stables and, after Sirhan had agreed to purchase one, Owen dropped him off at the Ambassador Hotel's kitchen entrance. Sirhan asked Owen if he would return to deliver the horse to the hotel's kitchen door the following night around midnight. But Sirhan's possible attempt to arrange a getaway vehicle failed when Reverend Owen got a call to preach in another city the following day and had to leave before he could meet Sirhan.

PB4Y Liberator

In July 1944, Lieutenant Joseph P. Kennedy, Jr., volunteered for an extremely dangerous mission piloting a large cargo plane called a PB4Y that had been turned into a drone. In a desperate attempt to stop the V-1 rocket bombings that were doing so much damage to England, the plane was to be loaded with explosives at an English base and flown to a point just miles away from the German rocket base. The pilot and copilot would parachute into the sea, where they would be picked up by waiting boats, and the plane would then be guided for the remaining few minutes by a remote control device located in an escort fighter.

On the morning of August 1, 1944, Joe Junior and his copilot, Lieutenant Wilford J. Willy, took off in the Liberator, code-named "Zoot-Suit Black." They successfully flew the PB4Y for several hours, to a spot at an altitude of about two thousand feet, just minutes away from the place at which they would have parachuted out. Then

Joe, Jr. during his pilot training in England. (Owen W.W., Black Star)

a sudden huge explosion destroyed the plane and killed the two aviators instantly. Many years later, analysis of German documents revealed that the Kennedy-Willy mission would have been pointless even if successful: The German rocket base had already been moved to another location. In 1972, parts of the fuselage and a wing were located buried in a wood in England.

PT Service

The PT (Patrol Torpedo) service was a branch of the Navy in World War II that manned a fleet of small, light combat craft considered ideal for use in the naval war against Japan in the Pacific. The boats were made of plywood, and measured about ninety feet long. The merit of the PT boats lay chiefly in their speed and great maneuverability. Jack Kennedy was only one of many wealthy young men whose childhood experience with pleasure boating led to enrollment in the PT service.

PT-59

After Lieutenant John F. Kennedy lost PT-109 in a collision with a Japanese destroyer in August 1943, he was given another command, a new type of PT boat that carried guns rather than torpedoes. His new craft was PT-59. Kennedy was relieved of that command on November 19, 1943, when he was directed to return to the States for medical treatment of injuries caused by the sinking of PT-109.

PT-109

PT-109 was the patrol torpedo boat commanded by Lieutenant (Junior Grade) John F. Kennedy in action in the fighting in the Solomon Islands during World War II. PT-109 was built by the Electric Boat Company in Bayonne, New Jersey, and had been delivered to the Brooklyn Naval Yard in the summer of 1942. Kennedy took command on April 25, 1943, replacing Ensign Leonard J. Thom, who remained aboard as a crew member. On the night of August 1, PT-109 was patrolling the waters of the Blackett Strait, looking for a convoy of four Japanese destroyers, when it collided with one of them, the *Amagiri*. As Kennedy told the story at the time, "It all happened so fast there wasn't a chance to do a thing. The destroyer hit our starboard forward gun station and sliced right through. I was in the cockpit. I looked up and saw a red glow and streamlined stacks. Our tanks were ripped open and gas was flaming on the water about twenty yards away."

Two of Kennedy's crew, Andrew Kirksey and Harold Marney, were killed outright, but Kennedy managed to save all ten of the men who survived the initial crash: Leonard Thom, Raymond Albert, Charles Harris, William Johnston, George Ross, Edgar Mauer, John McGuire, Patrick McMahon, Ray Starkey, and Gerald Zinser. Kennedy towed several of the injured crew members from the water to the half of the PT boat that was still afloat, and later he got them all to land on nearby Plum Pudding Island. Kennedy then organized the efforts for survival and himself swam for long hours in the Pacific trying to flag down passing American ships. The group moved from one small island to another in the hope of getting closer to passing ships, living on coconuts and hope. After four days, Lieutenant Kennedy succeeded in contacting a group of natives, to whom he gave a coconut with a message scratched on the shell. The natives returned with food and a kerosene stove, and later that night, all eleven survivors were picked up by a PT boat dispatched to their location. John F. Kennedy returned to base to find that he had become a hero.

PT-109: *The Book*

During the Kennedy presidency, author Robert J. Donovan proposed writing a book on John F. Kennedy's wartime experiences as commander of PT-109. President Kennedy tried to discourage Donovan from the undertaking, telling him there was no real story to be found. Donovan went ahead with the project, and his dedication to accurate research was so great that he personally went out to the Solomon Islands and swam the same waters in which Kennedy's adventures had taken place. The book, entitled simply *PT-109*, was a best-seller when it was published in 1962, and rights were then sold for a film of the same name.

PT-109: *The Movie*

The movie version of President John F. Kennedy's wartime exploits was called *PT-109* and based on the book of the same name by Robert J. Donovan. It was Joseph P. Kennedy who proposed the idea of a movie to Jack Warner, at Warner Brothers. It was also Joe Kennedy who negotiated the contract on behalf of author Donovan and the crew members of the PT boat. He later approved the script and selected handsome Cliff Robertson to play the role of his son, young Lieutenant Kennedy. The movie was released in 1963, at the height of President Kennedy's popularity in the White House. Not surprisingly, the movie portrayed young Lieutenant Kennedy in a completely favorable light.

"PT-109": *The Song*

In the spring of 1962, one of the songs topping the charts was the Columbia recording of "PT-109," by country singer Jimmy Dean. The song, written by Marijohn Wilkin and Fred Burch, recounted President Kennedy's experience as a commander of a PT boat in the Pacific theater during World War II. The lyrics began, "In 43, they put to sea, Thirteen men and Kennedy, Aboard the PT-109, To fight the brazen enemy."

P

Cliff Robertson as Lt. John F. Kennedy in an anxious moment from P.T. 109 (Movie Star News)

Ruth Paine

Ruth Paine was the Quaker and pacifist who in 1962–63 took an interest in the problems of a young Russian immigrant to Dallas, Marina Oswald, and her moody and difficult husband. Paine, at that time thirty-one and separated from her husband, Michael, became friendly with Marina Oswald and was distressed to see how badly her husband treated her. "I thought Marina was a wonderful person. We were both young mothers and liked to talk about families and housework. I thought that I could teach her English and she could help me with my Rus-

sian. I didn't like her husband at all, though. It was almost as if he were daring you to like him and hoping you wouldn't."

On several occasions in 1962 and 1963, Marina left Lee and took shelter with Ruth, but she always ended up returning when he begged her, and she even moved with him to New Orleans for a brief stay in the spring of 1963. When the couple returned to Dallas in mid-1963, Ruth offered a home to Marina, then pregnant with the couple's second child, and Marina's daughter, June, in Ruth's suburban Dallas home, while Lee lived in a Dallas rooming house and looked for work. Even after Oswald obtained a job at the Texas School Book Depository through the recommendation of Ruth Paine, he continued to live apart from his family. On October 20, Marina gave birth to the couple's second child, another daughter. He visited them at Ruth Paine's house the day before the assassination.

Providencia Parades

Providencia Parades, usually called "Provy," was Jacqueline Kennedy's personal maid while she was in the White House. A native of the Dominican Republic, Provy had been hired as a "second-floor maid" not long after Jacqueline married the Senator, and she stayed with Mrs. Kennedy until the family moved to New York in 1964. Provy's main duties were to keep Mrs. Kennedy's clothes cleaned, mended, and pressed, and to help her dress for her public appearances. A special task was looking after Mrs. Kennedy's huge wardrobe of long twenty-button kid gloves, a particular trademark of her style.

Paramount Pictures

In 1936, Paramount Pictures hired Joseph P. Kennedy as a financial consultant to help stop their large quarterly losses. He was so helpful that the head of Paramount, Adolph Zukor, tried to get Joe to stay on in some capacity, but Kennedy refused to be anyone else's employee, no matter how good the job offer.

Park Agency, Inc.

Park Agency is one of the companies set up by Joseph P. Kennedy in the 1940s to act as a holding company for his real estate investments, including the Merchandise Mart in Chicago. Park Agency invested heavily in midtown Manhattan, especially along Lexington Avenue, and routinely sold properties for three or four times what they had cost. Park Agency also invested in land on Pelham Parkway in the Bronx, in office buildings in White Plains and Albany, and in various shopping centers. Today the offices of Park Agency are located in Manhattan's Pan Am building.

Pathé

Pathé was a leading film studio that was owned by the Keith-Albee-Orpheum chain of theaters, in which a controlling interest was purchased by Joseph Kennedy in 1928. Pathé's chief asset was director Cecil B. deMille, who made his profitable high-budget epics at the studio. Joe

Kennedy decided not to interfere with deMille's operation at Pathé, but the studio ran in the red for 1928, '29, and '30. Kennedy retained his interest in Pathé even after he sold RKO, and late in 1930, after the studio had just released three successful pictures, he negotiated a deal to sell Pathé and all its assets to RKO. Joseph Kennedy walked away from the deal with five million dollars in cash and notes, but some small stockholders were badly hurt by his deal and instituted a suit against him, claiming the deal defrauded them. In the end, Joe Kennedy won the case, which dragged on for years.

The Peace Corps

On March 1, 1961, President John F. Kennedy signed an executive order directing the State Department to establish and administer the Peace Corps. Three days later, the President named his brother-in-law, R. Sargent Shriver, as the director. Shriver resigned in 1966, as required by a five-year limit set on administration positions. At that time, the Peace Corps had more than fifteen thousand volunteers, idealistic young people who wanted to serve their government and help people in underdeveloped countries. Bill Moyers summed up the appeal of the organization: "The Peace Corps is to the American Government what the Franciscans in their prime were to the Roman Catholic Church: a remarkable manifestation of a spirit too particular and personal to be contained by an ecclesiastic (read: bureaucratic) organization."

Under the Republican administrations of Nixon and Ford, the Peace Corps declined to under six thousand volunteers by 1976 and lost its autonomy along with most of its budget. But with the leadership of the new director appointed by President Reagan in 1981, Loret Miller Ruppe, the Peace Corps began to regain some of its old vitality. It is once again an independent agency, bipartisan support for its activities has developed in Congress, and it plans to increase its staff of volunteers to about ten thousand people by 1992.

Peapack, New Jersey

One of the four homes presently owned by Jacqueline Kennedy Onassis is a country house near Peapack, New Jersey, which she uses for weekend getaways. She chose the location because it is within the area where the Essex Hunt Club fox-hunts. She sometimes participates in the hunts, and she also competes in the riding events at the Club's annual meet. Fellow members include C. Douglas Dillon and Murray McDonnell.

Victoria Frances Lawford Pender

Victoria Frances Lawford is the third child of Peter and Pat Kennedy Lawford, born in Santa Monica, California, on November 4, 1958, the same day her uncle, John F. Kennedy, won re-election to the Senate by an enormous margin. Her name was chosen to celebrate that victory, and Jack became her godfather; her middle name honors Lawford family friend Frank (Francis) Sinatra. Vicki graduated from the Lycée Français de New York and received her Bachelor of Arts Degree from Mount Vernon College in Washington in 1981. She worked in Washington covering congressional news for cable TV and is now a television coordinator for Very Special Arts, a nonprofit affiliate of the John F. Kennedy Center for the Performing Arts in Washington that sponsors programs for disabled people. On June 13, 1987, she married attorney Robert Beebe Pender, Jr., of the Washington law firm of Nixon, Hargrave, Devane and Doyle. Their first child, Alexandra Lawford Pender, was born in 1988.

Dr. Malcolm Perry

Dr. Malcolm Perry was the young surgeon on duty at Parkland Hospital in Dallas who treated President John F. Kennedy when he was brought in suffering from gunshot wounds. For all intents and purposes, the President was dead on arrival, but Perry and other doctors tried for some minutes to revive him before they acknowledged that the task was hopeless. By an ironic coincidence, Dr. Perry was also on duty at Parkland two days later, when Lee Harvey Oswald was brought in after being shot by Jack Ruby. Again, the efforts to save the victim were in vain.

Phone Sex

Maria Shriver and her husband, Arnold Schwarzenegger, are often separated by the demands of their two careers, as she usually works in television on the East Coast and he usually works in movies on the West Coast. When asked how the couple manages to survive the long separations, Arnold teasingly told an interviewer, "We've taken phone sex to new heights."

The Pink Chanel Suit

On the day of President John F. Kennedy's assassination in Dallas, his wife was wearing a hot pink suit of nubby wool with a matching pillbox hat. The suit was from the French couture house of Chanel, with characteristic Chanel touches of brass buttons and navy trim on the collar facings, the sleeves, and the pockets. In the minutes of anguish after President Kennedy was shot, Jacqueline Kennedy cradled his wounded head on her lap, so that her skirt and her stockings were stained by his blood. Friends tried to get her to change aboard Air Force One during the return trip to Washington with her husband's body, but she refused. She wore the suit throughout the night as she stayed at Bethesda Naval Hospital during the postmortem and the preparation for burial, and she was still wearing the suit the following morning as an ambulance bore the coffin of the slain President back to the White House. It was not until later that morning that she finally agreed to remove the suit, which was eventually carefully folded and stored in a box next to the dress she wore at her wedding to John F. Kennedy.

Plane Crash Injures Edward M. Kennedy

On June 19, 1964, less than a year after the death of President John F. Kennedy, his brother Senator Edward M. Kennedy took off in a chartered plane from the Washington Airport on his way to the Massachusetts Democratic State Convention. Flying near the landing field outside Springfield in dense fog, the twin-engine Aero-Commander hit the tops of some tall trees and crashed. The pilot was killed instantly, and Kennedy's administrative assistant, Edward Moss, died of his injuries a few days later. Passengers Senator and Mrs. Birch Bayh were thrown clear and thus escaped serious injury, but Ted Kennedy was in critical condition with a spine fractured in six places. It was more than six months before he had recovered sufficiently to be able to resume his duties. When he walked into the Senate unaided, his colleagues applauded his effort and courage.

A Poem for a President

At the request of President Kennedy, Robert Frost had written a poem especially for the President's inauguration on January 20, 1961. The poem read:

Summoning artists to participate
In the august occasions of the state
Seems something artists ought to celebrate.
It makes the prophet in us all presage
The glory of a next Augustan age
Of a power leading from its strength and pride,
Of young ambition eager to be tried,
Firm in our free beliefs without dismay,

In any game the nations want to play.
A golden age of poetry and power
Of which this noonday's the beginning hour.

The glare of the sun was so bright that the poet was only able to read the first three lines; even a makeshift shield provided by Vice-President Johnson's hat failed to remedy the situation. Frost chose to conclude by reciting from memory one of his most famous poems, "The Gift Outright," with its moving opening line, "The land was ours before we were the land's."

The Porcellian

The Porcellian was for decades the most elite of the seven private clubs at Harvard University, with membership restricted largely to the sons of old New England families. New members were chosen in the winter of their sophomore year, and it was the most coveted social distinction in the university. In the winter of 1910, sophomore Joseph P. Kennedy, although he was popular with his classmates and a natural leader, was not elected to the Porcellian, nor any of the six other clubs, because of his background and his Catholicism. Intimates believed that Kennedy never forgot or forgave the slight.

Marina Nicholaevna Oswald Porter

Marina Nicholaevna was a young Russian woman working as a pharmacist when she met American defector Lee Harvey Oswald. She married Oswald in 1961, and their first child, June Lee, was born in 1962. In that same year, Marina's husband decided he wanted to return to the country of his birth, and the U.S. government provided financial assistance to help the family travel to Fort Worth. Unable to find work immediately because of the language barrier, Marina devoted herself to raising her daughter and learning to speak English. Marina frequently lived apart from her husband, and she appears to have known little or nothing about his plans to assassinate President John F. Kennedy. Marina gave birth to her second daughter only a few weeks before the assassination, and she was still living with a woman friend, Ruth Paine, at the time of the event that shocked the nation. Despite their de facto separation, she was hard-hit by her husband's own death at the hands of Jack Ruby. After Oswald's funeral, Marina soon remarried and then purposely slipped into obscurity, resurfacing only in 1978, when she was called to testify by the Senate subcommittee investigating the assassinations of John and Robert Kennedy.

Portraits of President and Mrs. Kennedy

It is traditional for Presidents to present an official portrait to the White House after leaving office. Jacqueline Kennedy debated for several years before choosing an artist for the Commission, and finally settled on New York-based Aaron Shikler. His portrait shows a thoughtful John Kennedy, with crossed arms; the accompanying portrait of Mrs. Kennedy captures something of the youthful radiance that won the hearts of the country.

One month before the official unveiling of the portraits, Jacqueline accepted the invitation of the Nixons to return to the White House for a private viewing. She and her two children inspected the paintings and then dined with the entire Nixon family. It was the first—and to date also the last—time she had returned to her former home.

Portsmouth Priory

Portsmouth Priory was the Catholic preparatory school, operated by the Benedictines, in Portsmouth, Rhode Island (on Narragansett Bay), to which Robert F. Kennedy was sent in 1939, when the Kennedy family returned from England on the eve of World War II. Students at Portsmouth, founded in 1936, followed a spartan regime similar to that of the Benedictine monks. Bobby stayed at the school for two and a half years, the only one of the Kennedy sons to attend a Catholic boarding school for more than a single term. His grades at Portsmouth Priory were low, but he absorbed much of the religious foundation in which the school specialized. Bobby left in 1942 to attend Milton Academy, thought by his father to be a better preparation for the academic rigors of Harvard. Bobby's younger brother, Edward M. Kennedy, later went to Portsmouth Priory for one term.

The Post-Inaugural Luncheon

After the Inauguration of President John F. Kennedy, dignitaries were invited to luncheon at the Capitol as guests of Chairman of the Joint Congressional Inaugural Committee John Sparkman and his wife. The menu included such delicacies as tomato soup with popcorn, New England broiled lobster, Texas prime rib, and hot garlic bread. One of the most memorable moments came when former President Truman thrust his menu at the new President and asked for an autograph.

Robert Sturgis Potter

Robert Sturgis Potter met Joseph P. Kennedy when they were both students at Harvard. Despite the fact that their backgrounds were greatly dissimilar, they became good friends. Potter came from an old Main Line Philadelphia family and had all the social credentials Joe Kennedy lacked; Kennedy had the fire and the will to win that Potter admired.

Dave Powers

Dave Powers was a political aide to John F. Kennedy. Their association went all the way back to the 1946 election for the eleventh Congressional District in Massachusetts. At the time they first met, in early 1946, Powers was considerably more experienced in politics than Kennedy, but he was immediately impressed with Kennedy's instincts and his impact on the voters. Although Powers had initially supported a rival candidate, he switched his allegiance to Kennedy—and remained loyal even years after his boss's death.

Powers functioned for Jack Kennedy rather as Eddie Moore had done for Jack's father, Joe: a combination secretary, valet, errand-runner, entertainer, and diplomat. Powers had a fantastic memory for sports statistics, which Jack Kennedy loved. He was with the presidential party on that fatal day in Dallas, and accompanied the body of his slain friend back to Washington. Thereafter, he helped Robert F. Kennedy with his political campaigns and remained close to the family. He is currently associated with the Kennedy Library in Boston, where he serves as a living link with the Kennedy political legacy.

A Present for Rose

Joseph P. Kennedy established the tradition of presenting his wife, Rose, with a gift each time she bore him another child. As time went by, and the size of both his fortune and their family increased, his gifts on these occasions became more and more expensive. When daughter Jean was born in 1928, Joe gave Rose a magnificent diamond bracelet. A friend asked teasingly what he would give his wife if she had another baby. Joe replied, "A black eye."

Four years later, the couple's last child, Edward M. Kennedy, was born. It is not recorded what Joe Kennedy gave Rose on this occasion.

Presentation at Court

On May 11, 1938, Ambassador Joseph P. Kennedy arranged for his two eldest daughters, Rosemary and Kathleen, to be presented at court to King George VI and Queen Elizabeth. Their mother took the girls to Paris to select their dresses: Kathleen's came from Lucien Lelong, a dress of white illusion net ornamented with puffs of netting and two net shoulder straps. Rosemary chose a Molyneux, also in white net, traditional for debutantes, with silver stripes. Both girls wore elbow-length white kid gloves and carried small bouquets of lilies-of-the-valley. Rose, who was to accompany her daughters as their sponsor, also chose a Molyneux, a white silk gown richly embroidered in silver. All three women wore the customary Prince of Wales feathers in their hair, and Rose topped hers off with a borrowed diamond tiara and carried a large feathered fan. A framed photo of that occasion, one of the most treasured mementoes of the Kennedy family, still hangs on the wall of Mrs. Kennedy's Hyannis Port house. Rose saved her dress and was able to wear it twenty-three years later to the Inauguration Ball when her son took office as President in January 1961.

President Reagan Comments on President Kennedy

In 1985, President Ronald Reagan spoke at the dedication of the John F. Kennedy Library Foundation, and revealed his own admiration for his predecessor. Said Reagan, "He seemed to grasp from the beginning that life is one fast-moving train and you have to jump aboard and hold onto your hat and relish the sweep of the wind as it rushes by."

Private Mass for the Kennedy Family

On Saturday morning, November 23, 1963, the Kennedy family gathered by the coffin that lay in state in the East Room of the White House, a member of the Armed Forces at each of the four sides. Two priests conducted a private mass for the family as they knelt by the flag-draped coffin with tall white candles burning at the corners.

Prix de Paris

In 1951, the winner of *Vogue*'s Prix de Paris contest was twenty-two-year-old Jacqueline Bouvier. All the contestants had to write four papers, draw up a plan for an issue of one magazine,

P

and write an essay on "People I Wish I Had Known." Jackie wrote that the three men she would most like to have met in person were French poet Charles Baudelaire, the English writer with the scandalous private life, Oscar Wilde, and Russian ballet impresario Serge Diaghilev. Jacqueline declined the prize she had won (defeating more than 1200 competitors), a job for a year in *Vogue*'s Paris office, saying that since she had just spent the previous year in school in Paris, she would prefer to stay in the United States. Instead, she took a job as the inquiring photographer for the Washington *Times-Herald*.

Profiles in Courage

While Senator John F. Kennedy was in Palm Beach during the fall and winter of 1954–55 convalescing from surgery on his bad back, he occupied himself by working on a book called *Profiles in Courage*. It was a series of portraits of American politicians who had stood firm against the wishes of their constituents and/or their colleagues to follow their own consciences; the book underlined the fact that such moral courage could make a difference to the entire country. His wife, Jacqueline, later commented, "This project saved his life. It helped him channel all his energies, while distracting him from pain." The book was dedicated to her:

This book could not have been possible without the encouragement, assistance and criticism offered me from the very beginning by my wife, Jacqueline, whose help during all my days of convalescence I cannot ever adequately acknowledge.

Published in the fall of 1955 by Harper and Brothers and featuring a foreword from distinguished historian Allan Nevins, *Profiles in Courage* struck a responsive chord in the nation, and it became an immediate best-seller. The following spring, it achieved the additional distinction of winning a Pulitzer Prize, which brought with it a significant addition to Kennedy's stature. Kennedy presented the five-hundred-dollar Pulitzer check to the United Negro College Fund.

Yet there was criticism at the time the Prize was awarded, and for years afterward, about the fact that Senator Kennedy had received help in writing the book. He never concealed the fact that various researchers, historians, and writers had made contributions to the final manuscript. It was undeniably John F. Kennedy's concept and vision behind the book, but the execution owed much to others.

Promises to Keep

A 1988 book by novelist George Bernau, called *Promises to Keep*, was based on the premise that the 1963 assassination of President John F. Kennedy had failed. The publication of the Warner book, on the twenty-fifth anniversary of the assassination, was a testimonial to the power the event still exerts over Americans.

P

The Pursuit of Justice

In October 1964, *The Pursuit of Justice* was published by Harper and Row. The author was Robert F. Kennedy, and the subject was one he cared about deeply, the inequitable treatment of minorities in the United States.

Pushinka

Pushinka was a pet dog of President John F. Kennedy's children while they were growing up in the White House. The dog was a descendant of the Russian dog, Laika, that traveled in space, and was a gift to the Kennedy children from Russian Premier Nikita Khrushchev.

Queen Kelly

Queen Kelly was the name of the movie that Joseph P. Kennedy and Gloria Swanson tried to make together. Production went on for months, but no final film ever emerged. As producer, Kennedy put at least eight hundred thousand dollars of his own money into the venture; Swanson, then at the peak of her fame, was to be the star. Kennedy hired the cantankerous German genius Erich von Stroheim to write the script and direct. Stroheim already had a reputation for devastating schedules and budgets, but Kennedy felt his own expertise as a business manager could keep the director under control.

The plot of the movie was extremely convoluted. It involved a Middle European prince who falls in love with an innocent young girl in a convent. The prince's evil mother, the queen, arrests him and forces the girl to leave the country. Through a string of strange coincidences, she ends up as the leading attraction (given the ironic name of "Queen Kelly") in a brothel in East Africa, from which the Prince eventually manages to rescue her. He then marries her and sets her on the throne of his country, making her a real queen at last.

Stroheim shot an immense amount of footage for *Queen Kelly*, but seemed unable to bring it to a conclusion. New endings were proposed, story changes made daily, and a series of assistant directors brought in to try to speed things up as the picture ran wildly over all of Kennedy's carefully planned constraints. Eventually Stroheim was fired, Gloria Swanson went on to another film, and Joe Kennedy tried to hire someone to salvage the film through editing. But *Queen Kelly* was never released. The project ended Stroheim's career and damaged Swanson's image and finances; it also probably brought an end to the romance between Joe and Gloria.

Years later, a clip from *Queen Kelly* was used in *Sunset Boulevard*, which starred Gloria Swanson as a fading movie queen and Erich von Stroheim as her former director. Together, they watch the films they made in their glory days—one of which proved to be a short excerpt from *Queen Kelly*. It was the kind of inside joke that Hollywood appreciates the most.

"Queen of the May"

When Joseph P. Kennedy became Ambassador to the Court of St. James, he moved into the beautifully decorated American embassy in Grosvenor Square, in the Mayfair section of London. Describing his office, he wrote to a friend, "I have a beautiful blue silk room and all I need to make it perfect is a Mother Hubbard dress and a wreath to make me Queen of the May."

R

The Race for the Eighth

In 1987, a book was published by two journalists who followed Joseph P. Kennedy II throughout his 1986 congressional campaign. The book was titled *The Race for the Eighth: The Making* *of a Congressional Campaign: Joe Kennedy's Successful Pursuit of a Political Legacy* and written by Gerald Sullivan and Michael Kenney.

Radio Corporation of America (RCA)

Radio Corporation of America (RCA) was one of the leaders in the sound industry in the late 1920s, when talking pictures first came on the market. In 1929, RCA's president David Sarnoff and Joseph P. Kennedy, president of FBO, struck a deal, through which FBO's films were made with the help of RCA technology and technicians and RCA acquired a substantial amount of stock in FBO. A year later, RCA was merged with FBO and another Kennedy acquisition, Keith-Albee-Orpheum, to form RKO, or Radio Keith Orpheum.

Prince Stanislaus Radziwill

The second husband of Lee Bouvier was Prince Stanislaus Radziwill (nicknamed "Stash"), a Polish nobleman twenty years her senior who immigrated to England in 1946 and founded a profitable construction and real estate investment business. The Radziwills settled in London, where Lee's sister, Jacqueline, was a frequent visitor, and they entertained many important figures in international society. They had two children: Antony and Anna Christine. The Radziwills owned a London townhouse around the corner from Buckingham Palace, a Queen Anne-style country estate in England, and a twelve-room duplex on New York's Fifth Avenue. The couple was divorced in 1974, and Prince Radziwill died in 1976.

The Real Truth about Joan Kennedy and Alcohol

Joan Kennedy has been courageously frank about her own struggle to beat the disease of alcoholism. Although some observers have blamed her drinking problem on the demands of marrying into the Kennedy family, Joan steadfastly denies that anyone else could "make" her alcoholic, pointing out that it is a complicated disease, thought in large part to be passed on from one generation to the next. Joan has entered a variety of treatment centers to find help in staying sober, and she continues to attend meetings of Alcoholics Anonymous, finding help and support in the company of other people with the same problem. Since her last hospitalization, in 1979, she has been for the most part in control of her own life, despite a number of pressures on her, such as the Senator's run for the presidency in 1980 and their divorce the following year.

Because Joan has been so open about her situation, it is inevitable that any slight lapse receives maximum publicity. There were reports of a brief relapse in 1986, and, in the summer of 1988, an automobile accident in which she was driving started a flurry of rumors of renewed drinking, reportedly brought on by the news of her younger son Patrick's plans to go into politics. Joan's valiant fight to stay sober continues to make her a sympathetic figure.

Timothy Reardon, Jr.

Timothy Reardon, Jr., always called Ted, was a classmate of Joe Junior at Harvard in the 1930s. During their college years, Ted often visited the Kennedy family, and he remained close to them even after Joe Junior died. Reardon worked for Jack Kennedy in his first political campaign for the seat in the Eleventh Congressional District in 1946. When John F. Kennedy entered the White House, Reardon became an assistant to the President.

Recalling the Horror

On the twenty-fifth anniversary of the assassination of President John F. Kennedy, the Arts and Entertainment cable network interrupted its regular programming at 1:56 P.M. on November 22 to broadcast in its entirety the first six hours of NBC's televised coverage of the 1963 assassination.

Report of the House Select Committee on Assassinations

More than a decade after the assassination of President John F. Kennedy, the House of Representatives formed a Select Committee on Assassinations to pursue the rumors about conspiracies that lay behind the deaths of President Kennedy, his brother Robert, and civil-rights leader Martin Luther King, Jr. The committee spent two and a half years in its investigations and amassed twenty-eight volumes of evidence. In July 1979 it released a final report. The committee concluded that Lee Harvey Oswald and James Earl Ray (convicted for killing King) probably did not act alone. The report pointed a finger at likely underworld involvement through mobsters Carlos Mercello of New Orleans and Santos Trafficante of Tampa, and also identified several other possible conspirators, among them some agents of the Cuban government and James R. Hoffa. Unfortunately, the committee was unable to find a "smoking gun," any hard evidence of a plot to kill President Kennedy. Acoustic evidence suggested that a shot had been fired at President Kennedy from a different source than the Texas Book Depository, and links were established between Oswald and a former airline pilot who worked for Carlos Mercello's lawyer. The evidence for a conspiracy was circumstantial—enough to comfort longtime conspiracy theorists but not enough to permit any criminal arraignments.

The Religious Issue

When Senator John F. Kennedy decided to run for President in 1960, one of the chief issues he had to face was public concern about his religion. No Catholic had yet been elected to the presidency, and there was a belief among some voters that the actions of a Catholic President would be too strongly influenced by Catholic religious leaders. At the time Kennedy announced his presidential candidacy, he made a statement that he hoped would lay the religious issue to rest. "I would think that there is really only one issue involved in the whole question of a candidate's religion—that is, does a candidate believe in the Constitution, does he believe in the First Amendment, does he believe in the separation of church and state. When the candidate gives his views on that question, and I think I have given my views fully, I think the subject is exhausted." But the subject kept resurfacing in questions asked by the press and in the political tactics of opponents. It was not until Kennedy defeated Hubert Humphrey in the May primary in West Virginia, where anti-Catholic sentiment had been expected to play a large role in the voting, that the issue of religion truly disappeared from politics of the election. Since that time, the issue of a candidate's religion has not been an issue in any presidential contest.

Resolute

The *Resolute* was the sailboat owned by RFK; it was used constantly by his entire family during the summers at Hyannis Port.

The Resolute *Desk*

When President John F. Kennedy moved into the Oval Office, he decided to replace the desk used by President Eisenhower and to use instead a desk Mrs. Kennedy had found in a basement storeroom. A gift to President Rutherford B. Hayes in 1880 from Queen Victoria, the desk was constructed from timbers that had once formed part of H.M.S. *Resolute*, a British naval vessel that got stuck in the ice and abandoned in 1854. An American whaling ship found the *Resolute* decades later and returned the timbers to Great Britain; hence the gift from the Queen. The desk had been used not only by Hayes but also by President Woodrow Wilson.

Caroline Kennedy and her cousin, Kerry Kennedy, play hide-and-seek in the Oval Office. (Courtesy of the Kennedy Library)

Rights for Americans

In December 1964 Bobbs-Merrill published a collection of speeches by Robert F. Kennedy entitled *Rights for Americans*. It was edited by Thomas Hopkins, who also provided a commentary.

Riverdale

In the fall of 1927, Joseph P. Kennedy moved his family from Brookline, Massachusetts, to the New York City neighborhood of Riverdale. The Kennedy's rented house at 5040 Independence Avenue, located by Joe's ubiquitous aide, Eddie Moore, was spacious and elegant, with thirteen rooms and a view of the Hudson River. The house had formerly been the home of Chief Justice Charles Evans Hughes. To ease the pain of leaving Brookline, where the family had lived for more than a decade, Joe made the move in a private railroad car he had rented for the occasion. The Kennedy family stayed in Riverdale only briefly. Soon Joe Kennedy bought the Joseph Goetz house in Bronxville, north of Riverdale.

Riverdale Country Day School

The Riverdale Country Day School was a private school located in Riverdale-on-Hudson, not far from Joseph P. Kennedy's home in Bronxville, New York. The school, situated on twelve acres near the river, was founded in 1907. Joe Kennedy, Jr., was a student there for two years, from 1927 to 1929. Jack Kennedy attended grades five, six, and seven at Riverdale Country Day, leaving in 1930 for Choate. Bobby Kennedy was also a student at the expensive and prestigious school, leaving in 1938 when his father became U.S. Ambassador to Great Britain and the Kennedy family moved to London.

Robert F. Kennedy Memorial

The Robert F. Kennedy Memorial is a foundation that was created after RFK's death in 1968 by his widow as an instrument to carry on some of his work. The foundation's programs include one that sends young people into disadvantaged communities to help improve the conditions that affect the children of the poor, and another that helps high school students organize their own antidrug programs. For a number of years, one of the best-known fund-raising activities of the foundation was the Pro-Celebrity Tennis Tournament that paired professional tennis players with famous celebrities in a widely publicized tournament. Among the friends of the Kennedy family who have become involved in the work of the Robert F. Kennedy Memorial are columnist Art Buchwald, Senator John Glenn, soccer star Pele, TV's Walter Cronkite and David Hartman, and actress Lauren Bacall.

Robert F. Kennedy Memorial Stadium

In January 1969, the District of Columbia Stadium in Washington was renamed the Robert F. Kennedy Memorial Stadium, in honor of the recently slain senator. The dedication was attended by many members of the Kennedy family.

Robert Kennedy in His Own Words

In 1988 Bantam published a selection of the oral history material Robert F. Kennedy recorded for the John F. Kennedy Library. Entitled *Robert Kennedy in His Own Words*, the book furnished a previously unpublished look inside the workings of the Kennedy administration.

Robin

Robin was the pet canary Caroline Kennedy had as a child growing up in the White House.

The Rocking Chair

Shortly after President Kennedy moved into his White House office, the press discovered that his favorite seat was a high-backed wooden rocking chair. He told reporters he liked it because it was good for his back, and his physician, Dr. Janet Travell, confirmed that he had seen a similar rocker in her office, providing comfort to the aching backs of her other patients, and had decided to order one for himself. Upon its arrival in the White House, the simple rocker was stained a darker color to match the mahogany furniture of the Oval Office and given a new pad in plain beige to match the upholstery of the sofas. The rocking chair became a familiar symbol of the Kennedy presidency. After the President's assassination, his widow gave the rocking chair to his valet, George Thomas.

Juan Romero

Juan Romero was a Mexican youth who was working as a dishwasher in the kitchen of the Ambassador Hotel in Los Angeles on the night of June 5, 1968. Senator Robert F. Kennedy passed near his workstation after giving a victory speech to his campaign workers in the California primary, and everyone wanted to shake the winner's hand. Kennedy was reaching out to shake hands with Romero when the shots were fired that ended his life.

Franklin Delano Roosevelt

Franklin Delano Roosevelt was the President who appointed Joseph P. Kennedy to a number of important government positions. The paths of Roosevelt and Kennedy first crossed during World War I, when Roosevelt was the assistant secretary of the Navy and Kennedy was the general manager of Bethlehem Steel's shipbuilding yard. By 1930, when Kennedy had made a fortune on the stock market and then fortuitously taken most of it out before the crash of October 1929, Roosevelt had been elected governor of New York and was already being spoken of as a possible candidate for the presidency in the 1932 election. Although Joe Kennedy had been an admirer of President Herbert Hoover, he concluded that Roosevelt might be better able to save the faltering American economy and preserve the free market system, so he announced his support of Roosevelt. Kennedy not only contributed funds to Roosevelt's campaign, but also helped bring in the endorsement of other businessmen and financiers.

When Roosevelt won the election, he surprised Kennedy by failing to name him immediately to a high government post. In 1933, Kennedy was made a member of the Securities and Exchange Commission and then became its chairman. In 1936, he took on the job of head of the Maritime Commission. It was not until late 1937, after a second presidential victory for Roosevelt, that Kennedy got the kind of reward he had been hoping for. Roosevelt appointed Kennedy his country's Ambassador to the Court of St. James. Kennedy held the post until early 1941 (and one more presidential election in which he supported Roosevelt), when it was clear he had lost the President's confidence. Kennedy had openly espoused a policy first of appeasement toward Hitler's Germany and then of American isolationism, but Roosevelt expected his Ambassador to express only the official policy of his government, not a personal opinion.

In all his dealings with Roosevelt, Joe Kennedy uncharacteristically wound up giving more than he got. His own loyal nature made him assume that Roosevelt would be grateful for his support and reward Kennedy accordingly. In fact, Roosevelt was an astute politician who had the invaluable knack of being able to recruit support without giving away anything in return. Joe Kennedy was deeply hurt by the President's unwillingness to support him during his last days in London, even though his outspoken advocacy of isolationism made him unpopular with the British and an undoubted political liability to the President.

Like most Americans, Joseph Kennedy reacted to President Roosevelt's death in 1945 with great sorrow. He released a public statement that said, "As a member of President Roosevelt's official family for many years, I know that he felt justice had been violated seriously by this war, and he had dedicated his life that the grave injuries to states and inhabitants should be rectified."

The Roosevelt Special

The *Roosevelt Special* was the campaign train that in 1932 took Presidential candidate Franklin Delano Roosevelt on a thirteen-hundred-mile trip to meet the voters in more than twenty states and ask for their support in his fight against the incumbent Republican President, Herbert Hoover. At Roosevelt's invitation, Joseph P. Kennedy boarded the train in Albany on September 13 and stayed with the train as it crisscrossed the country for more than three weeks. Kennedy, formerly a Republican, had contributed money and advice to Roosevelt's Democratic campaign, and he had used his influence to get other prominent people in the financial community to support his choice of candidate. The invitation to ride the *Roosevelt Special* was Kennedy's reward, and he greatly enjoyed the camaraderie that developed among Roosevelt's entourage of advisors and supporters.

The Roped Horse

In Gloria Swanson's 1980 autobiography, *Swanson on Swanson*, she recounts her memory of her first romantic encounter with Joseph P. Kennedy. It came in late 1928, several months after Joe had started to act as her financial advisor. Gloria, then at the height of her movie fame, decided to travel to Palm Beach for some winter sunshine. Joe first met her at the train station, and then hours later visited her luxurious suite at the Royal Poinciana Hotel. Too passionate to wait any longer, Joe quickly entered her bedroom and shut the door behind him. Recalled Gloria:

He moved so quickly that his mouth was on mine before either of us could speak. With one hand, he held the back of my head, with the other he stroked my body and pulled at my kimono. He kept insisting in a drawn-out moan, "No longer, no longer. Now." He was like a roped horse, rough, arduous, racing to be free. After a hasty climax he lay beside me, stroking my hair. Apart from his guilty, passionate mutterings, he had still said nothing cogent.

Rose Garden

In the spring of 1961, President John F. Kennedy asked his wife's friend, expert horticulturalist Mrs. Paul ("Bunny") Mellon, to redesign the garden that was outside his office window. Said Jacqueline Kennedy, "It was absolutely atrocious before Bunny took over ..." Mrs. Mellon decided to plant roses there, and by the following spring, the White House Rose Garden was a beautiful and serene spot, the perfect tranquil-izer for a worried or stressed President. The Johnsons officially named it the Jacqueline Kennedy Rose Garden, and it has been a favorite with all administrations since. In fact, President Jimmy Carter liked it so well he was nicknamed by critics the "prisoner of the Rose Garden," because he spent a great deal of time there during the height of the Iran hostage crisis.

Rosemont College

Rosemont College, located in Pennsylvania, was the alma mater of Patricia Kennedy Lawford. She enrolled in 1941 and graduated in 1945 from the suburban Philadelphia college, a small Catholic liberal arts school for women.

Caroline Lee Bouvier Canfield Radziwill Ross

Caroline Lee Bouvier was the second child of Janet Lee and John Vernou Bouvier III, born on March 3, 1933, in New York City. Like her older sister Jacqueline, Lee attended the Chapin School in New York and then Miss Porter's in Farmington, Connecticut. She was named Debutante of the Year in 1950, when she enrolled in Sarah Lawrence College. After working briefly at *Harper's Bazaar* and taking voice lessons for a career as a singer, in April 1953, Lee married Michael Temple Canfield, son of the socially prominent publisher at Harper and Row. The wedding took place at Holy Trinity Church in Washington, with a reception at Merrywood, the estate of Hugh Auchincloss, Lee's stepfather; her sister, Jackie, was her maid of honor. The groom was a Harvard graduate and World War II veteran who worked in his father's publishing company until he took a job at the American embassy in London. It was there that Lee met her second husband, exiled Polish Prince Stansilaus Radziwill; they were married in 1959 (and Lee was officially granted an annulment of her first marriage by the Vatican in 1964). The Radziwills had two children: Antony, born in 1959, and Anna Christine, born in 1960. The Radziwills were divorced in 1974. After attempts at a career as an actress and a television talk show hostess, Lee opened her own interior design business in Manhattan, where she currently resides. In 1979, she announced her engagement to Newton Cope, a California millionaire, but decided against the wedding only hours before the ceremony. In 1988, she married veteran Hollywood director Herbert Ross in the living room of her New York apartment, with a small reception afterward at her sister's home.

Herbert Ross

In September 1988, Lee Bouvier Canfield Radziwill married her third husband, Hollywood director Herbert Ross. Ross, born in 1927, is a former dancer and choreographer. Among his directing credits are *The Sunshine Boys, The Turning Point, The Goodbye Girl*, and *California Suite*. He was previously married to ballerina Nora Kaye.

Jack Ruby

Jack Ruby was the fifty-two-year-old nightclub operator who shot and killed presidential assassin Lee Harvey Oswald as he was being transferred from the city to the county jail. He had been born in Chicago on March 25, 1911, to Orthodox Jewish parents who named him Jack Leon Rubenstein; he later changed his last name legally to Ruby. He moved to Dallas in 1948 and began running a nightclub owned by his sister. By 1963, he himself owned two clubs, the Carousel and the Vegas, and his income was said to be in six figures.

Jack Ruby's face was well known to local police, as he frequently visited the municipal building in which the jail was located, and he had twice been arrested for carrying a concealed weapon. Ruby mingled with throngs of onlookers for the day and a half Oswald had been held for interrogation and even attended a press conference held by the Dallas police chief; he also passed out to policemen cards advertising one of his nightclubs. Finally, he saw his opportunity when Oswald and his guards moved through the crowds, and Ruby shot the President's assassin with a nickel-plated Colt .38. Ruby was charged with Oswald's murder and found guilty. He claimed to have committed the crime because he had loved the President, and because he didn't want Mrs. Kennedy to have to face the ordeal of returning to Dallas for Oswald's homicide trial. There were suspicions that Ruby might have been part of a conspiracy that decided Oswald must be killed so he wouldn't talk. But subsequent investigations turned up no proven links between Ruby and possible co-conspirators. On March 14, 1964, Ruby was convicted of the murder of Lee Harvey Oswald, but the conviction was overturned in October 1966, because the defendant's jailhouse confession was illegally introduced into his trial. Ruby died of cancer on January 3, 1967, while awaiting a retrial. His death occurred in Parkland Hospital, where President Kennedy and Lee Harvey Oswald had also died.

Mary Courtney Kennedy Ruhe

Mary Courtney Kennedy is the fifth child of Robert F. and Ethel Skakel Kennedy, born on September 9, 1956. She attended the University of California and then studied history and literature at Trinity College in Dublin. On June 14, 1980, Courtney married television sports producer Jeffrey R. Ruhe in the Holy Trinity Church in Georgetown, with a lavish reception afterward at the Kennedy family home, Hickory Hill; the match was in large part sponsored by Kennedy family friend Lem Billings, whom Courtney remembers fondly. Courtney is currently in charge of fund-raising for the RFK Memorial and is also a member of the Kennedy Library board. Courtney also acts as a fundraiser for her brother Joe's political campaigns.

"Rules for Visiting the Kennedys"

In 1957, a friend of the Kennedy family jokingly wrote the following rules for being a guest of the family:

Prepare yourself by reading the *Congressional Record, US News & World Report, Time, Newsweek, Fortune, The Nation, How To Play Sneaky Tennis,* and *The Democratic Digest.* Memorize at least three good jokes. Anticipate that each Kennedy will ask you what you think of another Kennedy's a) dress, b) hairdo, c) backhand, d) latest public achievement. Be sure to answer, "terrific." This should get you through dinner. Now for the football field. It's "touch" but it's murder. If you don't want to play, don't come. If you do come, play, or you'll be fed in the kitchen and nobody will speak to you. Don't let the girls fool you. Even pregnant, they can make you look silly. If Harvard played Touch, they'd be on the varsity. Above all, don't suggest any plays, even if you played quarterback at school. The Kennedys have the signal-calling department all sewed up, and all of them have A-pluses in leadership. If one of them makes a mistake, keep still . . . But don't stand still. Run madly on every play and make a lot of noise. Don't appear to be having too much fun, though. They'll accuse you of not taking the game seriously enough. Don't criticize the other team, either. It's bound to be full of Kennedys, too, and the Kennedys don't like that sort of thing. To become really popular you must show raw guts. To show raw guts, fall on your face now and then. Smash into the house once in a while, going after a pass. Laugh off a twisted ankle, or a big hole torn in your best suit. They like this. It shows you take the game as seriously as they do.

Fun and games at Hyannis Port, left to right: *Jack, Jean, Rose, Joe, Teddy, Pat, Bobby, and Eunice. (Courtesy of the Kennedy Library)*

Rumors of Suitors for the Hand of Jacqueline Kennedy

As soon as the world began to recover from the shock of President Kennedy's death, speculation began to focus on the future of his widow. It was inevitable that rumors would circulate about suitors for the hand of Jacqueline Kennedy. Among the men the press attempted to link with her romantically were: composer/conductor Leonard Bernstein; Secret Service man Clint Hill; architect John Carl Warnecke; former Deputy Defense Secretary Roswell Gilpatric; former British Ambassador to the U.S. Lord Harlech; actor/director Mike Nichols; poet Robert Lowell; financier Andre Meyer; Secretary of Defense Robert S. McNamara; Spanish Ambassador Antonio Garrigues; former presidential aide Arthur Schlesinger. According to a remark attributed to Jackie by her biographer, C. David Heymann, her own standards for suitors were simple: "He must weigh more and have bigger feet than I do."

Runnymede, England

On May 14, 1965, Queen Elizabeth II dedicated a shrine honoring the late President John F. Kennedy in ceremonies that were attended by Kennedy's widow and his young son, John. The location was Runnymede, a site near London where in 1215, the Magna Carta was signed. The inscription on the Kennedy shrine read:

This acre of English ground was given to the United States of America by the people of Britain in memory of John F. Kennedy (born 29 May 1917) President of the United States 1961–1963. Died by an assassin's hand on 22 November 1963. "Let every nation know whether it wishes us well or ill that we shall pay any price, bear any burden, meet any hardship, support any friend, or oppose any foe to assure the survival and success of liberty."

Dean Rusk

Dean Rusk held the position of secretary of state in the Kennedy Cabinet. Rusk was born in 1909 in Cherokee County, in rural Georgia and attended Davidson College in North Carolina as a scholarship student. A Rhodes scholar who did his graduate work at Oxford, Rusk taught political science at Mills College and rose to the position of dean. Rusk served in the Far East in World War II and then worked briefly in the Pentagon. Afterward, he joined the State Department under President Harry S. Truman, eventually becoming assistant secretary for Far Eastern Affairs. He left Washington in 1952, when Eisenhower became President, to run the Rockefeller Foundation, and returned in 1961 as secretary of state. He held that position throughout the Kennedy administration, and then served Kennedy's successor, President Lyndon Johnson, in the same post. He left office in January 1969, when the Nixon administration took office. By then, Rusk was completely identified in the public mind with the unpopular war in Vietnam. He returned to Georgia as a professor of international law at the University of Georgia.

Rusty

Rusty was the small poodle that was the family pet of the children of Edward and Joan Kennedy.

S

S Street

Robert F. and Ethel Kennedy, with their two young children Kathleen and Joe, moved to Washington in January 1953, when RFK began working for Senator Joseph McCarthy's Subcommittee on Investigation. The Kennedy's first Washington home was a rented house in Georgetown, on S Street. It had four bedrooms and a small garden in the rear. The Kennedys paid four hundred dollars a month rent.

Sable Underwear

When John F. Kennedy was campaigning for the presidency, one of the issues that emerged was the question of his wife's expensive—and foreign—fashion preferences. It had been widely reported that Jacqueline Kennedy ordered couture clothes from Givenchy and Balenciaga, and one well-researched magazine article claimed that she and her mother-in-law each spent at least thirty thousand dollars a year buying clothes in Paris. In an interview with *The New York Times*, Jackie pooh-poohed the notion that she ever spent such sums on clothes—"I couldn't spend that much unless I wore sable underwear," she derided. Jackie also emphasized the fact that she bought many of her clothes from American designer Norman Norell, and that she sometimes wore fashions made by a "little" dressmaker in Washington. She contrasted herself with the wife of the Republican candidate, Pat Nixon, who shopped at "expensive stores" such as Elizabeth Arden.

In fact, the reports on what Mrs. Kennedy spent and where she spent it were probably more or less accurate; she did wear couturier clothes, and thirty thousand dollars was a reasonable sum for a woman in the public eye to spend on her wardrobe. Interest in Mrs. Kennedy's wardrobe never died down, but in time she and the President's staff came to recognize that Mrs. Kennedy's chic wardrobe and excellent taste in clothes were among her husband's greatest assets in the White House.

St. Aidan's Catholic Church

St. Aidan's was the Brookline, Massachusetts, church near the home of Rose and Joseph Kennedy where the family usually attended Mass. Their son John Fitzgerald Kennedy was baptized at St. Aidan's on June 19, 1917. Most of the other Kennedy children were also baptized at St. Aidan's. Only Jean and Edward, born after the family moved to New York, were baptized elsewhere.

St. Coletta's

St. Coletta's is a Catholic home for the mentally retarded in Jefferson, Wisconsin, where Rosemary Kennedy has lived since 1941. She has her own house there, her own car—all the material comforts that she needs or wants—and the nuns of St. Coletta's look after her devotedly. Over the years, the Kennedy family has given a great deal of money to St. Coletta's, the largest single gift coming in 1983 (one million dollars) as a commemoration of Rose Kennedy's ninety-third birthday.

St. Francis Xavier

The Catholic church the Kennedy family attends when they are at Hyannis Port is St. Francis Xavier, in the nearby town of Hyannis, Massachusetts. The small white clapboard church captures something of the spirit of New England, and inside it is very simple, almost austere. The Kennedys have long been closely connected with this church, the site of family worship, christenings, and weddings. During the days of the Kennedy presidency, photos often showed the President and his family leaving St. Francis Xavier on Sunday morning, and today there is a plaque to mark the pew in which the First Family regularly sat. St. Francis Xavier was also the much-photographed site of Maria Shriver's wedding to Arnold Schwarzenegger in 1986. For many years Rose Kennedy went to mass there every morning that she was in residence at the Hyannis Port house. After she became too feeble to make the daily trip, the priest of the church, Father Edward Duffy, visited the Kennedy home in Hyannis Port to conduct a weekly mass for his faithful parishioner.

St. Francis Xavier was the location Joseph and Rose Kennedy chose for a memorial to their oldest son, Joseph P. Kennedy, Jr., after he was killed in World War II. The altar they donated in his memory was dedicated on June 29, 1946.

The plaque reads:

The Main Altar
presented by
Mr. and Mrs. Joseph P. Kennedy
in Memory of their son
Lt. Joseph Patrick Kennedy, Jr., U.S.N.R.
Killed in Action
August 12, 1944

On one side of the carved wooden altar is St. George of England; on the other is the French Saint Joan of Arc. The two figures symbolize the flight from England to France on which young Kennedy was killed.

St. Joseph's Roman Catholic Church

St. Joseph's Roman Catholic Church was the church regularly attended by the Kennedy family when they lived in Bronxville, New York. Bobby Kennedy received his first communion there on April 30, 1933, and he later became an altar boy at the church. Edward and Joan Kennedy were married at St. Joseph's in 1958.

St. Stephen's Church

St. Stephen's Church was the old Catholic church in Boston's North End, designed by eminent eighteenth-century architect Charles Bulfinch and originally housing the Boston Congregationalists. St. Stephen's was where the great-grandparents of President Kennedy worshipped and where his grandfather John Fitzgerald was baptized. When the President and his brothers and sisters were small, Rose Fitzgerald Kennedy often took her children to St. Stephen's, with its large congregation and old-fashioned ritual, to celebrate special feast days.

Pierre Salinger

Pierre Salinger was press secretary to John F. Kennedy, starting with his 1960 campaign and continuing throughout his entire presidency. The French-speaking Salinger was a journalist working for *Collier's* magazine when he first met Jack Kennedy at the 1956 Democratic convention. A few months later, when the magazine ceased publication, Salinger was offered a job working for Robert F. Kennedy during the Senate Select Committee hearing on labor racketeering. That led to an offer to work as press liaison for John F. Kennedy and eventually to the appointment as White House Press Secretary. The jovial and witty cigar-smoking Salinger seemed the perfect spokesman for the Kennedy administration; he conducted press conferences with a light touch combined with a keen awareness of what would—and wouldn't—make his boss look good in the media.

After President Kennedy's death, Salinger served briefly as press secretary to President Lyndon B. Johnson but resigned because, he said, "the memory of JFK was too overpowering." In 1964, he ran for a Senate Seat in California but lost the election. Salinger wrote his own reminiscences of the Kennedy years in the best-selling book, *With Kennedy*. Salinger presently works as a European correspondent for ABC.

Sandy the Seal

In a large enclosure near the swimming pool at Hickory Hill lived a seal named Sandy when the children of Ethel and Robert F. Kennedy were growing up there. Sandy ate ten pounds of fish a day and did tricks to entertain family guests. One day he flipped himself over the chain-link fence and waddled off to a store about a mile away, frightening startled patrons by his entrance. Soon thereafter, the Kennedys gave Sandy to the Washington Zoo.

Sardar

Sardar was the name of the magnificent Arabian horse given to Jacqueline Kennedy by President Ayub Khan of Pakistan during her 1962 visit to his country. The First Lady loved the horse, which was kept at nearby Glen Ora, and decreed that no one but herself should ever ride him.

Arthur Schlesinger, Jr.

Arthur Schlesinger, Jr., born in Columbus, Ohio, in 1917, served as a special assistant to President John F. Kennedy. Schlesinger was a Harvard graduate who studied at Cambridge and then taught history at Harvard. Although he had known Kennedy since 1947, Schlesinger worked in Adlai Stevenson's 1952 campaign. He was contacted in 1956 by Kennedy aide Ted Sorensen to ask for help in making Kennedy the Stevenson running mate; thereafter, Schlesinger remained politically close to Jack Kennedy.

The winner of the Pulitzer Prize for History in 1946 for his book *The Age of Jackson*, Schlesinger won the Prize again in 1966 for the virtually definitive history of the Kennedy administration, *A Thousand Days: John F. Kennedy in the White House*. More than a thousand pages long, it chronicles the events of 1961–63 against a background of historical perspective. In 1978, Schlesinger published another massive work, *Robert Kennedy and His Times*. Schlesinger holds the position of Albert Schweitzer Professor of the Humanities at City University of New York.

Caroline Bouvier Kennedy Schlossberg

Caroline Bouvier Kennedy was the first child of John F. Kennedy and his wife, Jacqueline Bouvier. The seven-pound, two-ounce Caroline was born on November 27, 1957, at the Lying-In Hospital in New York City. She was named after her mother's sister, Caroline Lee, who is also her godmother. Her godfather was the late Robert F. Kennedy, and she was christened (wearing the same dress her mother had worn) by Archbishop Cushing at St. Patrick's Cathedral. Her first school was a private class organized by her mother in the White House. Later she attended the Brearley School in New York and graduated from Concord Academy in Concord, Massachusetts, in 1975. After a year in London enrolled in Sotheby's Works of Art program, Caroline did her undergraduate work at Radcliffe College, receiving a Bachelor of Arts degree in 1980, and worked for a time in the Film and Television Development Office of the Metropolitan Museum of Art. In 1985, she enrolled in law school at Columbia University.

In 1986, Caroline Kennedy married Edwin Schlossberg in a ceremony at the Church of Our Lady of Victory, in Centerville, Massachusetts, near the Kennedy compound on Cape Cod. Caroline passed her law school final exams in 1988 just before her first child, Rose Kennedy Schlossberg, was born on June 25. The Schlossbergs live in a twelve-room apartment on Park Avenue at Seventy-eighth Street, which they bought in early 1988 for a price estimated at $2.65 million.

Portrait of Caroline Kennedy. (Rick Friedman, Black Star)

Edwin Arthur Schlossberg

Edwin Arthur Schlossberg is the husband of Caroline Kennedy. Born in 1946, the son of textile manufacturer Alfred Schlossberg grew up in an Orthodox Jewish home. He attended the Birch Wathen School and Columbia University from which he subsequently earned his Ph.D. A "conceptive theorist," Ed is the founder and head of Edwin Schlossberg, Inc., a firm that specializes in designing and building educational and interactive environments. His firm had under-

taken assignments for many museums and is currently working on commercial projects for amusement parlors for adults. His electronic games include Food Fight and Beat the System. In 1988, he and his wife had their first child, a daughter named Rose. He told the press he was working on a model constellation that glows in the dark to hang on the ceiling of the new baby's nursery.

Rose Kennedy Schlossberg

Rose Kennedy Schlossberg is the first child of Edwin and Caroline Kennedy Schlossberg, born on June 25, 1988. The seven-pound, twelve-ounce baby, named after Caroline's grandmother, was the first grandchild of President Kennedy and his wife, Jacqueline. According to published reports, Caroline timed her contractions with an egg-timer before she was taken by limousine to New York Hospital-Cornell Medical Center. To protect her privacy, she was listed on hospital records only as "Mrs. Sylva."

Arnold Schwarzenegger

Kennedy in-law Arnold Schwarzenegger was born in 1948 in Austria, where he took up the sport of bodybuilding. His championship form won thirteen major titles in the sport, and gave him the chance to move to the United States, where he studied at the University of Wisconsin. In 1977, he parlayed his athletic fame into a movie role in *Pumping Iron*, playing himself. The 1982 flick *Conan the Barbarian* was the one that brought Hollywood stardom, and today he is one of the highest paid of all screen actors. In March 1986, Arnold (a Republican) wed long-time sweetheart Maria Shriver. In the 1988 election, Schwarzenegger campaigned for George Bush, who nicknamed him "Conan the Republican."

Maria Owings Shriver Schwarzenegger

Maria Owings Shriver was the second child of R. Sargent and Eunice Kennedy Shriver, born in Chicago on November 6, 1955. She spent her first two years of college at Manhattanville and then transferred to Georgetown University, from which she graduated in 1977. Maria then embarked on a career in television, working first at KYW-TV in Philadelphia and then WJZ-TV in Baltimore. Among her credits are a stint as a national correspondent on *PM Magazine* from 1981 to 1983, and an assignment from 1985 to 1986 as co-anchor, with Forrest Sawyer, on the ill-fated *CBS Morning News*. She currently co-anchors the NBC *Sunday Today* program, with veteran newsman Garrick Utley. Maria also anchors a monthly news magazine for young people on the NBC network, called *Main Street* and hosts new specials, such as her highly acclaimed show on women in prison. On April 26, 1986, Maria married actor and former bodybuilder Arnold Schwarzenegger.

Securities and Exchange Commission

After Franklin D. Roosevelt was elected to his first term as President, in 1932, one of his top priorities was setting up a Securities and Exchange Commission to regulate activities on the stock market, which was still the source of much economic bad news as the Depression of the

Arnold Schwarzenegger as Conan the Barbarian. (Movie Star News)

A pensive Maria Shriver. (Courtesy of NBC/Roger E. Sandler)

Maria conducts interviews for her TV program about women in prison. (Courtesy of NBC)

1930s deepened. The SEC was established in 1933. Despite advice to the contrary, FDR took the bold step of naming financial speculator Joseph P. Kennedy to the Commission, which then acceded to Roosevelt's wishes and named Kennedy chairman. Roosevelt later said the intention behind the Kennedy appointment was to set a thief to catch a thief, since only an insider who had used and abused all the loopholes could possibly know how to plug them up.

Joseph P. Kennedy was sworn in on July 2, 1934, and remained at the SEC until September 1935. Contrary to some people's expectations, he was unanimously acknowledged to have done an excellent job on a tough assignment. At the time of Kennedy's resignation, one of his harshest critics, liberal John Flynn, wrote in the *New Republic*, "I think it but fair to him to say that he disappointed the expectations of his critics. He was, I firmly believe, the most useful member of the Commission."

Senate Election of 1952

In 1952, Congressman John F. Kennedy, a veteran of six years in the House of Representatives, decided to seek the Senate seat for Massachusetts. Kennedy had to run against the incumbent, Senator Henry Cabot Lodge, a liberal Republican who was closely associated with the Eisenhower presidential campaign. Most analysts predicted that Lodge, with his experience and his connection to a popular presidential candidate, would easily defeat Kennedy. But as the weeks went by and the Kennedy campaign gathered momentum, it was clear that Jack would put up a good fight. With the aid of the many relatives who were willing to help him campaign —and especially his brother Bob who took time off from his own job to manage the campaign— John F. Kennedy won a surprise victory. In a state that voted heavily for the Eisenhower ticket, Kennedy pulled off a Democratic victory by more than one hundred thousand votes. Lodge conceded the following morning with a telegram that said, "I extend my congratulations and hope that you will derive from your term in the Senate all the satisfaction that comes from courageous and sincere efforts in public service."

Senate Foreign Relations Committee

One of the most prized assignments in the Senate is membership on the Foreign Relations Committee. When Massachusetts Senator John F. Kennedy decided in late 1956 that he would run for the presidency in 1960, he and his advisors agreed that a seat on that committee would be a big boost to his political career. It was the Senator's father, Joseph P. Kennedy, who approached the man who could give his son that seat, Senate Majority Leader Lyndon B. Johnson, using his own combination of flattery and promised gratitude. In January 1957, Senator Kennedy became a member of the Foreign Relations Committee.

Senate Select Committee on Improper Activities in the Labor and Management Field

In 1954, Robert F. Kennedy accepted the post of chief counsel to the Senate Select Committee on Improper Activities in the Labor and Management Field, at the invitation of Chairman John S. McClellan. Kennedy's long fight against racketeering was the basis of his national reputation.

Senate Subcommittee on Investigations

In January 1953, Robert F. Kennedy went to work as assistant to the general counsel to the Senate Subcommittee on Investigations of the Committee of Government Operations. Soon the post of general counsel was vacated and Kennedy was working for the chief counsel, Roy

Cohn. The chairman of the subcommittee was Senator Joseph R. McCarthy, and RFK got the job because his father, Joseph P. Kennedy, had been a big contributor to McCarthy's 1952 re-election campaign. Bobby left his forty-two-hundred-dollar-a-year job with the subcommittee within six months, presumably due to a personality conflict with Cohn.

The Sexiest Man Alive (1988)

In September 1988, *People* magazine announced that John F. Kennedy, Jr., was the sexiest man alive. The article made repeated reference to his "well-defined" thighs and reminded readers that Liz Smith had referred to his "gorgeous buns." There was, of course, no official response to the article by the Kennedy family, but insiders say the subject of the adulatory article found it most amusing.

Maud Shaw

Maud Shaw was the English-born nanny engaged by John F. and Jacqueline Kennedy eleven days after their daughter, Caroline, was born in 1957. Miss Shaw went with the Kennedy family to the White House, where she looked after both Caroline and John, and after the assassination she remained in the employ of Mrs. Kennedy for several years. She later wrote a book called *White House Nanny*, published in 1966 by New American Library, about her experiences with the First Family. Through her press secretary, Mrs. Kennedy said that the book violated her consistent effort to preserve the children's privacy. "It is a disappointment that one so close would write about them, regardless of what is written."

Ships Christened by the Kennedys

President Polk, christened by Patricia Kennedy in Newport News, Virginia, on June 27, 1941.

U.S.S. *Joseph P. Kennedy, Jr.*, christened by Jean Kennedy in Quincy, Massachusetts, on July 26, 1945.

Lafayette, christened by Jacqueline Kennedy in Groton, Massachusetts, on May 8, 1962.

John F. Kennedy, christened by Caroline Kennedy in Newport News, Virginia, on May 27, 1967.

Anthony Paul Shriver

Anthony Paul Shriver is the fifth child of R. Sargent and Eunice Kennedy Shriver, born on July 20, 1965. He attended St. Alban's in Maryland, then the Potomac School, Georgetown Prep, and Georgetown University in Washington.

Eunice Kennedy Shriver

Eunice Kennedy was the fifth child of Joseph P. and Rose Fitzgerald Kennedy. She was born on July 10, 1921, in the family's new and larger home on Naples Avenue in Brookline, Massachusetts. Eunice attended the Sacred Heart convent school at Noroton and finished high school at a Sacred Heart convent in Roehampton, England, after her father was appointed U.S. Ambassador to Great Britain. She spent two years of college at another Sacred Heart institution, Manhattanville, and then transferred to secular Stanford, in Palo Alto, California. Eunice graduated from Stanford in 1943 with a degree in sociology and for a time held a job as a social worker in Harlem. In the mid-1940s Eunice worked in Washington, as executive secretary to the Juvenile Delinquency Committee of the Justice Department. She has been called one of the most able of the Kennedys, and it was reported that her father once said of her, "If that girl had been born with balls, she would have been a hell of a politician."

On May 23, 1953, Eunice married Robert Sargent Shriver, a member of her father's staff, whom she had known for many years. The Shrivers have five children: Robert (1954), Maria (1955), Timothy (1959), Mark (1964), and Anthony (1965). Eunice has long been deeply involved in helping the handicapped, especially through the activities of the Joseph P. Kennedy, Jr., Foundation, which she serves as president. It is Eunice's drive and organizational ability that lies behind the success of the Special Olympics for the handicapped.

Mark Kennedy Shriver

Mark Kennedy Shriver is the fourth child of R. Sargent and Eunice Kennedy Shriver, born on February 17, 1964. Like his brothers, he attended preparatory school at St. Alban's, near the family's Maryland home. Mark later attended Georgetown Prep and Holy Cross College and currently works for the state of Maryland, setting up programs for inner-city kids in Baltimore.

Robert Sargent Shriver

Robert Sargent Shriver is the husband of Eunice Kennedy. The descendant of a signer of the Declaration of Independence, "Sarge" was born in Westminster, Maryland, on November 9, 1915, and attended Canterbury Prep in New Milford, Connecticut, during the brief period young Jack Kennedy went to that school, although the two seem not to have remembered one another. Sarge was a cum laude graduate of Yale in 1938 and subsequently attended Yale Law School. He worked briefly in a law firm before he entered the military during World War II. Shriver served in the Navy, rising to the rank of lieutenant commander. When the war was over, Shriver returned to Washington and a job as assistant to the editor of *Newsweek*. He met Eunice Kennedy at a Washington dinner party, and she recommended him to her father, who was looking for someone to edit Joe Junior's letters for private publication. Seven years later, on May 23, 1953, Eunice and Sarge were married. The couple has five children: Robert Sargent III

(1954), Maria (1955), Timothy (1959), Mark (1964), and Anthony (1965).

Shriver directed the Kennedy-owned Merchandise Mart in Chicago and also served as president of the Chicago Board of Education. In 1961, his brother-in-law, President John F. Kennedy, asked Sargent Shriver to direct the Peace Corps. President Johnson later named him director of the Office of Economic Opportunity, and from 1968 to 1970, Shriver served as United States Ambassador to France. He was the running mate of George McGovern on the national Democratic ticket in 1972, selected to fill the vice-presidential spot after the withdrawal of Senator Thomas Eagleton, who had unwisely concealed the fact that he had once been treated for depression. Shriver made a short-lived bid for the presidential nomination in 1976, and there was later talk that he might run for governor of Maryland, but he has stayed out of the public eye for the past decade. He is currently a partner in the Maryland office of the law firm of Fried, Frank, Harris, Shriver and Kampelman, which handles some of the affairs of the Kennedy family and the family trusts.

Robert Sargent Shriver III

Robert Sargent Shriver III is the first child of R. Sargent and Eunice Kennedy Shriver, born April 29, 1954. He graduated from Yale in 1976 and then went on to study at Yale Law School, getting his law degree in 1981. Currently, he is attorney for the venture capital firm of Jim Wolfinson Company in New York. Bobby acted as producer of the Special Olympics telecast in 1987. In partnership with his father and other investors, Bobby bought the Baltimore Orioles baseball team in early 1989.

Timothy Perry Shriver

Timothy Perry Shriver is the third child of R. Sargent and Eunice Kennedy Shriver, born on August 29, 1959. He attended St. Alban's preparatory school in Maryland. After graduation from Yale in 1981, he studied for a master's in spirituality and education at Catholic University. Tim settled in the New Haven area and was married in 1986 to the former Linda Potter, an attorney. They have one daughter, Sophie. Tim now works for the New Haven school system, administering a program to help abused children. He says, "True social service is what we all do for one another. It's not just a profession."

Sign on Joe Kennedy's Desk

During the 1930s, when Joseph P. Kennedy worked in Washington's frustrating bureaucracy, he displayed a sign on his desk that read, "After you've done your best, the hell with it."

Frank Sinatra

Frank Sinatra was a friend of Peter Lawford in Hollywood, a fellow member of the famed "Rat Pack." So when Lawford's brother-in-law, Senator John F. Kennedy, decided to run for President, Sinatra agreed to lend his support. When a reporter once asked Lawford what Jack Kennedy and Frank Sinatra had in common, Lawford answered, "Let's just say that the Kennedys are interested in the lively arts and that Sinatra is the liveliest art of all." Sinatra campaigned for Kennedy in 1960 and also recruited other Hollywood figures to endorse Kennedy. After the November 1960 victory, Sinatra was named as one of the chief organizers of the Inaugural Gala, an event that President Kennedy obviously enjoyed thoroughly. It was also Sinatra who later organized a 1962 birthday party for President Kennedy at Madison Square Garden, with Marilyn Monroe singing "Happy Birthday."

But after FBI wiretaps established the fact that Judith Campbell, the woman having an affair with the President, was also the mistress of mobster Sam Giancana, those around the President felt that he had to put a stop to his intimacy with Sinatra, who had introduced him to Judith. In a slap in the face for Sinatra, President Kennedy made a 1962 visit to Palm Springs and pointedly stayed at the home of Bing Crosby rather than with Sinatra, who had already installed a helicopter pad and bank of phones in the expectation of a presidential visit. It was Lawford who had to break the bad news to Sinatra, an act that put an end to the long friendship between the fellow members of the Rat Pack. Throughout most of the 1980s, Sinatra was again a welcome guest at the White House, thanks to his long friendship with Republican President Ronald Reagan and his wife, Nancy.

Frank Sinatra. (Movie Star News)

Sinking of the Athenia

On September 4, 1939, just hours after Great Britain had declared war on Germany, German submarines sank the British ocean liner the S.S. *Athenia*. Most of the fourteen hundred passengers were British, but there were three hundred Americans aboard, twelve of whom went down with the ship. The United States Ambassador to Great Britain, Joseph P. Kennedy, sent his son John, not yet returned to college for his senior year, to the scene. Young Kennedy's mission was to find out from the survivors how the sinking had actually happened, and to provide the help they needed. Although Jack Kennedy was not able to offer the one thing the survivors demanded anxiously—a naval escort to return them to the United States—he was generally agreed to have handled the situation well. There were no government funds available to answer the flood of telegrams from friends and relatives inquiring about the welfare of specific passengers, but Ambassador Kennedy paid for the responses out of his own pocket.

Sirhan Bishara Sirhan

Sirhan Bishara Sirhan was the twenty-four-year-old assassin of Senator Robert F. Kennedy. Sirhan was born to Jordanian parents in the city of Jerusalem on March 19, 1944. His father had a job in the local waterworks but lost it when Palestine was partitioned to create the new state of Israel. The Sirhan family came to the United States in 1957 under the sponsorship of a church in Pasadena, California, with passage provided by funds from the United Nations Relief and Welfare Agency. Sirhan's father, Bishara Sirhan, soon abandoned his family to return to his native Jordan, where he bought an olive grove. The small and slight Sirhan, an unemployed dropout who wanted to be a jockey, blamed his own troubles on the state of Israel and all the politicians who backed it. In a diary found later by the Los Angeles police, he wrote that Kennedy must be killed by the fifth of June, the first anniversary of the first day of the Six Day War between Egypt and Israel.

In the early morning of June 5, 1968, Sirhan pushed close to Senator Kennedy in a crowd at the Ambassador Hotel in Los Angeles after Kennedy's victory in the California presidential primary and shot the Senator with a .22-caliber Iver-Johnson revolver. Sirhan was immediately wrestled to the ground by members of the Kennedy entourage, including athletes Rosie Grier and Rafer Johnson, who then protected him from the wrath of the crowd. Police removed Sirhan, suffering from a broken finger and a sprained arm, and booked him on six counts of assault. Sirhan refused to give his name, but police identified him by tracing the gun to its purchaser, Sirhan's brother. He was indicted for murder on June 7, the day after RFK's death. Sirhan's father was interviewed in Jordan shortly thereafter and said, "I don't know how this happened, and I don't know who pushed him to do this. I raised him to love. I tell you frankly: Now I am against him." The assassin's mother sent a telegram to the Kennedy family, saying, "It hurts us bad what has happened."

Sirhan's trial began in January 1969, and he was found guilty of first-degree murder on April 17. The jury recommended a death sentence, but Senator Edward M. Kennedy asked the district attorney for mercy, and Sirhan appealed the sentence. While the appeal was going forward, the California Supreme Court abolished the death penalty in that state. On June 17, 1972,

Sirhan's sentence was officially commuted to life imprisonment. In May 1982, the state parole board revoked the scheduled first hearing of Sirhan's parole, due in September 1984, on the grounds that even behind bars he continued to threaten the lives of members of the Kennedy family. As of this writing, there have been nine hearings on the subject of parole for Sirhan Sirhan, who is serving his time at Soledad prison. Each time, parole has been denied.

636 Chain Bridge Road

The gray shingle house at 636 Chain Bridge Road in McLean, Virginia, is the home of Senator Edward M. Kennedy. He and his wife, Joan, bought the house in suburban Washington in the 1960s, attracted by the space for their young children and the nearness to his brother Robert and his family, a mile away at Hickory Hill. The one-story house overlooks the Potomac River, and the sixteen rooms have old paneling and elegant decor with antique furniture upholstered in damask and brocade. Tennis courts and a pool, with pool house complete the amenities. When Joan and Ted Kennedy divorced, she left the house on Chain Bridge Road, but Senator Kennedy continues to make it his Washington-area residence.

A Sixtieth-Birthday Party for Ethel

When Ethel Kennedy turned sixty in 1988, she threw a party to mark the occasion at her home in suburban Washington, Hickory Hill. More than two hundred guests attended, asked to dress in what they'd worn when Ethel first met them. The theme of the evening was the travels of Ethel and her late husband, Bobby. The place cards were luggage tags, tables were named after the countries the couple had visited, and a desk placed in the entrance hall bore the sign "Ethel Air." After the party was over, Ethel and her children gathered for a private mass celebrated in the pool house.

Shriver Day Camp

The Shriver Day Camp for the Mentally Retarded was founded by Eunice Shriver as part of her ongoing work for the mentally retarded. The camp, which gives retarded children a chance to experience the fun of outdoor activities, is funded by the Joseph P. Kennedy, Jr., Foundation. Mrs. Shriver's nephew Christopher Kennedy worked there for two summers as a counselor.

Sloane Street School for Boys

The Sloane Street School for Boys was the private school in London's Chelsea area that Bobby Kennedy attended when his father, Joseph P. Kennedy, was the United States Ambassador to Great Britain and the family lived in London.

George M. Smathers

George M. Smathers was a congressman from Florida who met Jack Kennedy when Jack went to Washington as representative from the Eleventh Congressional District of Massachusetts in 1947. Later Smathers, like Kennedy, was elected to the Senate, and the two men kept up a personal friendship as well as a political link.

Amanda Smith

Amanda Smith is the third child of Stephen E. and Jean Kennedy Smith, an adopted daughter, born April 30, 1967. Amanda attended the Spence School in New York and graduated from Harvard.

Jean Ann Kennedy Smith

The eighth child of Joseph P. and Rose Fitzgerald Kennedy, Jean was born on February 20, 1927, at St. Margaret's Hospital in Boston, where Rose went to await the birth so she could be under the care of her regular obstetrician. Jean's godfather was her older brother Joe, and she later took Ann as her confirmation name. Like her older sisters, Jean attended school at various Sacred Heart convents. She graduated from the Convent of the Sacred Heart at Eden Hall, in Pennsylvania. Jean enrolled in Manhattanville in 1945 and graduated in 1949.

Jean Kennedy married Stephen E. Smith, a New York executive, on May 19, 1956. The couple has four children: Stephen, Jr., born in 1957; William, born in 1960; Amanda, born in 1967; and Kym, born in 1972. They reside in New York City. Jean remains active in the various Kennedy family charitable organizations.

Kym Maria Smith

Kym Maria Smith is the fourth child of Stephen E. and Jean Kennedy Smith, an adopted daughter, born November 29, 1972. Kym attends Marymount School in New York.

Stephen Edward Smith

Stephen Edward Smith is the husband of Jean Kennedy. He was born in Brooklyn on September 24, 1927, into an Irish Catholic family that owned a small fleet of barges and tugboats that plied the Hudson River. Steve attended Polytechnic Prep and then Georgetown University; he was an Air Force lieutenant during World War II. At the time of his marriage to Jean Kennedy in 1956, Smith was employed as an executive in the family business. He helped raise funds for the 1960 presidential campaign of brother-in-law John F. Kennedy and then managed the 1964 senatorial campaign of RFK as well as his 1968 presidential campaign. Since the death of Joseph Kennedy in 1969, Steve has become the chief overseer of the Kennedy financial empire, including foundations, family trusts, and charitable bequests. In 1972, Smith briefly entertained the notion of running for governor of New York but quickly learned that his support was limited and withdrew from thoughts of public life.

Stephen Edward Smith, Jr.

Stephen Edward Smith, Jr., is the first child of Stephen E. and Jean Kennedy Smith, born on June 28, 1957. He attended Harvard College, graduating in 1979, and then received a law degree from Columbia Law School in 1984. He has worked as an assistant district attorney in the Bronx, as a member of Senator Paul Simon's legislative staff, and as an attorney with the Senate Foreign Relations Committee. Steve is now a teaching assistant at Harvard.

William Kennedy Smith

William Kennedy Smith is the second child of Stephen E. and Jean Kennedy Smith, born on September 4, 1960. Willy graduated from Duke University in September 1983 and worked for a time in the field of investment banking. He currently attends Georgetown University Medical School.

Some Magazine Articles Written by Members of the Kennedy Family

The Kennedys often use magazines as a forum from which to address various issues they deem important. Among the many articles penned by members of the Kennedy family are:

Joan Bennett Kennedy, "What It's Like to Marry a Kennedy," in *Ladies' Home Journal*

John F. Kennedy, "The Old Navy," in *Life*

John F. Kennedy, "Take the Academics Out of Politics," in *The Saturday Evening Post*, 1956

Joseph P. Kennedy, "The U.S. and the World," in *Life*, 1946

Robert F. Kennedy, "Our Climb Up Mount Kennedy," in *Life*, 1965

Robert F. Kennedy, "What We Can Do to End the Agony of Vietnam," in *Look*, 1967

Peter Lawford, "The White House Is Still Wondering What to Do with Me," in *McCall's*, 1961

Eunice Kennedy Shriver, "Hope for the Mentally Retarded," in *The Saturday Evening Post*

S

Some Recipients of Gifts from the Joseph P. Kennedy, Jr., Foundation

The Franciscan Missionaries of Mary, $600,000 in 1946 to establish a convalescent home for children of poor families

Assumption College, $150,000 in 1953, to help reconstruct school buildings damaged in a tornado

Boston College, $150,000 in 1953

Manhattanville College, $300,000 in 1956, for building a new dormitory and gymnasium

Boston College, $150,000 in 1959

The New Bedford Building Fund, $500,000 in 1959

Massachusetts General Hospital, $500,000 in 1960 for research into mental retardation.

Stanford University School of Medicine, $1,123,000, in 1964, for the study of mental retardation

University of Chicago, $1,500,000, in 1964, for the study of mental retardation

Albert Einstein College of Medicine, $1,450,000, in 1964, to establish the Rose Kennedy Institute for the Study of Mental Retardation

Georgetown University, $1,040,000, in 1966, for study of ways to improve training of the mentally retarded

George Peabody College, $960,000, in 1966, for study of ways to improve training of the mentally retarded

Georgetown University, $1,348,000, in 1971, to establish the Joe and Rose Kennedy Institute of Ethics

The Somerset Company

The Somerset Company was a liquor-importing firm established by Joseph P. Kennedy in the fall in 1933, as the end of Prohibition drew near. Using the influence of President Roosevelt's son Jimmy, Kennedy had concluded a deal to act as distributor for both Haig & Haig and Dewar's scotch, and his Washington connections had further allowed him to obtain permits to import liquor for "medicinal purposes" before Prohibition ended. The day that Americans were once more able to buy liquor legally, Joe Kennedy had warehouses full of the very best scotch whiskey to sell them.

The Somerset Company again made huge profits several years later when it stockpiled scotch during World War II and released it at the time of postwar shortages. Soon thereafter, Joe Kennedy was able to sell the company he had established at a cost of just one hundred thousand dollars for the price of eight million dollars. The Somerset Company was one of the most profitable enterprises in Kennedy's entrepreneurial career.

The Sorbonne

The Sorbonne is the leading French university in Paris where Jacqueline Bouvier spent her junior year of college, learning, among other things, to speak impeccable French.

Theodore Chaikin Sorensen

Theodore Chaikin Sorensen, usually called Ted, was an aide to John F. Kennedy, hired in 1953 when Kennedy took his seat in the Senate. Sorensen, born in Lincoln, Nebraska in 1928, received his law degree from the University of Nebraska in 1951; his father had been a crusader for liberal causes. The idealistic and hard-working Sorensen became both the conscience and the voice of John Kennedy, writing most of the speeches Kennedy delivered in his campaigns and during the White House years; the much-acclaimed Inaugural Speech was in large part Sorensen's work. The success of Sorensen's writing lay in the fact that he understood the way Kennedy talked and thought, so the speeches he devised for his boss genuinely reflected the personality and principles of the man who would deliver them. Sorensen left the White House after the assassination of President Kennedy and currently practices law in New York City.

Special Olympics

The Special Olympics is a program created and sponsored by the Joseph P. Kennedy, Jr., Foundation, the charitable foundation established by Joseph P. Kennedy in 1946 and named in honor of his oldest son, who was killed in World War II. Like many programs of the Kennedy foundation, it is aimed at helping the mentally retarded. The Special Olympics gives retarded people of all ages a national competition in track and field events. The motto of the Special Olympics is, "Let me win, but if I cannot win, let me be brave in the attempt." Eunice Kennedy Shriver has been instrumental in the success of the Special Olympics, and many members of the Kennedy family, along with their famous friends, such as Rafer Johnson, George Plimpton, and Roosevelt Grier, help out.

Spinal Cord Tumor

In the spring of 1988, Patrick, the younger son of Edward and Joan Kennedy, underwent an operation at Massachusetts General Hospital in Boston to remove a tumor on a spinal nerve just below his neck. The twenty-year-old Patrick had experienced increasing difficulty in walking, along with severe headaches, before the problem was discovered. Doctors said the tumor was benign, and Patrick was expected to make a full recovery.

Squaw Island

Not long after their marriage, Edward and Joan Kennedy built a rambling oceanfront house on Squaw Island, a few miles away from the Kennedy compound at Hyannis Port but only a short walk over the sand at low tide. The gray-shingled colonial is decorated in the blues and greens of the ocean, and like all Kennedy residences, contains family photos and memorabilia framed on walls and tabletops. When Joan and Ted divorced in 1981, Joan kept the Squaw Island house and continued to spend weekends and summers there with the children. Ted moved into his mother's house at the Compound.

Stanford University

After John F. Kennedy graduated from Harvard in June 1940, he decided he wanted to go to graduate school. He enrolled in the prestigious School of Business Administration at Stanford University, in Palo Alto, California, with the intention of obtaining an MBA. But by early 1941, Jack dropped out. October of that year found him in the navy. That same fall, his sister Eunice transferred from Manhattanville to Stanford. She graduated in April 1944.

Adlai Stevenson

Adlai Stevenson was one of the most important political figures in the Democratic party in the 1950s—by turns a mentor, a colleague, and a rival to John F. Kennedy. At the 1956 convention, Jack Kennedy made the speech that nominated Stevenson as the party's candidate for the presidency, and then Stevenson took the unprecedented step of throwing open the vice-presidency for the convention to decide. Kennedy came close to winning, but in the end the convention's choice was Tennessee Senator Estes B. Kefauver. In 1960, it seemed that Stevenson might be the man who could block Kennedy's drive for the White House, but by the spring of the year, Stevenson announced that he would not be a candidate. Although Stevenson and Kennedy shared many of the same political policies, they were personally dissimilar and never became close friends. Kennedy passed Stevenson over for a Cabinet position in his administration, but did appoint him to the position of ambassador to the United Nations, where he served with distinction. Adlai Stevenson went to Dallas only a few weeks before the President's scheduled trip in November 1963; he was spat upon and heard crowds chanting, "Kennedy will get his reward in hell, Stevenson is going to die." He reported back to the White House that Dallas might be a dangerous place for the President to visit.

The Story of Films

The Story of Films was a book edited by Joseph P. Kennedy that was published in 1927 by A. W. Shaw Company. It was a collection of transcribed talks given to students of the Harvard Business School by motion picture executives. The talks were organized by Kennedy, using his Hollywood contacts, and the association with Harvard, along with the publication of a book, gave him great prestige in the movie industry.

The Strange Case of the Disappearing Sound

On July 22, 1959, Robert F. Kennedy, then working for the Senate Committee investigating labor racketeering, made an appearance on the *Jack Paar Show*. In the prerecorded show, Kennedy made a number of accusations against teamsters' union president James Hoffa and then went on to mention names of racketeers associated with Hoffa. In the single minute that Robert Kennedy recited the list of names, the sound portion of the television show went dead four times. No plausible explanation for this "accident" was ever advanced.

The Suit Button Problem

In 1988, the state of Massachusetts commissioned sculptor Isabel McIlvain to create a bronze statue of the late President John F. Kennedy, to be placed outside the Massachusetts statehouse. The sculptor ran into an unexpected controversy—about the buttons on the President's suit. An aide to Senator Edward M. Kennedy asked if the suit could be left unbuttoned, the way it would be worn by a man concerned about the way his suits hang. The legislators who commissioned the statue examined photographs of the President and announced that he usually buttoned both buttons on his two-button suits. The sculptor, however, claims that Kennedy buttoned only the bottom button, and that is the way she intends to represent him.

Summit Meeting with Khrushchev

The summit meeting between President John F. Kennedy and Russian Premier Nikita Khrushchev took place in Vienna in June 1961. The atmosphere was acrimonious from the outset, and at several points during the discussions, the situation deteriorated to the point of the principals' banging on the table and delivering ultimatums involving nuclear missiles. The world press generally portrayed the summit meeting as a victory for the older, wilier Russian and a loss of face for the youthful and naive American President.

Sunday Today

In the 1987–88 season, NBC-TV inaugurated a new Sunday morning news magazine television show called *Sunday Today*. Co-anchors of the hour-long program were Garrick Utley and Maria Shriver, in her first regular assignment since she went to NBC in 1987. Maria calls her co-host Utley "a gentleman . . . very dignified, very bright, a fine writer."

S

"Survival"

"Survival" was an article written by journalist John Hersey about the sinking of PT-109 during the fighting against the Japanese in World War II and the heroic conduct of Lieutenant John F. Kennedy. The article was first published in *The New Yorker* on June 17, 1944, and then reached a broader audience when it was reprinted in the August issue of *Reader's Digest*. The article focused national attention on Kennedy, which proved to be helpful when Kennedy embarked on his political career several years later. Ironically, Hersey was the husband of a former girlfriend of JFK's, named Frances Ann Cannon. "Survival," was reprinted again in the *Reader's Digest* in February 1961, after John Kennedy entered the White House.

"Susie Glotz"

Shortly after the 1940 election that gave President Franklin D. Roosevelt his third term, Joseph P. Kennedy gave an interview to three journalists in Boston's Ritz-Carlton Hotel. The Ambassador to the Court of St. James, back in the U.S. to confer with his government, first restated his position that America should not get involved in a European war, and then went on to talk off-the-cuff about the President and his wife in more personal terms. Eleanor Roosevelt, he confided candidly, "bothered us more on our jobs in Washington to take care of the poor little nobodies who hadn't any influence than all the rest of the people down there together. She's always sending me a note to have some little Susie Glotz to tea at the embassy." Read in the context of the entire interview, it seems that Kennedy was trying to make the point that Mrs. Roosevelt worked hard to help ordinary people, but when his edited remarks appeared in the newspaper, they seemed to criticize the First Lady for being a busybody. The interview eroded the last links between Joe Kennedy and President Roosevelt, and Kennedy resigned his post as Ambassador soon afterward.

Gloria Swanson

In the fall of 1927, Joseph P. Kennedy met movie queen Gloria Swanson, then at the height of her fame yet struggling to find enough money to support her lavish lifestyle. Gloria, born in 1897, had been one of Mack Sennett's leading film comediennes and then went on to star in a number of sultry roles that made her the glamor queen of the silent screen. She married and divorced actor Wallace Beery, and at the time she met Joe Kennedy, she was on her third husband, a French marquis.

Joe Kennedy entered Gloria Swanson's life as a much-needed financial counselor, but by the winter of that year, Gloria and Joe had become lovers. For nearly two years, they continued their affair, despite the fact that both were married to other people. Curiously, Joe attempted to involve Gloria with his family, introducing her to his children as a glamorous movie star and to his wife as a confused protégé who needed his help. In return, Gloria dazzled the children and took Rose shopping in Paris and helped her learn how to dress more elegantly. According to Gloria's account, Joe even took her to Paris on the same ocean liner as his wife! Eventually, after several failed movies, Joe left Gloria, apparently in a bigger financial mess than he found her. She then divorced her husband and tried to reestablish her career, but her former level of success eluded her, and she decided to retire in 1934. She made a memorable comeback when she starred as Norma Desmond in *Sunset Boulevard* in 1950 and was rewarded with an Oscar nomination. Near the end of her life, Gloria wrote a frank autobiography, *Swanson on Swanson*, that recounted many details of her romance with Joe Kennedy. Gloria Swanson died in 1983.

Swearing-in of President Johnson

After the assassination of President Kennedy, the immediate concern of high government officials was an orderly transfer of power. The new President, Lyndon B. Johnson, decided to be sworn in on Air Force One before it returned to Washington with the body of the slain President. The five-minute ceremony was presided over by sixty-seven-year-old Judge Sarah T. Hughes, a Kennedy appointee, as the presidential jet stood on a secluded part of the runway of Love Field. Standing in the private cabin of the plane beside Johnson were his wife, Lady Bird, and Jacqueline Kennedy, the widow of the President, still wearing her blood-splattered pink suit. Kennedy staffers at the back of the conference room where the ceremony was held included Dave Powers, Larry O'Brien, and Kenny O'Donnell. The precise time that Johnson officially became the new President of the United States was 2:38 P.M., Central Standard Time, on November 22, 1963. After taking the oath of office, President Johnson embraced his wife and Mrs. Kennedy and gave the order for the plane to return to Washington.

"Sweet Adeline"

The sentimental ballad "Sweet Adeline," with all its possibilities for soul-satisfying harmonies, was a favorite of President Kennedy's grandfather, Boston politician John F. Fitzgerald, and it became one of his campaign trademarks. He often asked the crowd to join him in singing the well-known song, and his daughter Rose liked to accompany him on the piano. When his grandson Jack won his first election in 1946, taking the seat in the Eleventh Congressional District of Massachusetts which Fitzgerald himself had once occupied, Fitzgerald stood on a tabletop at the victory party and jubilantly burst into the old familiar song. The tune remains a Kennedy family favorite, always sung at high volume by the entire clan when they gather to celebrate Rose Fitzgerald Kennedy's birthday every summer at Hyannis Port.

T

The Tax Cut

The Kennedy administration adopted an innovative economic policy in early 1963, advocating a tax cut to improve the performance of the economy, especially in regard to full employment. The Kennedy program of induced deficit spending is now regarded as one of the most influential economic policies of the postwar period. As economic advisor Walter Heller later explained, it was the first time a President had told the country that a deficit could be good for its economic health.

At the last minute, four days before it had to be printed, I took 22 typewritten double-spaced pages to the President. I thought I'd just give them to him, tell him a little bit about it and then let him read it and tell me what changes to make. But he was a speed reader, and by now he was pretty savvy on the economic front. Of course, economic advisors always claim their President is savvy, but Kennedy really was. Although, always within limitations. But instead of having a little conversation and dismissing me, he said, "No, I'll go over it right now."

Now you have to remember that the tax cut was a totally innovative thing, because we had no recession. The economy was moving up. We had a substantial deficit, and never before had any President had the wit or wisdom to put in a tax cut in an expanding economy with a big budget deficit. Anyway, we were standing there—he on one side of his desk and I on the other—and he flipped through the speech in perhaps no more than 10 minutes, and then tossed it to me and said, "That's fine." I said, "My God, Mr. President, you're sure showing a lot of confidence in me."

He said, "Sure, why not."

I said, "Don't you know I have you saying something no other President has ever said—that a deficit under certain circumstances can be a good thing; that there are constructive deficits and destructive deficits and it depends on the circumstances?"

He said, "Well, let me take another look at that." So he went back and he looked at that part and he changed one sentence very slightly, and then he tossed it back to me and said, "Let's go."

Maxwell D. Taylor

Maxwell D. Taylor was the head of the Joint Chiefs of Staff during the Kennedy Administration. He later served under President Johnson as ambassador to Vietnam. The ninth child of Ethel and Robert Kennedy, Matthew Maxwell Taylor Kennedy, was named after him.

Tea Parties

During John F. Kennedy's 1952 campaign for the U.S. Senate, he and his advisors came up with the bright idea of holding a series of tea parties at which tens of thousands of women voters were invited to be honored guests of the Kennedy family. The Kennedy political organization rented large rooms in hotels, and covered the tables with real lace clothes and silver tea sets. All of the Kennedys were there to shake the guests' hands and speak a few personal words to each woman, just as if the event had truly been a society party rather than a political reception. The star of the tea parties turned out to be the candidate's mother, Rose Kennedy, always elegantly dressed in couturier clothes and impeccably groomed. When Jack won the election, reporters asked his opponent, incumbent Senator Henry Cabot Lodge, how he accounted for his own defeat. Answered Lodge, "It was those damn tea parties," he said. "Kennedy swam into the Senate on a sea of tea." Kennedy's own political staff agreed, so when he ran for President eight years later, he again used the tea parties as part of his successful campaign strategy. Later other members of the family, including Edward Kennedy, Sargent Shriver, and, most recently, the President's nephew, Joseph P. Kennedy II, have also adapted the tea party tactic to their own campaigns.

The Teddie-Eddie Debates

In 1962, Edward M. Kennedy decided to become a candidate for the Senate seat from Massachusetts. His chief competitor in the Democratic primary was Edward J. McCormack, Jr. The two agreed to appear in two televised debates, which were members of the press could not resist labeling the "Teddie-Eddie debates."

Teddy Has a Birthday

In recent years, Senator Edward M. Kennedy has hosted an annual birthday bash at his home in McLean, Virginia. Guests at his fifty-sixth birthday party, in 1988, were invited to come as the historical figure of their choice. The host chose to appear as an ancient Irish king, in skin-hugging tights and a laurel wreath; his sister-in-law Ethel arrived riding on a chariot, dressed as Cleopatra. A moat was constructed around the front of the house for the occasion, and filled with dry ice to send up wisps of vapor. Guests entered the house by crossing a drawbridge, which was raised and lowered by two guards at the front door.

Televised Debates

In the fall of 1960, at the height of the presidential campaign, candidates Senator John F. Kennedy and Vice-President Richard M. Nixon agreed to appear in a series of televised debates

T

(an event that has turned into a political tradition in subsequent elections.) Vice-President Nixon, a champion debater in high school and college, felt confident he could defeat Kennedy in such a forum, and he prepared by going over the points he intended to make at the expense of his less experienced opponent. Those who happened to hear the debates on radio agreed with Nixon that he was a superior debater. But the seventy million Americans who watched the first debate on television were impressed by Jack Kennedy's cool imperturbability, his steady gaze at the camera, and his slightly ironic distance from the heat of the campaign. They contrasted these qualities with Nixon's scowling demeanor, his five o'clock shadow, and the painful intensity of his desire to win. Many analysts believe the TV debates were the reason that John F. Kennedy won the election.

Maurice Tempelsman

Maurice Tempelsman has been Jacqueline Kennedy Onassis's most frequent escort throughout the 1980s. Born to an Orthodox Jewish family in Belgium in 1929 (making him the same age as Jackie), Maurice speaks fluent French and is at home in the world of arts and letters inhabited by Jackie. Often referred to by the press as a "diamond merchant," Tempelsman in fact is the owner of several mining companies as well as a diamond trading business. In 1949, he married his wife, Lily, now a marriage counselor. In 1982, the couple separated, but there has been no divorce, and the couple's West Side apartment in New York remains Tempelsman's official residence.

Tenovus *and* Onemore

In the late 1920s, Joseph P. Kennedy bought a boat for his children to sail in the summer races at Hyannis Port, Massachusetts. He named it the *Tenovus*, in reference to the size of his family at the time, with eight children and two parents. In 1932, the last child in the family, Edward Moore Kennedy, was born. Joe responded by buying a second, larger boat, which he called the *Onemore*.

Frank V. Teti

Frank V. Teti was a photojournalist specializing in political and entertainment personalities. In 1966, at the age of eighteen, his first coverage of a Kennedy family wedding in Newport, Rhode Island, led to subsequent opportunities to photograph private family functions. His 1983 book, *Kennedy: The New Generation*, contained over two hundred pictures of the twenty-nine grandchildren of Joseph and Rose Kennedy. Teti died in 1988 at age forty. In his will, his twenty-two-year collection of more than 10,000 Kennedy family photographs was bequeathed to

Melody Miller, Senator Kennedy's deputy press secretary, under whose supervision the Frank Teti Collection is available through the Kennedy Library archives.

That Shining Hour

After the death of Robert F. Kennedy, his sister Patricia Kennedy Lawford collected various personal reminiscences of RFK into a book called *That Shining Hour*. Following the family tradition, the book was privately printed and given to Kennedy family and friends.

George Thomas

George Thomas was President John F. Kennedy's valet, the man responsible for keeping the President's clothes in order and bringing him his breakfast in bed. Thomas began working for Jack Kennedy when he was a congressman, and he remained with him until the day Kennedy died. Thomas did his best to keep the often disheveled President looking neat and well-groomed, and chided him for skipping meals or wearing mismatched socks. After the President's assassination, Jacqueline Kennedy gave Thomas his rocking chair from the Oval Office as a memento of the man he had served so faithfully for so many years.

Sylvia "Sissy" Thomas

Sylvia "Sissy" Thomas was the daughter of Hugh Lloyd Thomas, who had been press secretary to the Duke of Windsor when he was Prince of Wales. Sissy met Kathleen Kennedy in early 1938, and the two struck up a friendship that lasted the rest of Kathleen's life. Sissy later married David Ormsby-Gore, the heir of Lord Harlech, and Kathleen was godmother to the couple's first child. Her husband was named Ambassador to the United States during the Kennedy presidency, and the Ormsby-Gores were part of the Washington circle of Kennedy insiders. Ormsby-Gore succeeded to the title of Lord Harlech in 1964. Lady Harlech was killed in a car crash in 1967. Rumors abounded that the widowed Jacqueline Kennedy would marry "old friend" and widower Lord Harlech—until she announced her intention of wedding Aristotle Onassis.

3017 N Street

After the death of President John F. Kennedy, his widow bought a Washington, D.C., house at 3017 N Street for herself and the children. Mrs. Kennedy paid $175,000 for the three-story, fourteen-room house, but quickly became aware that it lacked the privacy they needed. It faced the street and curious passersby could look right into the windows; it even became a popular destination for Washington tour buses. The house on N Street, only a few doors away from the Kennedys' old house in Georgetown, where they lived at the time of Jack's election to the presidency, was an interim solution, allowing the children to finish out the school year and remain close to their Kennedy cousins in McLean. By the following fall, the family moved to New York, where they were able to find the privacy they sought.

3307 N Street

In January 1958, Senator and Mrs. John F. Kennedy and their daughter, Caroline, moved into a red-brick townhouse built in 1812, at 3307 N Street, N.W., in Georgetown, D.C. The three-story house, with its high ceilings and airy rooms, would later be familiar to all the nation as the place where President-elect Kennedy often stood on the doorstep to announce appointments for his new administration.

Thirteen Days: A Memoir of the Cuban Missile Crisis

In January 1969, W. W. Norton and Company published *Thirteen Days: A Memoir of the Cuban Missile Crisis*, by Robert F. Kennedy. Senator Kennedy had completed the work before his death the previous June. There were forewords from Robert S. McNamara and former British Prime Minister Harold Macmillan.

To Seek a Newer World

In November 1967, Doubleday published *To Seek a Newer World*, a collection of speeches made by Senator Robert F. Kennedy.

"Toodles"

"Toodles" was the nickname of Elizabeth Ryan, a beautiful young woman who worked as a cigarette girl at the Ferncroft Inn in Middleton, Massachusetts, in the years preceding World War I. Boston Mayor John F. Fitzgerald often visited the inn for a relaxing evening of drinking, gambling, and dancing. He became one of the acknowledged admirers of the vivacious Toodles, although there was never any concrete evidence to suggest that the relationship actually went beyond public flirtation. In 1913, when Fitzgerald attempted to run for another term as mayor, his opponent James Michael Curley sent a black-bordered letter to Mrs. Fitzgerald, warning her that her husband's relationship with the twenty-three-year-old woman would soon be made public. At the same time, Curley publicly announced that he would be giving a series of lectures to all interested Bostonians. The first lecture, which Curley actually did deliver, was entitled "Graft in Ancient Times Versus Graft in Modern Times" and focused on the fact that one of the mayor's brothers had never paid any water bills while Fitzgerald was in office—a mere pinprick that Fitzgerald was able to laugh off. It was the subsequent lectures that could do the real damage: "Great Lovers in History: From Cleopatra to Toodles" and "Libertines in History from Henry the Eighth to the Present Day." Thanks to the Toodles threat, Fitzgerald withdrew from the race to protect his family, and the lectures were never delivered.

Tour of the White House

In February 1962, Jacqueline Kennedy conducted a televised tour of the White House to share its special history with the nation. Wearing a simple wool suit, she walked through the public rooms of the home of American Presidents and reeled off an impressive string of facts about the building and its contents. Mrs. Kennedy was accompanied by journalist Charles Collingwood of CBS. More than forty-six million viewers tuned in to take the tour. Jackie also taped introductions in French and Spanish, and the program was distributed in 106 countries.

Kathleen Hartington Kennedy Townsend

Kathleen Hartington Kennedy is the first child of Robert F. and Ethel Skakel Kennedy. She was born on July 4, 1951, in Hyannis, Massachusetts and named after her father's sister, who had died only a few years earlier. Kathleen attended the Sacred Heart Country Day School in Bethesda, Maryland, the Putney School, and Radcliffe College. She holds a law degree from the University of New Mexico School of Law. She wrote her final law school thesis on Emma Goldman, the controversial feminist and social activist. Her favorite quote from Goldman says, "Woman's development, her freedom, her independence, must come from and through herself."

In 1972, Kathleen Kennedy met her husband, David Lee Townsend, on a rafting trip down the Mississippi. They were married on November 17, 1973. They are the parents of three daughters: Meaghan, born in 1977; Maeve, born in 1979; and Rose Katherine, called Kate, born in 1984. The Townsends live in an old Victorian house in Baltimore. In 1986, Kathleen ran for a congressional seat from Maryland but lost her bid. She currently directs a program that enables teenagers to work on literacy, environmental, and health care projects in exchange for high school credits, while husband, David, teaches in the Great Books program at St. John's University.

Maeve Fahey Townsend

Maeve Fahey Townsend is the second child of David L. and Kathleen Kennedy Townsend, born on November 1, 1979, at her parents' home in New Haven, Connecticut. Maeve's godfather was her uncle Michael Kennedy, her godmother aunt Courtney.

Meaghan Ann Townsend

Meaghan Ann Townsend is the first child of David L. and Kathleen Kennedy Townsend, born on November 7, 1977, at the home of her parents in Santa Fe, New Mexico.

Rose Katherine Kennedy Townsend

Rose Katherine Kennedy Townsend is the third child of David L. and Kathleen Kennedy Townsend. Kate was born on December 17, 1984.

Dr. Janet Travell

Dr. Janet Travell was the physician who treated John F. Kennedy for his back problems. He became her patient not long after the second operation on his back, in 1954. The New York pharmacologist was able to relieve much of Kennedy's chronic back pain through injections of novocaine, and she also introduced him to cortisone pills as a way of combatting the adrenal insufficiency caused by Addison's disease. It was at Dr. Travell's office that Kennedy first encountered the rocking chair that was to be a part of his back therapy—and part of his image in the public mind.

Trip to Ireland

On June 26, 1963, President Kennedy's jet touched down in Dublin for a four-day trip to Ireland. He was on his way back to the White House after a triumphant visit to West Berlin, and he had decided to unwind with a return to the land of his forefathers. Everywhere he was greeted by signs that said "Welcome Home," as well as the traditional Irish greeting, "Cead Mile Failte," or "A Hundred Thousand Welcomes." Kennedy had a wonderful time in Ireland, and his face expressed deep emotion as he told those who had gone to the Shannon Airport to see him off, "I am going to come back and see old Shannon's face again."

T

247

Nancy Tuckerman

Nancy Tuckerman was a classmate of Jacqueline Bouvier at boarding school who was also one of her bridesmaids at her wedding to the senator from Massachusetts. Nancy later became Mrs. Kennedy's social secretary in the White House, replacing Letitia Baldridge, and she continued to work for the former First Lady after President Kennedy's assassination. She remains the spokesperson chosen to release most of Mrs. Onassis's statements. She also works as a publicist at Doubleday, the publishing firm Jacqueline Onassis joined in 1978.

Tulagi

During World War II, one of major naval bases in the Solomon Islands was at Tulagi. Lieutenant John F. Kennedy was stationed there, arriving on April 14, 1943, to take command of PT-109.

Twentieth Anniversary of the Assassination

On November 22, 1983, the twentieth anniversary of the assassination of President John F. Kennedy, a service was held in the slain President's honor at the Holy Trinity Church in Washington. President Ronald Reagan attended, as did members of the Kennedy family, and Caroline Kennedy read excerpts from her father's speeches. Later, the Kennedy family gathered at the President's grave.

U

U.S.S. Joseph P. Kennedy, Jr.

In December 1945, a little more than a year after Lieutenant Joseph P. Kennedy, Jr.'s death, the Navy launched Destroyer 850, which it named in his honor, as a tribute to the courage and heroism he displayed in flying his final mission. Joseph and Rose Kennedy, with children Jean, Bobby, and Teddy, as well as Rose's father, John F. Fitzgerald, attended the ceremony at which the twenty-two-hundred-ton vessel was launched from the Quincy, Massachusetts, shipyard of Bethlehem Steel, where the elder Joe had worked during World War I. Jean officially christened the ship with the ritual bottle of champagne. Subsequently young Robert F. Kennedy left the Naval Officer's Training School at Harvard to serve as an able-bodied seaman on board the destroyer named after his brother.

Years later, when John F. Kennedy was President, the U.S.S. *Joseph P. Kennedy, Jr.* was one of the ships that participated in the American blockade of Russian ships bearing nuclear missiles to Cuba.

"Uncle Cornpone"

"Uncle Cornpone" was reportedly the unkind nickname given Vice-President Lyndon B. Johnson by Kennedy staffers. Lady Bird was sarcastically referred to as his "little pork chop."

United Nations Conference of 1945

On April 25, 1945, only a few weeks before the formal end of World War II in Europe, delegates from European nations met with Americans in San Francisco to try to agree on a new world-wide organization that could help shape the postwar future. Thanks to a suggestion made by Joseph P. Kennedy to his friend William Randolph Hearst, the Hearst-owned *Chicago Herald-American* decided to send young naval veteran Lieutenant John F. Kennedy as their reporter to cover the conference. Jack's assignment was to look at the proceedings through the eyes of the returning serviceman who had fought the war, and his series of columns from San Francisco were so well received that the paper asked him to go to England the following month, to cover the British elections scheduled for June.

United States Maritime Commission

The United States Maritime Commission was established in 1937, not long after Franklin D. Roosevelt was inaugurated for his second term as President. Roosevelt asked Joseph P. Kennedy to serve as its first chairman. Initially, Kennedy felt it was too lowly a post in reward for his services, but he accepted the challenge and served until the end of 1937, when he was appointed Ambassador to the Court of St. James.

University of Virginia Law School

In the fall of 1948, after graduating from Harvard College, Robert F. Kennedy enrolled in the University of Virginia Law school in Charlottesville, Virginia. The admissions office had told him "in view of your record at Harvard College, you are unlikely to be admitted to this Law School unless you do well on the Law Aptitude Test," but he was finally accepted, and proved to be a better student in law school than he had been in college. He graduated in the middle of his class in June 1951. His chief distinction at law school came when, as president of the Student Legal Forum, he invited the distinguished black educator Dr. Ralph Bunche to address a gathering of students. The news was met with dismay from many students, and administrators as well, on the segregated campus. But Bobby stood firm and Dr. Bunche appeared before an integrated audience, a first for the university. Bobby's brother Ted attended the law school several years later.

In the next generation, Robert Kennedy's sons Robert, Jr., and Michael also received their law degrees from the University of Virginia Law School.

Unusual Awards Received by John F. Kennedy

In 1952, he was selected the "handsomest member of Congress" by reporters from *Capitol News*.

In 1952, he received the Iupa Romana award, given by the city of Rome to people who contribute to the city's welfare.

In 1959, he was named Man of the Year by the *Polish Daily News*.

U

Vassar

Jacqueline Bouvier attended Vassar College, in
Poughkeepsie, New York, for her first two years
of college.

Réné Verdon

Réné Verdon was the head chef at the White
House during the Kennedy presidency. Recommended by Joseph P. Kennedy, the French chef
was largely responsible for the renewed interest of White House guests in the food served
there. There was criticism at the time that the
White House should serve American, not French,
food, but the quality of the dishes served, and
the evident enjoyment of the guests, eventually
silenced the critics.

The Vice-Presidential Contest

When Senator John F. Kennedy went to the
Democratic convention in the summer of 1956,
he hoped only to make a good impression as a
party leader for the future. Thanks to his recent
Pulitzer Prize for the book *Profiles in Courage*
and his narration of the film about the history
of the Democratic party that opened the convention, Kennedy happened to be in the lime-
light. Thus when the convention's choice of a
presidential candidate, Adlai Stevenson, announced that he would ask the convention to
vote on the choice of a running mate, many

delegates decided they would like to see the youthful Kennedy on the ticket. Before going to the convention, Kennedy and his advisors had concluded that 1956 was not the right year for him to consider a bid for national office, but when they observed the groundswell of Kennedy support, they swung into action and did their best to win the vice-presidential nomination. On the first ballot, Kennedy's strength was respectable, and on the second ballot, he actually came within a handful of votes of winning. But his support began to erode on the third ballot, and he understood it was time to concede and let Senator Estes Kefauver of Tennessee win a clear victory. It was those few feverish hours of the 1956 convention that made Kennedy a viable candidate for President in the 1960 election.

Afterward, Jack Kennedy once compared his performance in the 1956 convention to what might have happened if his older brother Joe had survived World War II and gone into politics, as the family had expected. He hypothesized that Joe would have run for Congress, just as he himself had done, and won. Then Joe would have run for the Senate, and won again. At the 1956 convention, when the vice-presidential nomination suddenly arose, Joe—always a winner —would have managed to make it onto the national ticket. "And then," mused Jack Kennedy, "he and Stevenson would have lost the national election and his political career would have been blighted."

Victura

John F. Kennedy's first boat was an eighteen-foot sailboat that he named the *Victura*, apparently under the mistaken impression that it was the Latin word for "victory." Jack often sailed the *Victura* in races on Nantucket Sound, and was known to be a zesty competitor.

Vietnam: The Beginning

During the Kennedy administration, the U.S. government continued the policy, established in 1954 at the time the French left Indochina, of involving itself in the political situation of Vietnam. Because of the "domino theory," which stated that if one country in the area toppled to Communism, all its neighbors would follow, it was deemed important to support the anti-Communist government of Premier Ngo Dinh Diem. It was, of course, troublesome that the shaky Diem regime was tyrannical and corrupt, but the Kennedy administration continued to back Diem; as one wit put it, the policy of the U.S. government was "sink or swim with Ngo Dinh Diem." In 1961, President Kennedy agreed to begin sending small contingents of American troops as "advisors" to assist Diem's soldiers in strategic areas. Yet Kennedy and his foreign policy team remained deeply suspicious of the motives of the Diem government and many of them were unconvinced of its long-run viability.

By early October 1963, U.S. intelligence sources had collected many rumors of an impending coup by Diem's military but took no action. On November 2, the coup occurred, and Diem and his brother-in-law Ngo Dinh Nhu were murdered. According to insiders, President Kennedy was badly shaken by the news.

Supports of JFK assert that if he had lived, the U.S. would not have become so deeply involved in Vietnam. Critics point to the fact that it was Kennedy who sent the first troops to the country.

"Vigah"

Accustomed to the midwestern accents of Presidents Truman and Eisenhower, the American public was startled to hear the regional New England accent of John F. Kennedy. They joked about a President who would "paak the caa in Haavaad yaad" and were especially tickled by his pronunciation of one of his favorite words, *vigor*, or as Kennedy called it, "vigah." It came to be a trademark of the Kennedy years in the White House.

Visit to Windsor Castle

In April 1938, King George VI and Queen Elizabeth invited the United States Ambassador to Great Britain, Joseph P. Kennedy, and his wife, Rose, to make their first visit to Windsor Castle, where the royal family liked to spend their weekends. That occasion was one of the highlights of Joe and Rose Kennedy's lives, and they were henceforth to remember every little detail of those two days. After they had arrived at Windsor and settled into their two-bedroom, two-bathroom suite, Joe took a long look around him at the royal surroundings and said to his wife in a satisfied tone, "Rose, this is a helluva long way from East Boston."

A Voice From Beyond

Arthur Schlesinger, Jr., ends his book about Robert F. Kennedy with a story about RFK's funeral. By the time the funeral train arrived in Washington, Arlington Cemetery was dark and shadowed, and the pallbearers were uncertain of the exact location of the grave. As they trudged on carrying the heavy coffin, elder statesman Averell Harriman finally said to Kennedy's brother-in-law, Stephen Smith, "Steve, do you know where you're going?" Smith admitted he wasn't sure. Then, Smith later reported, he could swear he distinctly heard a voice coming out of the coffin, saying "Damn it, if you fellows will put me down, I'll show you the way."

Helga Wagner

Helga Wagner is a jewelry designer in Palm Beach with whom Senator Edward M. Kennedy was rumored to have had a long-term liaison. According to a book written by Joan Kennedy's secretary Marcia Chellis, Ted called Helga to discuss the problem of Chappaquiddick before he even broke the news to his wife, Joan.

Adam Walinsky

Adam Walinsky was a member of Senator Robert F. Kennedy's staff. He was a graduate of Cornell in 1957, spent a year in the Marines, and then went to Yale Law School, from which he graduated in 1961. Walinsky had briefly clerked for Judge Carroll C. Hincks at the Second Circuit Court of Appeals in New York and then joined the Justice Department when Kennedy was attorney general. Once he was hired for the senator's staff, Walinsky became RFK's chief speech-writer, and to some extent his conscience, even his alter ego. Today he practices law in New York City.

William Walton

William Walton was a friend of President John F. Kennedy and his wife, Jacqueline, who had the distinction of being the first private individual with whom Kennedy dined outside the White House after his Inauguration. Born in Illinois, Walton was a journalist who went to Washington to work for the *New Republic*. Later, he abandoned journalism for art and became a noted abstract painter. A close friend of Ernest Hemingway, he gave notable parties in Washington during the early 1950s, with an impressive array of guests. It was his friend John White who introduced Walton to Jacqueline Bouvier, who later introduced him to the man she married. Bill Walton served as coordinator of Jack Kennedy's presidential campaign. The President later appointed him chairman of the Fine Arts Commission.

The Warren Commission

After the assassination of President Kennedy and the death of the man accused of killing him, Lee Harvey Oswald, talk about a conspiracy to kill the President began to surface. Rumors became widespread. Some said it was a Communist plot, others laid it to the Mafia, still others to Kennedy enemies such as the officials of the teamsters' union. There was even a suspicion that President Lyndon B. Johnson was somehow behind the plot. To clear the air, President Johnson established a President's Commission on the Assassination of President John F. Kennedy and asked it to make a full investigation of the matter. The commission was headed by Chief Justice Earl Warren and included Senators Richard B. Russell of Georgia and John Sherman Cooper of Kentucky; Representatives Hale Boggs of Louisiana and Gerald R. Ford of Michigan; and Allen W. Dulles and John J. McCloy of the CIA.

The Warren Commission issued its report in September 1964, less than a year after the assassination. After interviewing 552 witnesses and examining hundreds of pieces of evidence, the commission concluded that Lee Harvey Oswald had acted alone. His motivation for the act was thought to be the "isolation, frustration and failure" of his life. Although the commission noted that it was impossible to prove conclusively that no conspiracy existed, the fact that no evidence of any sort of conspiracy had been uncovered made the members of the commission conclude that the theory was unlikely.

Washington Times-Herald

The Washington *Times-Herald* was a newspaper published in the nation's capital. Under the leadership of owner Cissy Paterson, the paper had a conservative political slant and tended to employ a young and socially prominent staff, the children of Cissy's own society friends. In 1941, Kathleen Kennedy worked at the *Times-Herald* as an inquiring reporter; her fellow employees included her close friend Page Huidekoper, who had worked for Joseph P. Kennedy at the London embassy; Lady Nancy Astor's niece, Dinah Bridge; John White, with whom Kathleen had a romantic entanglement; and Inga Arvad, who was seriously involved with Kathleen's brother Jack.

Twelve years later, another socially prominent young woman began to work at the *Times-Herald* as a reporter/photographer: Jacqueline Bouvier. Her job was the same one Kathleen Kennedy once held. Camera in hand, she went out on the streets of Washington asking people what they thought about a specific question, and then photographed her respondents. Jackie's questions were often personal and provocative: "What age do you think men should be when they marry?" is an example. By the time she resigned, she was earning a salary of $56.75 a week.

A Wedding Anniversary Calendar for the Kennedy Family

FEBRUARY 3
Sheila Rauch and Joe Kennedy

MARCH 14
Victoria Gifford and Michael Kennedy

APRIL 3
Emily Black and Robert Kennedy, Jr.

APRIL 24
Pat Kennedy and Peter Lawford

APRIL 26
Maria Shriver and Arnold Schwarzenegger

MAY 6
Kathleen Kennedy and Billy Cavendish

MAY 19
Jean Kennedy and Steve Smith

MAY 23
Eunice Kennedy and Sargent Shriver

JUNE 13
Victoria Lawford and Robert Pender

JUNE 14
Courtney Kennedy and Jeffrey Ruhe

JUNE 17
Ethel Skakel and Bobby Kennedy

JULY 19
Caroline Kennedy and Ed Schlossberg

SEPTEMBER 12
Jacqueline Bouvier and Jack Kennedy

SEPTEMBER 17
Sydney Lawford and Peter McKelvy

OCTOBER 7
Rose Fitzgerald and Joe Kennedy

NOVEMBER 17
Kathleen Kennedy and David Townsend

NOVEMBER 23
Mary Hickey and P. J. Kennedy

NOVEMBER 30
Joan Bennett and Ted Kennedy

Wedding: Rose Elizabeth Fitzgerald and Joseph Patrick Kennedy

Rose Elizabeth Fitzgerald and Joseph Patrick Kennedy were married on October 7, 1914. The ceremony was conducted by William Cardinal O'Connell in the private chapel connected to his Boston residence and the guest list was limited to the immediate families of the bride and groom. The bride was attended by her sister Agnes; the best man was Joseph Donovan, a friend from Joe's student days at Harvard. The bride wore a Dutch cap of lace with an illusion net veil, and a gown of rose-patterned brocade with a dropped waist and a long train. Her fashionably long-stemmed bouquet was composed of orange blossoms and lilies. Rose was given in marriage by her father, former Boston Mayor John F. Fitzgerald. The groom wore a cutaway and top hat. Afterward, there was a wedding breakfast for seventy-five guests at the home of the bride's parents in Dorchester. Rose's engagement ring was a flawless two-carat diamond.

Wedding: Janet Norton Lee and John Vernou Bouvier III

On July 7, 1928, Janet Norton Lee was married to John Vernou Bouvier III in St. Philomena Church, the local Catholic Church in fashionable East Hampton on New York's Long Island. The bride, in a floor-length dress of satin, lace, and silver was given away by her father, James T. Lee, and attended by six bridesmaids in spring-yellow dresses and green hats, and her two sisters as matron and maid of honor. Bud Bouvier, Jack's younger brother, was the best man. After the ceremony there was a reception for 500 guests on the grounds of the Lees' rented summer estate, which featured dancing to music provided by the Meyer Davis Orchestra.

Wedding: Kathleen Kennedy and William Cavendish, The Marquess of Hartington

Kathleen Kennedy and the Marquess of Hartington were married on May 6, 1944, in a registry office in the London district of Chelsea. The dreary location was a result of the couple's religious differences. The Protestant Billy would not convert to Catholicism, nor agree to have his children raised in the Catholic faith; and Kathleen, although she was willing to marry without the recognition of her own Catholic faith, was not willing to be married in another faith. The simple ceremony took place in the morning, and Joseph P. Kennedy, Jr., the sole member of the Kennedy family to attend the wedding, gave his sister away. The wedding ring was a family heirloom given by the groom's parents, the Duke and Duchess of Devonshire. The bride and groom had no attendants; the best man was the Duke of Rutland. Kathleen wore a pale pink crepe dress with a diamond pin at the neck, and a charming bright feathered hat with a wisp of a veil. She carried a nosegay of pink camellias and a small jeweled evening purse lent by family friend Marie Bruce as "something old." Billy wore his military uniform as an officer of the Coldstream Guards. Lady Nancy Astor and Marie Bruce were the only other people invited by Kathleen. Billy's parents, two sisters, and an aunt were also in attendance, throwing rose petals at the happy newlyweds (rice was rationed for the duration of the war). Afterward, there was a gala reception at the home of Lady Hambleden, a neighbor of the Duke and Duchess of Devonshire at Eaton Place; the Devonshires' own house had been badly damaged in the bombing. More than two hundred guests, some of them soldiers from Kathleen's Red Cross Canteen, ate plain fruit cake without frosting (sugar was also rationed).

Wedding: Ethel Skakel and Robert Francis Kennedy

Ethel Skakel and Robert Francis Kennedy were married on June 17, 1950, at St. Mary's Roman Catholic Church on Greenwich Avenue in Greenwich, Connecticut, the prosperous New York

City suburb where Ethel grew up. The ceremony was conducted by the Reverend Terence L. Connolly of Boston College, and John F. Kennedy (at the time still unmarried himself) served as his brother's best man. Ethel wore a traditional white satin gown with a fitted bodice embroidered with seed pearls, a bateau neckline, and a lace bertha; a small string of pearls was her only jewelry. Her matron of honor was her older sister Pat, who had been the object of Bobby's devotion before her marriage. Ushers included many members of the Harvard foot-ball team on which Bobby had played, captained by Kenny O'Donnell; Arthur Schlesinger, Jr., later joked that they were all so big they could hardly get down the aisle side by side. The football team had also been guests at a bachelor dinner the night before at the Harvard Club in Manhattan, which later sent the Kennedys a bill for the wreckage. After the wedding, there was a lavish reception at the Skakel home in Greenwich. Music was provided by Irish tenor Morton Downey, a friend of the Kennedy family and neighbor in Palm Beach.

Wedding: Eunice Mary Kennedy and Robert Sargent Shriver

Eunice Mary Kennedy and Robert Sargent Shriver were married in New York City, in St. Patrick's Cathedral. The date was May 23, 1953. The bride was given in marriage by her father, and the ceremony was presided over by Kennedy family friend Francis Cardinal Spellman. The bride wore a white net dress from Christian Dior with a fitted bodice and a skirt ornamented by bands of ruching. Eunice had elbow-length gloves, and wore only a single strand of pearls. Guests of note included Supreme Court Justice William O. Douglas, Margaret Truman, and Senator Joseph McCarthy, who had once dated the bride's sister Pat. At the luncheon reception held at the Waldorf-Astoria Hotel, guests were served slices of a seven-foot wedding cake, a rich moist confection incorporating cooked carrots. Eunice fondly toasted her groom with the following speech: "I searched all my life for someone like my father, and Sarge came closest."

Wedding: Jacqueline Lee Bouvier and John Fitzgerald Kennedy

Jacqueline Lee Bouvier and John Fitzgerald Kennedy were married on the morning of September 12, 1953, in picturesque St. Mary's Roman Catholic Church in Newport, Rhode Island. The more than eight hundred guests included such notables as Governor Roberts of Rhode Island and Senator Leverett Saltonstall of Massachusetts. The bride, given in marriage by her stepfather, Hugh D. Auchincloss, wore a dress of ivory tissue silk, with a portrait neckline, fitted bodice, and a bouffant skirt embellished with bands of more than fifty yards of flounces. Her rosepoint lace veil, worn first by her grandmother Lee, was draped from a tiara of lace and orange blossoms. Jacqueline wore a choker of pearls and a diamond bracelet that was a gift from the groom. The bride's bouquet was of pink and white spray orchids and gardenias.

Her attendants, dressed in pink taffeta, included her sister, Lee, then Mrs. Michael T. Canfield, as matron of honor; her stepsister Nina G. Auchincloss as maid of honor; and a bevy of ten bridesmaids, among them the groom's sister Jean and sister-in-law Ethel, and the bride's former boarding school roommate Nancy Tuckerman. Half-sister Janet Auchincloss was flower girl and half-brother James Auchincloss served as a page. Senator Kennedy's best man was his brother Robert, and among the ushers were brother Edward Kennedy, brother-in-law Sargent Shriver, cousin Joe Gargan, brother-in-law Michael Canfield, Lem Billings, Red Fay, Torbert MacDonald, Senate colleague George Smathers, and Charles Bartlett, who had introduced the couple. Most of the men—and one woman, the groom's sister Pat—had attended a stag dinner for 350 at Boston's Parker House Hotel a few nights earlier.

The ceremony was performed by Archbishop Cushing, a friend of the Kennedy family, and he was assisted by four other priests, including the former president of Notre Dame and the head of the Christopher Society. Before the mass, a special blessing from Pope Pius XII was read: "Holy Father on occasion of marriage cordially imparts Hon. John F. Kennedy and Mrs. Kennedy his paternal apostolic blessing in pledging enduring Christian happiness in married life." Tenor soloist Luigi Vena from Boston sang Gounod's "Ave Maria." (Vena would sing the "Ave Maria" again ten years later at the funeral of President John F. Kennedy.) The bride's engagement ring, slipped on again after the ceremony, was a beautiful emerald-and-diamond creation from Van Cleef and Arpels.

The reception was held on the huge terrace of the three-hundred-acre Auchincloss oceanfront estate, Hammersmith Farm, for more than twelve hundred guests, many of whom had to wait more than two hours to get through the receiving line. The wedding cake, four feet tall, had been ordered by Joseph Kennedy from an Irish bakery in Quincy, Massachusetts. Meyer Davis and his orchestra played under a huge canopy.

Wedding: Patricia Kennedy and Peter Lawford

Patricia Kennedy and Peter Lawford were married on April 24, 1954, at the Roman Catholic Church of St. Thomas More in New York City. Pat's only attendant was her younger sister, Jean, dressed in pink-and-blue taffeta. Her three brothers and family friend Lem Billings acted as ushers. Best man was J. Robert Neal of Houston, Texas. The wedding ceremony was performed by the Reverend John J. Cavanaugh, former president of the University of Notre Dame. Thanks to the groom's Hollywood stardom and the Kennedy family's celebrity, it required police barricades to restrain the crowd of more than three thousand spectators waiting to get a glimpse of the newlyweds.

The bride wore a chiffon veil and a white satin trained dress with a portrait neckline and tightly fitted bodice with three-quarter-length sleeves. Pat carried a bouquet of white orchids and wore a pearl choker. The small reception following the wedding was held at the Terrace Room of the Plaza Hotel.

Wedding: Jean Ann Kennedy and Stephen Edward Smith

Jean Ann Kennedy and Stephen Edward Smith were married in New York on May 20, 1956. It was an intimate ceremony in the Lady Chapel of St. Patrick's Cathedral, conducted by Kennedy family friend Francis Cardinal Spellman. Jean later told a friend, "Daddy gave me a choice of a big wedding and a small present, or a small wedding and a big present"; Jean chose a sizable diamond pin. Her dress was champagne satin, with a design almost identical to that of her sister Pat's, and she carried a bouquet of orange blossoms and stephanotis. Eunice Shriver was the matron of honor and her sister's only attendant; the groom's brother, Philip Smith, was his best man. Ushers included the bride's three brothers and Lem Billings. The reception was held at the Crystal Room of New York's Plaza Hotel.

Wedding: Virginia Joan Bennett and Edward Moore Kennedy

Virginia Joan Bennett married Edward Moore Kennedy on November 30, 1958. Ted was the last of his generation to wed. The ceremony was held at St. Joseph's Roman Catholic Church in Bronxville, New York, where both bride and groom had attended church as children, and conducted by Kennedy family friend Francis Cardinal Spellman. The bride was given in marriage by her father. Her sister Candace was her maid of honor, and sister-in-law Jean Kennedy Smith was one of her attendants. The best man was the groom's brother, Senator John F. Kennedy. Robert Kennedy served as an usher, along with family friend Lem Billings and Ted's cousin Joe Gargan.

The bride's ivory satin gown had long sleeves and a sweetheart neckline trimmed with lace. Joan wore a family veil of rosepoint lace pinned to her hair with a sprig of orange blossom. Her bouquet was of white roses, stephanotis, and stock. The reception after the wedding was held at the nearby Siwanoy Country Club.

Wedding: Jacqueline Bouvier Kennedy and Aristotle Onassis

Jacqueline Bouvier Kennedy married Aristotle Onassis in a Greek Orthodox ceremony held in the small neoclassic Chapel of the Little Virgin, located in a secluded cypress grove on the Onassis private island of Skorpios on October 10, 1968. The marriage ceremony was conducted by a Greek Orthodox archimandrite, Father Polycarpos Athanassion. As on the occasion of her first marriage, the bride was given away by her stepfather, Hugh D. Auchincloss. She was dressed in a knee-length beige chiffon and lace dress designed by Valentino, with a matching ribbon in her bouffant hairdo. According to Kitty Kelley, the dress was not purchased new for the wedding but was one she had worn some months earlier to the wedding of the daughter of her good friend, Mrs. Paul Mellon. Both bride and groom wore ceremonial garlands of lemon buds, and the chapel was decorated with masses of tulips flown in from Holland.

The bride's children, Caroline and John Kennedy, were her attendants at the thirty-minute ceremony. Among the twenty-one guests at the ceremony were the bride's mother and her former sisters-in-law Pat Lawford and Jean Smith, as well as the Onassis children, Alexander and Christina. The wedding ring was a large cabochon ruby surrounded by one-carat diamonds, valued at $1.2 million.

The gala wedding reception was held aboard the white-hulled Onassis yacht, the *Christina*. The new Mrs. Onassis showed the guests her wedding ring and the matching heart-shaped ruby earrings and massive gold ram's head bracelet set with rubies. Pink champagne was served, and then the party sat down to an exquisite dinner. The following morning the guests were flown back to their homes aboard Olympic Airways, the groom flew to Athens to continue an important business negotiation, and the new Mrs. Onassis called New York decorator Billy Baldwin to ask him to come help her redecorate the house on Skorpios.

Wedding: Kathleen Hartington Kennedy and David Lee Townsend

On November 17, 1973, Kathleen Hartington Kennedy, the daughter of Ethel Skakel and the late Senator Robert F. Kennedy, married David Lee Townsend. The wedding was held at Holy Trinity Church in Washington, conducted by a Jesuit priest, the Reverend James English. The bride was given in marriage by her uncle, Senator Edward M. Kennedy. She wore a simple floor-length dress of white lace and had a wreath of stephanotis in her hair. Singer Andy Williams,

a Kennedy family friend, provided the vocal music, and the rings exchanged were handmade by the groom. The maid of honor was the bride's sister Courtney Kennedy; the matron of honor her aunt Jean Smith. Sister Kerry Kennedy and cousin Caroline Kennedy were bridesmaids, dressed in dark green velvet. Six of the bride's brothers were ushers, and the seventh (Douglas) was a ring bearer. Her cousin John Kennedy was an altar boy.

Wedding: Maria Owings Shriver and Arnold Schwarzenegger

Maria Owings Shriver and Arnold Schwarzenegger were married on April 26, 1986, at St. Francis Xavier's Roman Catholic Church in Hyannis, Massachusetts, before a group of 450

guests. The bride was given in marriage by her father R. Sargent Shriver. She wore a pearl-edge dress of white satin with an eleven-foot train, designed by Marc Bohan of Christian Dior. Ma-

Kathleen Kennedy on the way to the altar, escorted by her uncle, Senator Edward M. Kennedy. (Dennis Brack, Black Star)

ria's bouquet, flown in from Paris, included lilies-of-the-valley, stephanotis, and pink roses. The maid of honor was cousin Caroline Kennedy; bridesmaids included cousins Sydney Lawford McKelvy, Courtney Kennedy Ruhe, the younger sister of Queen Noor of Jordan, and a granddaughter of Winston Churchill. The best man was former Mr. Universe Franco Columbu. Guests included Jacqueline Kennedy Onassis, Senator Edward M. Kennedy, Andy Warhol, Tom Brokaw,

Susan St. James and husband Dick Ebersol, and Oprah Winfrey, who read a poem by Elizabeth Barrett Browning at the ceremony.

The wedding reception was held on the lawn of the Kennedy compound in Hyannis Port. Music was provided by the orchestra of Peter Duchin, and guests feasted on oysters and cold lobster. The 425-pound wedding cake was a replica of the one served at the wedding of the bride's parents.

Wedding: Caroline Bouvier Kennedy and Edwin Schlossberg

Caroline Bouvier Kennedy, daughter of the late President, was married to Edwin Schlossberg on July 19, 1986. The wedding took place at the Church of Our Lady of Victory, in Centerville, Massachusetts, near Hyannis Port. More than two thousand onlookers stood outside the church, in addition to the several hundred invited guests who watched the intimate ceremony. In deference to the groom's Jewish faith, there was no formal wedding mass. The bride wore a wedding dress designed by Carolina Herrera, made of white silk organza with a bodice appliquéd with white shamrocks, and an elegant tulle train, petticoat, and veil. Caroline's only jewelry was a pair of pendant pearl earrings borrowed from her mother. She was given in marriage by her uncle, Senator Edward M. Kennedy. Caroline was attended by a bevy of bridesmaids (in cheerful floral prints), including cousins Sydney Lawford McKelvy and newly married Maria Shriver Schwarzenegger as matron of honor. The groom wore a navy linen suit designed by Willi Smith; he chose as his best man the bride's brother, John F. Kennedy, Jr. The mother of the bride, Jacqueline Kennedy Onassis, wore a pistachio-green dress also designed by Carolina Herrera, detailed with a string of small buttons down the back.

The reception was held on the lawn of the Kennedy compound, under a white tent. The wedding cake was yellow and topped with little Godzillas dressed as brides and grooms. To entertain the wedding guests, Carly Simon, a neighbor of Mrs. Onassis on Martha's Vineyard, sang "Chapel of Love" and George Plimpton staged a fireworks display over the water, based on the theme, "What Ed Schlossberg Does."

Wedding: Victoria Lawford and Robert Beebe Pender, Jr.

Victoria Lawford married lawyer Robert Beebe Pender, Jr., in a ceremony on Long Island on June 13, 1987. The wedding took place at the Roman Catholic Church of the Sacred Hearts of Jesus and Mary, followed by a reception at the Southampton estate of the bride's mother, Pat Lawford. The bride, given in marriage by her brother Christopher, wore an ivory dress with puffed sleeves and a sweetheart neckline, ornamented by a single strand of pearls. Her attendants were sisters Robin Lawford and Sydney Lawford McKelvy, as well as cousins Kara Kennedy and Kerry Kennedy. Guests included Senator Edward M. Kennedy, Joan Kennedy escorted by her son Ted, Jr., Jacqueline Kennedy Onassis in a chic black-and-white print suit escorted by her son, John, and Caroline and Ed Schlossberg.

J. B. West

J. B. West was for many years the chief usher of the White House, serving in that capacity during the Kennedy presidency as well as others. The chief usher is in effect the manager of the President's mansion, and First Families soon learn that he is their best support in times of crisis. West was a great help to Jacqueline Kennedy when the Kennedys entered the White House, and she was grateful for his advice and support. West later wrote a discreet book about his experiences with all the First Families he had served.

Wexford

Wexford was the weekend residence at Atoka, in the Middleburg hunt country of Virginia, that President and Mrs. John F. Kennedy were just building at the time of his assassination in 1963. They bought the land from friends Paul and Bunny Mellon, whose estate adjoined Wexford. The Kennedys gave up the lease at Glen Ora and planned to use Wexford, named after the Irish county from which the first Kennedys emigrated to the New World, as their retreat from the pressures of the White House. After the death of the President, Mrs. Kennedy continued to use the country place while she and the children lived in Washington. It went on the market in 1964 when they moved to New York. The purchase price was $225,000, and the buyer had to sign an agreement not to permit any publicity about the former Kennedy house for ten years.

What Does the President Do?

Caroline Kennedy's most frequently quoted remark came when she wandered into the White House communications room one quiet Sunday during her father's administration. When a reporter idly asked the little girl what her father was doing at that moment upstairs in the family's private quarters, Caroline replied candidly, "He's not doing anything. He's just sitting up there with his shoes and socks off, doing nothing."

What to Call Bobby Kennedy

Journalist Jack Newfield once made a list of the twenty adjectives most often used to describe Robert F. Kennedy.
They were:

intolerant	simplistic	vindictive	courageous	pragmatic	ambitious
spoiled	tense	honest	emotional	authoritarian	restless
			rude	competitive	moralistic
			moody	tough	ruthless
			cold	loyal	

"Where Were You?"

All over the world, people still remember the answer to the question, "Where were you when President Kennedy was shot?" The impression of that moment was burned into our memories.

Byron Raymond White

Byron Raymond White, nicknamed "Whizzer" because of his speed on the football field, was a friend of John F. Kennedy's. The two young men traveled extensively together in Berlin on the eve of World War II. White, born in Colorado in 1917, graduated from the University of Colorado and was a Rhodes scholar. He received his law degree from Yale in 1946 and then clerked for Chief Justice Frederick M. Vinson. White worked in the 1960 Kennedy campaign, organizing a group called Citizens for Kennedy. After President Kennedy appointed his brother attorney general, Robert Kennedy selected Byron White as his deputy attorney general. It was White who then recruited many of the men who made the Justice Department the effective and efficient unit it became under the Kennedys. In March 1962 President Kennedy appointed White to fill in a vacancy on the bench of the Supreme Court; the President attended his swearing-in ceremony on April 16.

John White

John White was a feature writer on the staff of the Washington *Times-Herald* in 1941, when Kathleen Kennedy went to work there. The two reporters were immediately attracted to one another, finding spice in their differences: John a Protestant, a skirt-chaser, a social rebel; Kathleen a devout Catholic with high moral standards behind her sense of fun. John was continually frustrated by the lack of a sexual element in his relationship with Kathleen, but their involvement continued for a number of months, until John enlisted in the Marine Corps in May 1942. Kathleen continued to write to him for some months thereafter.

Some years later, John White befriended another socialite with a job at the *Times-Herald*, Jacqueline Bouvier. By that time, he was working at the State Department.

Theodore H. White

Journalist Theodore H. White followed Jack Kennedy's 1960 campaign for the presidency and later wrote a best-selling book about it, called *The Making of a President, 1960*. The book was such a success that White later wrote similar volumes about subsequent presidential campaigns.

The White Whale

One of the ways President John F. Kennedy liked to entertain his children was to tell them stories about the White Whale. The constantly elaborated stories were about a small whale that was able to follow the presidential yacht unseen, by lurking in its white wake. According to Kennedy, the whale's favorite food was men's socks, and often he asked male guests (including Vice-President Johnson) to remove their socks and throw them overboard as a snack for the White Whale. Family friend Lem Billings later remarked, "We all learned that when Jack began telling Caroline about the White Whale, it was time to move to another part of the yacht."

Why Bobby Couldn't Be a Boy Scout

When the Kennedy family moved to England after Joseph P. Kennedy became the American ambassador in 1939, Bobby Kennedy wanted to join a boy scout troop there. Then he learned that in England, the oath included a pledge of allegiance to the British king. The patriotic Bobby gave up the idea of becoming a boy scout.

Why England Slept

In his last year of college at Harvard, John F. Kennedy was required to write a senior thesis. He chose as his topic the subject of Great Britain's lack of preparation for entering World War II. Of course, as the son of the United States ambassador to that country, Jack had access to information not available to the average undergraduate. His Harvard thesis was so well received that his father suggested it might be turned into a book and asked his friend, journalist Arthur Krock, to lend Jack some assistance. They decided to call the book *Why England Slept*, an allusion to the book earlier published in Great Britain by Prime Minister Winston Churchill about the build-up of Nazi Germany, called *While England Slept*.

John F. Kennedy's first book turned out to be a critical success as well as a best-seller. With a foreword by magazine magnate Henry R. Luce, it was published by Wilfred Funk, Inc., in August 1940, and sold for two dollars. The book earned its author a total of forty thousand dollars in royalties. He used some of the money to buy himself a Buick, and donated his English royalties to the town of Plymouth, which had been hard hit by German bombing early in the war. Ambassador Joseph P. Kennedy was delighted with the book's success and wrote his son, "You would be surprised how a book that really makes the grade with high-class people stands you in good stead for years to come."

Patricia Wilson

In October 1943, Joseph P. Kennedy, Jr., stationed at an American naval air base in an English town called Mudville Heights, met Patricia Wilson during a dinner party at the Savoy Hotel in London. At that time, the Australian-born beauty was married to Robin Wilson, a banker who was a major in the British Army, stationed in Libya. Wilson was her second husband; her first had been the Earl of Jersey. Joe and the youthful mother of three children fell deeply in love, and he spent all of his leaves with her at her country cottage. Pat Wilson was waiting for Joe to return when he was killed by the explosion of his plane on August 12, 1944. When she wrote to his parents to express her own sorrow, as well as her pride in Joe, she was rebuffed. Joe's brother Jack did look her up several years later when he visited London after the war. Her own husband was killed not long after Joe's death.

Oprah Winfrey

One of the closest friends of Maria Shriver is talk-show host Oprah Winfrey. The two women worked together in television for two years at station WBZ-TV in Baltimore, and during that period they were also neighbors in the same apartment complex. Oprah was one of the guests at Maria's wedding to Arnold Schwarzenegger, and she read a poem by Elizabeth Barrett Browning during the ceremony.

The Woman in the Polka-Dot Dress

Sometime after the assassination of Senator Robert F. Kennedy on June 5, 1968, reports began to surface that a young woman in a polka-dot dress was seen running away from the Ambassador Hotel shouting, "We shot him!" Police files released twenty years later indicate that many eyewitnesses came forward to say they had indeed seen gunman Sirhan Sirhan with a woman, and one of these reports described the woman as wearing a polka-dot dress. But it seems that the investigation never went any further, the woman in the polka-dot dress was never located, and Sirhan's contention that he acted alone became the official version of the assassination.

Words Jack Loved

Words Jack Loved was a privately printed book that Edward M. Kennedy put together as a 1976 Christmas present for Kennedy family members. It had anecdotes about President Kennedy's lifelong interest in reading, as well as excerpts from his favorite books.

Writing About the Kennedys

As of 1989, more than one hundred books about the Kennedy family are in print, and hundreds more have been published and then gone out of print. At least twenty-four books were published in 1988 to mark the twenty-fifth anniversary of the President's assassination. Among the new titles:

85 Days: The Last Campaign of Robert Kennedy, by Jules Witcover, published by Morrow/Quill

A Time to Remember, by Stanley Shapiro, published by NAL/Signet

JFK For Beginners, by Errol Selkirk, published by Putnam/Perigee

Contract on America: The Mafia Murder of President John F. Kennedy, by David E. Scheim, published by Shapolsky Publishers.

The Kennedy Legacy: A Generation Later, by Jacques Lowe and Wilfred Sheed, published by Viking Studio.

John F. Kennedy, by Judie Mills, published by Franklin Watts

Life in Camelot: The Kennedy Years, edited by Philip B. Kunhardt, Jr., published by Little, Brown

Remembering America: A Voice from the Sixties, by Richard Goodwin, published by Little, Brown

James Browning Wyeth

James Browning Wyeth ("Jamie") was the artist who painted the official posthumous portrait of President John F. Kennedy. Wyeth, born in Wilmington, Delaware, in 1946, is the son of artist Andrew Wyeth, and has had a number of highly acclaimed one-man shows.

Wyoming

In the balloting to select a presidential candidate at the 1960 Democratic convention, the Kennedy team put its best effort into getting John. F. Kennedy chosen on the first ballot, for they feared that his support might erode if his candidacy did not appear to have overwhelming momentum. Kennedy campaign managers listened tensely throughout the first ballot, constantly recalculating the total number of votes for Jack and hoping to attain the magic number, a majority of 761 votes. Near the end of the balloting, sensing the drift of events, Edward Kennedy went down on the convention floor and shouted at the chairman of the Wyoming delegation, yet to vote, "You have in your grasp the opportunity to nominate the next President of the United States. Such support can never be forgotten by a President." Jack Kennedy's moment came shortly thereafter. The committeeman from Wyoming rose and said, "Wyoming casts all fifteen votes for the next President of the United States, John F. Kennedy."

The Yacht Christina

The yacht *Christina* belonged to Aristotle Onassis and was named after his daughter. Onassis bought the ship, formerly a Canadian frigate called the *Stormont*, in 1954, and spent $2.5 million converting it into a "floating palace". One of the largest private yachts in the world, the *Christina* had a number of luxury touches: gold-plated fixtures on the Siena marble bathtubs; lapis lazuli fireplaces; a dance floor that could be rolled back to reveal a swimming pool tiled with mosaics copied from the Palace of Minos; El Greco's "Madonna and Child" hanging in the salon; forty-two phones; a hospital equipped with x-ray machine and surgical supplies; a children's playroom containing dolls dressed by Dior; and, most unusual, bar stools covered with the tanned skins of whale testicles. The ship required a full-time crew of fifty, including two chefs, one French and one Greek. Jacqueline Kennedy vacationed aboard the *Christina* in October 1963, after the death of her newborn son Patrick, and when she later married Onassis, many of the Kennedy family cruised on the *Christina*. Today, in accordance with a clause in Onassis's will that directed his heirs that if upkeep on the vessel proved prohibitive they were to present it to the Greek treasury, the fabled Onassis yacht belongs to the Greek government and is used for official entertaining.

A Year in France for Jacqueline

In early 1949, Vassar student Jacqueline Bouvier applied for the Junior Year Abroad program and was accepted to study in France. She arrived in mid August and first went to the University of Grenoble, in the south of the country, for a six-week intensive program in the French language. In September, she enrolled in the Sorbonne, France's most prestigious educational institution. Rather than living in the dormitory that housed most of the other American students, she boarded with a French family, Countess Guyot de Renty and her children. The De Rentys apartment at 78 Avenue Mozart had no central heating, a single bathroom shared by the family and boarders, and hot water only on rare occasions. When Hugh and Janet Auchincloss visited Jackie that winter, they were appalled by the lack of convenience, but she refused to leave the typically French apartment. Her year in France made Jacqueline a lover of all aspects of French culture for the rest of her life.

The Yellow Cab Company

One night in 1923, Walter Howey of the *Boston American* knocked on the door of Joseph P. Kennedy's home in Brookline, Massachusetts, and asked his friend Joe if he would look into the problems of the Yellow Cab Company, in which Howey had invested his life savings. The following day, Kennedy went to New York to meet with founder and president John Hertz, who explained that a rival firm was manipulating the price of his stock to force it down, in the hope of preventing the merger of Yellow Cab with another cab company and the subsequent expansion of the new and larger firm into the New York market. Hertz gave Kennedy carte blanche and a "war chest" of five million dollars.

Kennedy shut himself up in a room in New York's Waldorf-Astoria Hotel with only trusted aide Eddie Moore at his side, and embarked on a month-long campaign of buying and selling Yellow Cab Company stock in such a confusing pattern that the rival manipulators, fearful of losing their own investment, pulled out of the market. It took another month of carefully calculated buying and selling to make the price of the stock return to a level that reflected its true value. John Hertz was then able to proceed with his plans (and the following year to found his car rental business), and Walter Howey's investment was saved. When it was all over, a tired Joe Kennedy went home to his family, to meet the new baby (Patricia) born while he was at work. His fee for this endeavor was a large cash sum, stock in Yellow Cab Company, and a chance to invest in the new Hertz car rental business on favorable terms.

The Zapruder Film

Businessman Abraham Zapruder was visiting Dallas on November 22, 1963, and decided to watch the presidential motorcade pass by. As fate would have it, he stationed himself near the Texas Book Depository, and as the President's limousine drew near, he turned on his eight-millimeter Bell & Howell movie camera. Zapruder thus recorded the terrible twenty-two seconds when President Kennedy was hit, and the frantic scramble in the back seat of the car. Zapruder's photos were sold for $150,000 to *Life*, which published them a week after the assassination, as horrified Americans were still trying to answer the question of how it had all happened. Zapruder donated part of his fee to Mrs. J. D. Tippett, widow of the policeman murdered by Oswald.

Abraham Zapruder died in 1970. In 1975, *Time* sold the film back to the Zapruder family for one dollar. The family charges fees of up to $30,000 for commercial use of the film, which prompted a lawsuit challenging the Zapruders' copyright to such an important historical document. The Zapruders won in court and thus retain their copyright.

BIBLIOGRAPHY

Baldridge, Letitia. *Of Diamonds and Diplomats.* New York: Ballantine Books, 1968.

Blair, Joan. *The Search for JFK.* New York: Berkley, 1976.

Brown, Gene, ed. *The Kennedys: A New York Times Profile.* New York: Arno Press, 1980.

Burns, James MacGregor. *Edward Kennedy and the Camelot Legacy.* New York: W. W. Norton, 1976.

Chellis, Marcia. *The Joan Kennedy Story.* New York: Simon and Schuster, 1985.

Collier, Peter, and David Horowitz. *The Kennedys: An American Drama.* New York: Summit Books, 1984.

Curl, Donald W. *Mizner's Florida: American Resort Architecture.* Cambridge, MA: The Architectural History Foundation at M.I.T., 1984.

David, Lester, and Irene David. *Bobby Kennedy: The Making of a Folk Hero.* New York: Dodd Mead, 1986.

Davis, John H. *The Bouviers.* New York: Farrar, Straus & Giroux, 1969.

Davis, John H. *The Kennedys: Dynasty and Disaster.* New York: McGraw-Hill, 1984.

Exner, Judith, as told to Ovid Demaris. *My Story.* New York: Grove Press, 1972.

Fay, Paul B. *The Pleasure of His Company.* New York: Harper and Row, 1966.

Four Days: The Historical Record of the Death of President Kennedy. Compiled by United Press International and American Heritage Magazine, 1964.

Frolick, S. J. *Once There Was a President for Children To Remember.* New York: Black Star, 1964.

Galbraith, John Kenneth. *A Life in Our Times: Memoirs.* Boston: Houghton Mifflin, 1981.

Gallagher, Mary Barelli. *My Life with Jacqueline Kennedy.* New York: David McKay, 1969.

Gardner, Gerald. *All the Presidents' Wits.* New York: William Morrow, Beech Tree Books, 1986.

Gibson, Barbara, with Caroline Latham. *Life with Rose Kennedy.* New York: Warner Books, 1986.

Goodwin, Doris Kearns. *The Fitzgeralds and the Kennedys: An American Saga.* New York: St. Martin's Press, 1987.

Hall, Gordon Langley, and Ann Pinchot. *Jacqueline Kennedy: A Biography.* New York: New American Library, 1964.

Heymann, C. David. *A Woman Named Jackie.* New York: Lyle Stuart, 1989.

Howar, Barbara. *Laughing All the Way*. New York: Stein and Day, 1973.

Kelley, Kitty. *Jackie Oh!* New York: Lyle Stuart, 1978.

Kennedy, Rose. *Times to Remember*. New York: Doubleday, 1974.

Koskoff, David. *Joseph P. Kennedy: A Life and Times*. New York: Prentice-Hall, 1974.

Lasky, Victor. *JFK: The Man and the Myth*. New York: Dell Publishing, 1977.

Let Us Begin: The First Hundred Days of the Kennedy Administration. New York: Simon and Schuster, 1961.

Lieberson, Goddard, ed. *John Fitzgerald Kennedy ... As We Remember Him*. New York: Atheneum, 1965.

Lincoln, Evelyn. *My Twelve Years with John F. Kennedy*. New York: David McKay, 1965.

McTaggart, Lynn. *Kathleen Kennedy: Her Life and Times*. New York: Dial, 1983.

Manchester, William. *The Death of a President*. New York: Harper and Row, 1967.

Manchester, William. *Portrait of a President*. Boston: Little, Brown, 1962.

Martin, Ralph G. *A Hero for Our Time: An Intimate Story of the Kennedy Years*. New York: Macmillan, 1983.

Newfield, Jack. *Robert Kennedy, A Memoir*. New York: New American Library, 1969.

O'Brien, Lawrence F. *No Final Victories*. New York: Doubleday, 1974.

O'Donnell, Kenneth P., and David Powers, with Joe McCarthy. *Johnny, We Hardly Knew Ye*. Boston: Little, Brown, 1972.

Rachlin, Harvey. *The Kennedys: A Chronological History*. New York: World Almanac, 1986.

Roberts, Allen. *Robert F. Kennedy: Biography of a Compulsive Politician*. Brookline, MA: Brandon Press, 1984.

Saunders, Frank, with James Southwood. *Torn Lace Curtain*. New York: Holt, Rinehart & Winston, 1982.

Schlesinger, Arthur M., Jr. *Robert Kennedy and His Times*. Boston: Houghton Mifflin, 1978.

Schlesinger, Arthur M., Jr. *A Thousand Days: John F. Kennedy in the White House*. Boston: Houghton Mifflin, 1965.

Searls, Hank. *The Lost Prince: Young Joe, the Forgotten Kennedy*. New York: World Publishing, 1969.

Shepard, Tazewell, Jr. *John F. Kennedy: Man of the Sea*. New York: William Morrow, 1965.

Sorensen, Theodore. *Kennedy*. New York: Harper and Row, 1965.

Strousse, Flora. *John Fitzgerald Kennedy: Man of Courage*. New York: Signet Press, 1964.

Teti, Frank with Jeannie Sakol. *Kennedy: The New Generation*. New York: Delilah Books, 1983.

Thayer, Mary Van Rensselaer. *Jacqueline Kennedy: The White House Years*. Boston: Little, Brown, 1967.

The Torch Is Passed ...: The Associated Press Story of the Death of a President. New York: The Associated Press, 1963.

Triumph and Tragedy: The Story of the Kennedys. New York: The Associated Press, 1968.

Whalen, Richard J. *The Founding Father: The Story of Joseph P. Kennedy*. New York: New American Library, 1964.

The White House: A Historic Guide. Washington: White House Historical Association, 1964.